2019 Medical Coding Start to Finish Semi

Created Exclusively by OBC

Samples & Seminar Examples

Sample Forms from Coding Kit 1-20

Example #1 - Diabetic Retinopathy 21

Example #2 - Glaucoma 33

Example #3 - AMD 45

Example #4 - Epiretinal Membrane 53

Example #5 - High Risk Med 65

Example #6 - Cataract 73

Example #7 - Dry Eye 87

Example #8 - Trichiasis Epilation 97

Example #9 - Cornea Foreign Body 103

Example #10 - Conjunctivitis 109

ISBN-13: 978-1792045448
© 2019 Optometric Billing Consultants - All Rights Reserved

Most people have vision insurance and medical insurance. They are very different in terms of the services they cover and it's important for our patients to understand those differences. Vision coverage (VSP, Spectera, EyeMed, Davis etc) is mainly designed to determine a prescription for glasses and is not equipped to deal with complex medical conditions and/or diagnoses. It does allow for screenings of conditions, but once they are determined, then medical insurance is filed on those services. When a medical condition is present (such as diabetes, cataracts, dry eye, floaters, etc.) it is necessary to file the visit with your major medical carrier (BCBS, Aetna, UHC, Cigna, etc) and the co-pays for that insurance will apply. Insurance carriers set these rules and our office is required to follow them. In most cases, there is no way to know prior to the examination which type of insurance our office will be able to file for you.

1. If you have ANY problems or complaints that MAY be attributable to a medical condition which requires a more in-depth investigation and additional medical decision-making to rule out any underlying eye disease, we will accordingly bill your MEDICAL insurance, NOT your vision plan. These include, but are not limited to:
- New or sudden blurry vision
- Eye pain or redness
- Flashes or floaters
- Headaches
- Dry or itchy eyes
- Loss of vision
- Eyestrain or double vision

2. There are a variety of systemic conditions that can profoundly and permanently affect a patient's vision that require a more in-depth investigation, which may include additional testing, follow up visits, and reports to your primary care physician. This type of examination is NOT covered under "vision" plans, and we will bill your MEDICAL insurance, NOT your vision plan. These include, but are not limited to:
- Diabetes
- Lupus or autoimmune disease
- Hypertension
- Diseases resulting in use of high risk medications like Placquenil
- Thyroid disease

3. If you have previously been diagnosed by another eye doctor for any eye issues that require medical decision-making, treatment or management, we will bill your MEDICAL insurance, NOT your vision plan. These include, but are not limited to:
- Cataracts
- Macular or retinal disease
- Amblyopic/lazy eye
- History of eye surgery
- Glaucoma/previous diagnosis of high eye pressure

We make every effort to be on every major carrier for your convenience and we will file those claims for you. In the event that we do not take your insurance we will provide you with an itemized receipt so that you may file with your carrier for reimbursement. If you have any questions, please let us know.

I understand the paragraph above & authorize Dr Botts & Associates to file my insurance by the above guidelines.

Signature: _____ Date: _____

<<PRACTICE NAME>> *Notice of Privacy Practices* Effective _____

This Notice describes how medical information about you may be used and disclosed and how you can get access to this information. Please review it carefully. If you have any questions please contact our office.

<<Practice Name>> is required by law to:
- Maintain the privacy of your protected health information;
- Give you this notice of our duties and privacy practices regarding health information about you;
- Follow the terms of our notice that is currently in effect.

HOW *<<Practice Name>>* MAY USE AND DISCLOSE YOUR HEALTH INFORMATION:

Described as follows are the ways *<<Practice Name>>* may use and disclose health information that identifies you (Health Information, or PHI). Except for the following purposes, we will use and disclose Health Information only with your written permission. You may revoke such permission at any time by writing to us and stating that you wish to revoke permission you previously gave us.

Treatment. *<<Practice Name>>* may use and disclose Health Information for your treatment and to provide you with treatment-related health care services. For example, we may disclose Health Information to doctors, nurses, technicians, or other personnel, including people outside our office, who are involved in your medical care and need the information to provide you with medical care.

Payment. *<<Practice Name>>* may use and disclose Health Information so that we may bill and receive payment from you, an insurance company, or a third party for the treatment and services you received. For example, we may give your health plan information so that they will pay for your treatment. However, if you pay for your services yourself (e.g. out-of-pocket and without any third party contribution or billing), we will not disclose Health Information to a health plan if you instruct us to not do so.

Health Care Operations. *<<Practice Name>>* may use and disclose Health Information for health care operation purposes. These uses and disclosures are necessary to make sure that all of our patients receive quality care and to operate and manage our office. For example, we may use and disclose information to make sure the care you receive is of the highest quality. Subject to the exception above if you pay for your care yourself, we also may share information with other entities that have a relationship with you (for example, your health plan) for their health care operations.

Appointment Reminders, Treatment Alternatives and Health Related Benefits and Services. *<<Practice Name>>* may use and disclose Health Information to contact you and to remind you that you have an appointment with us. We also may use and disclose Health Information to tell you about treatment alternatives or health-related benefits and services that may be of interest to you. We will not, however, send you communications about health-related or non health-related products or services that are subsidized by a third party without your authorization.

Individuals Involved in Your Care or Payment for Your Care. When appropriate, *<<Practice Name>>* may share Health Information with a person who is involved in your medical care or payment for your care, such as your family or a close friend. We also may notify your family about your location or general condition or disclose such information to an entity assisting in a disaster relief effort.

Research. Under certain circumstances, *<<Practice Name>>* may use and disclose Health Information for research. For example, a research project may involve comparing the health of patients who received one treatment to those who received another, for the same condition. Before we use or disclose Health Information for research, the project will go through an approval process. Even without approval, we may permit researchers to look at records to help them identify patients who may be included in their research project or for other similar purposes, as long as they do not remove or take a copy of any Health Information.

Fundraising and Marketing. Health Information may be used for fundraising communications, but you have the right to opt-out of receiving such communications. Except for the exceptions detailed above, uses and disclosures of Health Information for marketing purposes, as well as disclosures that constitute a sale of Health Information, require your authorization if we receive any financial remuneration from a third party in exchange for making the communication, and we must advise you that we are receiving remuneration.

Other Uses. Other uses and disclosures of Health Information not contained in this Notice may be made only with your authorization.

SPECIAL SITUATIONS:

As Required by Law. *<<Practice Name>>* will disclose Health Information when required to do so by federal, state or local law.

To Avert a Serious Threat to Health or Safety. We may use and disclose Health Information when necessary to prevent a serious threat to your health and safety or the health and safety of the public or another person. Disclosures, however, will be made only to someone who may help prevent the threat.

Business Associates. We may disclose Health Information to our business associates that perform functions on our behalf or provide us with services if the information is necessary for such functions or services. For example, we may use another company to perform billing services on our behalf. All of our business associates are obligated to protect the privacy of your information and are not allowed to use or disclose any information other than as specified in our contract.

Organ and Tissue Donation. If you are an organ donor, we may use or release Health Information to organizations that handle organ procurement or other entities engaged in procurement; banking or transportation of organs, eyes, or tissues to facilitate organ, eye or tissue donation; and transplantation.

Military and Veterans. If you are a member of the armed forces, we may release Health Information as required by military command authorities. We also may release Health Information to the appropriate foreign military authority if you are a member of a foreign military.

Workers' Compensation. We may release Health Information for workers' compensation or similar programs. These programs provide benefits for work-related injuries or illness.

Public Health Risks. We may disclose Health Information for public health activities. These activities generally include disclosures to prevent or control disease, injury or disability; report births and deaths; report child abuse or neglect; report reactions to medications or problems with products; notify people of recalls of products they may be using; a person who may have been exposed to a disease or may be at risk for contracting or spreading a disease or condition; and the appropriate government authority if we believe a patient has been the victim of abuse, neglect or domestic violence. We will only make this disclosure if you agree or when required or authorized by law.

- **Health Oversight Activities.** We may disclose Health Information to a health oversight agency for activities authorized by law. These oversight activities include, for example, audits, investigations, inspections, and licensure. These activities are necessary for the government to monitor the health care system, government programs, and compliance with civil rights laws.
- **Lawsuits.** If you are involved in a lawsuit or a dispute, we may disclose Health Information in response to a court or administrative order. We also may disclose Health Information in response to a subpoena, discovery request, or other lawful process by someone else involved in the dispute, but only if efforts have been made to tell you about the request or to obtain an order protecting the information requested.
- **Law Enforcement.** We may release Health Information if asked by a law enforcement official if the information is: (1) in response to a court order, subpoena, warrant, summons or similar process; (2) limited information to identify or locate a suspect, fugitive, material witness, or missing person; (3) about the victim of a crime even if, under certain very limited circumstances, we are unable to obtain the person's agreement; (4) about a death we believe may be the result of criminal conduct; (5) about criminal conduct on our premises; and (6) in an emergency to report a crime, the location of the crime or victims, or the identity, description or location of the person who committed the crime.
- **Coroners, Medical Examiners and Funeral Directors.** We may release Health Information to a coroner or medical examiner. This may be necessary, for example, to identify a deceased person or determine the cause of death. We also may release Health Information to funeral directors as necessary for their duties.
- **National Security and Intelligence Activities.** We may release Health Information to authorized federal officials for intelligence, counter-intelligence, and other national security activities authorized by law.
- **Protective Services for the President and Others.** We may disclose Health Information to authorized federal officials so they may provide protection to the President, other authorized persons, or foreign heads of state, or to conduct special investigations.
- **Inmates or Individuals in Custody.** If you are an inmate of a correctional institution or under the custody of a law enforcement official, we may release Health Information to the correctional institution or law enforcement official. This release would be if necessary: (1) for the institution to provide you with health care; (2) to protect your health and safety or the health and safety of others; or (3) the safety and security of the correctional institution.

YOUR RIGHTS:

You have the following rights regarding Health Information *<<Practice Name>>* have about you:

- **Right to Inspect and Copy.** You have a right to inspect and copy Health Information that may be used to make decisions about your care or payment for your care. This includes medical and billing records, other than psychotherapy notes. To inspect and copy this Health Information, you must make your request, in writing, to our office.
- **Right to Amend.** If you feel that Health Information we have is incorrect or incomplete, you may ask us to amend the information. You have the right to request an amendment for as long as the information is kept by or for our office. To request an amendment, you must make your request, in writing, to our office.
- **Right to an Accounting of Disclosures.** You have the right to request a list of certain disclosures we made of Health Information for purposes other than treatment, payment and health care operations or for which you provided written authorization. To request an accounting of disclosures, you must make your request, in writing, to our office.
- **Right to Request Restrictions.** You have the right to request a restriction or limitation on the Health Information we use or disclose for treatment, payment, or health care operations. You also have the right to request a limit on the Health Information we disclose to someone involved in your care or the payment for your care, like a family member or friend. For example, you could ask that we not share information about a particular diagnosis or treatment with your spouse. To request a restriction, you must make your request, in writing, to our office. **We are not required to agree to all such requests.** If we agree, we will comply with your request unless the information is needed to provide you with emergency treatment.
- **Right to Request Confidential Communication.** You have the right to request that we communicate with you about medical matters in a certain way or at a certain location. For example, you can ask that we only contact you by mail or at work. To request confidential communication, you must make your request, in writing, to our office. Your request must specify how or where you wish to be contacted. We will accommodate reasonable requests.
- **Right to a Paper Copy of This Notice.** You have the right to a paper copy of this notice. You may ask us to give you a copy of this notice at any time. Even if you have agreed to receive this notice electronically, you are still entitled to a paper copy of this notice. You may obtain a copy of this notice at our web site, www._____. To obtain a paper copy of this notice please request it in writing.
- **Right to Electronic Records.** You have the right to receive a copy of your electronic health records in electronic form.
- **Right to Breach Notification.** You have the right to be notified if there is a Breach of privacy such that your Health Information is disclosed or used improperly or in an unsecured way.

CHANGES TO THIS NOTICE:

<<Practice Name>> reserve the right to change this notice and make the new notice apply to Health Information we already have as well as any information we receive in the future. We will post a copy of our current notice at our office. The notice will contain the effective date on the first page, in the top right-hand corner.

COMPLAINTS:

If you believe your privacy rights have been violated, you may file a complaint with our office or with the Secretary of the Department of Health and Human Services. All complaints must be made in writing. **You will not be penalized for filing a complaint.**

I acknowledge having been provided this Notice. Signed: _____.

EXAMINATION

5

Patient _____ Date _____ Sex: M F DOB _____ Age _____ Last Exam _____
Chief Complaint _____

History
HPI:
Symptoms   Allergies
Location
Quality   Medications
Severity
Duration   Ocular ROS
Timing
Context   Medical History & ROS from ___/___/___ reviewed: ☐ no changes
Modifiers   Dr. Initials _____

Examination Head/Face ☐ nl   Psych: Mood/Affect (anxiety/depression) ☐ nl   Neuro: Oriented (person/time/place) ☐ y ☐ n

VA: sc<   cc<   ph<   near<

K: OD _____   OLD RX: OD _____   add _____ △
         OS _____   OS _____   add _____
R-scopy: OD _____   REF: OD _____ 20/_____ add _____
             OS _____   OS _____ 20/_____ add _____

Perimetry: ☐ nl   CF ☐ nl   Color ☐ nl ☐ RG defect   **ADNEXA** ☐ nl
Motility: ☐ Full   Stereo Animals /3 WD /9   **EYELIDS:** ☐ Blepharitis   OD OS OU
Cover Test: ☐ Eso _____ ☐ Exo _____ ☐ Ortho   ☐ Meibomianitis OD OS OU

Pupils: ☐ no afferent defect   ☐ round OU   Size: OD _____ OS _____   ☐ 20D
                                                                                 ☐ 90D/78D
                                                                                 ☐ 3 Mirror
                                                                                 ☐

SLE: OD   OS   **RETINA: OD   OS**
☐ nl ☐ FBUT:____ TEAR FILM ☐ nl ☐ FBUT:____   ☐ nl ☐ drusen   MACULA   ☐ nl ☐ drusen
☐ nl ☐ arcus   CORNEA   ☐ nl ☐ arcus   ☐ nl ☐ RPE chgs   ☐ nl ☐ RPE chgs
☐ nl ☐ pterygium   ☐ nl ☐ pterygium   ☐ nl ☐ cotton wool POST POLE ☐ nl ☐ cotton wool
☐ nl ☐ infiltrate   ☐ nl ☐ infiltrate   ☐ nl ☐ hemes   ☐ nl ☐ hemes
☐ nl ☐ spk   ☐ nl ☐ spk   ☐ nl ☐ DME   ☐ nl ☐ DME
☐ nl ☐   SCLERA   ☐ nl ☐   ☐ nl ☐   VESSELS   ☐ nl ☐
☐ nl ☐ injection CONJ.   ☐ nl ☐ injection   ☐ nl ☐ PVD   VITREOUS ☐ nl ☐ PVD
☐ nl ☐ pinguecula   ☐ nl ☐ pinguecula   ☐ nl ☐ strands   ☐ nl ☐ strands
☐ D&Q ☐   AC   ☐ D&Q ☐   ☐ nl ☐   PERIPHERY ☐ nl ☐
☐ nl ☐ rubeosis IRIS   ☐ nl ☐ rubeosis   **OPTIC DISCS: OD   OS**
☐ clear ☐ cat ☐ ns LENS   ☐ clear ☐ cat ☐ ns   ☐ nl   SIZE/APPEARANCE/NFL ☐ nl
                                                                ☐ ____ C/D   ☐ ____

NCT / @ _____   Pachymetry: OD _____
TAG / @ _____   OS _____   Dilated: M .5% 1% PA 1%/0.25% C 1% 2% Ph 2.5% 10% OU@ _____

Diagnosis/Plan   MDM 1 2 3 4   Order: ☐ HRT/GDX/OCT   RTO: ___ day
                                                        ☐ Photo   ___ week
                                                        ☐ VF   ___ month
                                                        ☐ Consult   ___ year

                                                          Dr. _____

Rev.11/11

MEDICAL HISTORY

Name _____ Date _____/_____/_____
Address _____ Phone _____
City_____ State _____ Zip_____ Cell Phone _____
Guardian (if applicable)_____ Email _____
Birthdate _____/_____/_____ Last Eye Exam _____/_____/_____ Occupation _____
Do you have vision insurance? ❏ No ❏ Yes   If yes, insurance carrier _____
Do you have health insurance? ❏ No ❏ Yes   If yes, insurance carrier _____
Do you have medicare?   ❏ No ❏ Yes

Medical History
List medications you take (including oral contraceptives, aspirin, over-the-counter medications, and home remedies)
_____
_____
_____

Check any of the following that you have had: ❏ age-related macular degeneration   ❏ inflammatory disorder
❏ cataract   ❏ strabismus   ❏ kerataconus   ❏ amblyopia   ❏ glaucoma suspect   ❏ glaucoma   ❏ surgery
❏ retinal degeneration/hole/detachment   ❏ patching   ❏ eye injury
Are you pregnant and/or nursing?   ❏ No   ❏ Yes
Do you wear glasses?   ❏ No   ❏ Yes   If yes, how old is your present pair of lenses? _____
Do you wear contact lenses?   ❏ No   ❏ Yes   If yes, what brand? _____
Type of contact lenses: ❏ Rigid   ❏ Soft   ❏ Extended Wear   ❏ Other   Are they comfortable? ❏ No ❏ Yes

Family History
Please note any family history (parents, grandparents, siblings, children; living or deceased) for the following conditions:

Disease/Condition	Yes	No	?	Relationship
Thyroid Disease	❏	❏	❏	_____
Diabetes	❏	❏	❏	_____
Hypertension	❏	❏	❏	_____
Cancer	❏	❏	❏	_____
Strabismus	❏	❏	❏	_____
Cataract	❏	❏	❏	_____
Glaucoma Suspect	❏	❏	❏	_____
Amblyopia	❏	❏	❏	_____
Severe Myopia	❏	❏	❏	_____
Macular Degeneration	❏	❏	❏	_____
Retinal Detachment/Disease	❏	❏	❏	_____
Glaucoma	❏	❏	❏	_____
Severe Hyperopia	❏	❏	❏	_____
Other	❏	❏	❏	_____

Social History
– This information is kept strictly confidential. However, you may discuss this portion directly with the doctor if you prefer.
❏ Yes, I prefer to discuss my Social History information directly with the doctor.
Do you drive?   ❏ No   ❏ Yes   If yes, do you have visual difficulty when driving?   ❏ No   ❏ Yes   If yes, please describe:
_____
Do you use tobacco products?   ❏ No   ❏ Yes   If yes, type/amount/how long _____
Are you a   ❏ Former Smoker   ❏ Current Occasional Smoker   ❏ Current Everyday Smoker
Do you drink alcohol?   ❏ No   ❏ Yes   If yes, type/amount/how long _____
Do you use illegal drugs?   ❏ No   ❏ Yes   If yes, type/amount/how long _____

– OVER –

Name _____ Date _____/_____/_____

Review of Systems
Do you currently, or have you ever had, any problems in the following areas:

	Yes	No		Yes	No
Eyes			**Respiratory (continued)**		
Itching	☐	☐	Sleep Apnea	☐	☐
Diplopia	☐	☐	Other_____		
Burning	☐	☐	**Gastrointestinal**		
Mattering	☐	☐	Celiac Disease	☐	☐
Loss of Vision	☐	☐	Crohn's Disease	☐	☐
Photophobia	☐	☐	Ulcer	☐	☐
Red	☐	☐	Colitis	☐	☐
Floaters	☐	☐	Acid Reflux	☐	☐
Loss of Sharpness	☐	☐	Other_____		
Flashes	☐	☐	**Genitourinary**		
Tearing	☐	☐	Kidney Disease	☐	☐
Other_____			STD - Herpetic/Chlamydia	☐	☐
Constitutional			Prostate Disease/Cancer	☐	☐
Developmental Disorders	☐	☐	Pregnant/Nursing	☐	☐
Cancer	☐	☐	Other_____		
Fatigue Syndrome	☐	☐	**Musculoskeletal**		
Other_____			Arthritis	☐	☐
Ear, Nose, Mouth, Throat			Ankylosing Spondylitis	☐	☐
Sinusitis	☐	☐	Fibromyalgia	☐	☐
Dry Mouth	☐	☐	Muscular Dystrophy	☐	☐
Hearing Loss	☐	☐	Osteoarthritis	☐	☐
Laryngitis	☐	☐	Gout	☐	☐
Other_____			Other_____		
Neurological			**Integumentary**		
Epilepsy	☐	☐	Herpes Simplex/Cold Sores	☐	☐
Multiple Seizures	☐	☐	Herpes Zoster/Shingles	☐	☐
Tumor	☐	☐	Rosacea	☐	☐
Cerebral Palsy	☐	☐	Psoriasis	☐	☐
Stroke/CVA	☐	☐	Eczema	☐	☐
Migraine	☐	☐	Other_____		
Other_____			**Endocrine**		
Psychiatric			Diabetes Type II	☐	☐
Depression	☐	☐	Thyroid Dysfunction	☐	☐
Bipolar	☐	☐	Hormonal Dysfunction	☐	☐
Anxiety	☐	☐	Diabetes Type I	☐	☐
Attention Deficit	☐	☐	Other_____		
Other_____			**Hematologic/Lymphatic**		
Vascular/Cardiovascular			Large Volume Blood Loss	☐	☐
Vascular Disease	☐	☐	Anemia	☐	☐
Stroke	☐	☐	Ulcer	☐	☐
Heart Disease	☐	☐	High Cholesterol	☐	☐
High Blood Pressure	☐	☐	Other_____		
Congestive Heart Failure	☐	☐	**Allergic/Immunologic**		
Other_____			Environmental Allergies	☐	☐
Respiratory			Lupus	☐	☐
Cigarette Smoker	☐	☐	Rheumatoid Arthritis	☐	☐
Bronchitis	☐	☐	Drug Allergies	☐	☐
COPD	☐	☐	If yes, what drug?_____		
Emphysema	☐	☐	Sjogrens Syndrome	☐	☐
Asthma	☐	☐	Other_____		

If you answered yes to any of the above, or have a condition not listed, please explain:
_____
_____
_____

Doctor's Signature_____ Date _____/_____/_____

Signature on File Form

• *RESPONSIBILITY STATEMENT* •

Your insurance is a method for you to receive reimbursement for fees you have paid to the optometrist for services rendered. Having insurance is not a substitute for payment. Many companies have fixed allowances or percentages based on your contract with them not with our office. It is your responsibility to pay in advance for the deductible, coinsurance, or any other balances not paid for by your insurance. We will assist you in receiving reimbursement as much as possible, but you are responsible in advance for your bill.

• *FINANCIAL RESPONSIBILITY* •

By signing this statement you agree to be financially responsible for all charges.

• *AUTHORIZATION TO RELEASE MEDICAL INFORMATION* •

I authorize any holder of medical information about me to release to the Health Care Financing Administration and its agents any information needed to determine benefits or the benefits payable for related services. This assignment will remain in effect until revoked in writing. A photocopy of this assignment is considered to be as valid as the original.

Patient Signature_____ Date_____

Witness _____ Date_____

A. Notifier:

B. Patient Name: C. Identification Number:

Advance Beneficiary Notice of Noncoverage (ABN)

NOTE: If Medicare doesn't pay for **D.** ⎯⎯⎯⎯⎯ below, you may have to pay.
Medicare does not pay for everything, even some care that you or your health care provider have good reason to think you need. We expect Medicare may not pay for the **D.** ⎯⎯⎯⎯⎯ below.

D.	E. Reason Medicare May Not Pay:	F. Estimated Cost
Because: Medicare does not pay for the following: ☐ The doctor did not prescribe this item or service as medically necessary. The doctor did not complete the Certificate of Medical Necessity, which is required in order for Medicare to pay for enhancements. ☐ We do not have a Medicare supplier number, therefore, Medicare will not pay for any materials which we furnish to you. ☐ The doctor does not have a Medicare provider number, therefore, Medicare will not pay for an examination. ☐ A lens processing fee. ☐ A refraction.		

WHAT YOU NEED TO DO NOW:
- Read this notice, so you can make an informed decision about your care.
- Ask us any questions that you may have after you finish reading.
- Choose an option below about whether to receive the **D.** ⎯⎯⎯⎯⎯ listed above.
  Note: If you choose Option 1 or 2, we may help you to use any other insurance that you might have, but Medicare cannot require us to do this.

G. OPTIONS: Check only one box. We cannot choose a box for you.

☐ **OPTION 1.** I want the **D.** ⎯⎯⎯⎯⎯ listed above. You may ask to be paid now, but I also want Medicare billed for an official decision on payment, which is sent to me on a Medicare Summary Notice (MSN). I understand that if Medicare doesn't pay, I am responsible for payment, but **I can appeal to Medicare** by following the directions on the MSN. If Medicare does pay, you will refund any payments I made to you, less co-pays or deductibles.

☐ **OPTION 2.** I want the **D.** ⎯⎯⎯⎯⎯ listed above, but do not bill Medicare. You may ask to be paid now as I am responsible for payment. **I cannot appeal if Medicare is not billed.**

☐ **OPTION 3.** I don't want the **D.** ⎯⎯⎯⎯⎯ listed above. I understand with this choice I am **not** responsible for payment, and **I cannot appeal to see if Medicare would pay.**

H. Additional Information:

This notice gives our opinion, not an official Medicare decision. If you have other questions on this notice or Medicare billing, call **1-800-MEDICARE** (1-800-633-4227/**TTY:** 1-877-486-2048).
Signing below means that you have received and understand this notice. You also receive a copy.

I. Signature:	J. Date:

According to the Paperwork Reduction Act of 1995, no persons are required to respond to a collection of information unless it displays a valid OMB control number. The valid OMB control number for this information collection is 0938-0566. The time required to complete this information collection is estimated to average 7 minutes per response, including the time to review instructions, search existing data resources, gather the data needed, and complete and review the information collection. If you have comments concerning the accuracy of the time estimate or suggestions for improving this form, please write to: CMS, 7500 Security Boulevard, Attn: PRA Reports Clearance Officer, Baltimore, Maryland 21244-1850.

Form CMS-R-131 (03/11)   Form Approved OMB No. 0938-0566

BILLING STATEMENT

Company Name
Doctor of Optometry

Address
City, State, Zip
Phone
Miscellaneous (Fax, Email, Etc.)

Patient's Name:_____ DOB:_____ ☐Male ☐Female
Address:_____ City:_____ State:_____ Zip:_____
Telephone:_____ Insured's Name:_____ Insured's DOB:_____
ID Number:_____ Secondary Ins:_____ Total:_____
Date of Service:_____ Refraction Paid:_____
Special Instructions:_____ Co-Pay/Deductible Paid:_____
Ins/Mcaid/Mcare Paid:_____
Secondary Paid:_____
Write Off:_____
Balance Due:_____

MODIFIERS: 24 25 26 50 55 59 79 RT LT E1 E2 E3 E4 1P 2P 8P TC GW QW

MISCELLANEOUS
- ☐ E10.65   Type 1 Diabetes w complications
- ☐ E10.9   Type 1 Diabetes wo complications
- ☐ E11.65   Type 2 Diabetes w complications
- ☐ E11.9   Type 2 Diabetes wo complications
- ☐ H27.0[1 2 3] Aphakia
- ☐ H53.8   Blurred Vision
- ☐ H57.1[1 2 3] Ocular Pain
- ☐ M06.9   Rheumatoid Arthritis
- ☐ Z79.899 High Risk meds
  {1-RT 2-LT 3-Bilateral}

UVEAL DISORDERS
- ☐ H20.01[1 2 3] Primary iridocyclitis
- ☐ H21.0[1 2 3]   Hyphema
- ☐ H21.23[1 2 3] Degeneration of Iris
- ☐ H21.26[1 2 3] Iris Atrophy
- ☐ H21.4[1 2 3]   Pupillary membranes
- ☐ H57.05[1 2 3] Tonic Pupil
  {1-RT 2-LT 3-Bilateral}

EYELIDS
- ☐ H00.023 Hordeolum internum RT eye
- ☐ H00.026 Hordeolum internum LT eye
- ☐ H00.13   Chalazion RT eye
- ☐ H00.16   Chalazion LT eye
- ☐ H01.023 Squamous blepharitis RT eye
- ☐ H01.026 Squamous blepharitis LT eye
- ☐ H01.113 Allergic dermatitis RT eye
- ☐ H01.116 Allergic dermatitis LT eye
- ☐ H02.033 Senile entropion RT eye
- ☐ H02.036 Senile entropion LT eye
- ☐ H02.053 Trichiasis wo entropion RT eye
- ☐ H05.056 Trichiasis wo entropion LT eye
- ☐ H02.133 Senile ectropion RT eye
- ☐ H02.136 Senile ectropion LT eye
- ☐ H02.40[1 2 3] Unspec ptosis of eyelid
- ☐ H02.833 Dermatochalasis RT eye
- ☐ H02.836 Dermatochalasis LT eye
  {1-RT 2-LT 3-Bilateral}

CATARACT/LENS
- ☐ H25.01[1 2 3] Cortical age-related cat
- ☐ H25.04[1 2 3] Post subcap polar age-related cat
- ☐ H25.1[1 2 3]   Age-related nuclear cat
- ☐ H25.89   Other age-related cat
- ☐ Z96.1   Presence of intraocular lens
  {1-RT 2-LT 3-Bilateral}

DISORDER OF REFRACTION
- ☐ H52.0[1 2 3]   Hypermetropia
- ☐ H52.1[1 2 3]   Myopia
- ☐ H52.22[1 2 3] Regular Astigmatism
- ☐ H52.4   Presbyopia
  {1-RT 2-LT 3-Bilateral}

VISUAL DISORDERS
- ☐ H51.11   Convergence insufficiency
- ☐ H51.12   Convergence excess
- ☐ H52.53[1 2 3] Spasm of accommodation
- ☐ H53.02[1 2 3] Refractive amblyopia
- ☐ H53.03[1 2 3] Strabismic amblyopia
- ☐ H53.14[1 2 3] Visual discomfort
- ☐ H53.41[1 2 3] Scotoma involving central area
- ☐ H53.42[1 2 3] Scotoma of blind spot area
- ☐ H53.43[1 2 3] Sector or arcuate defects
- ☐ H53.46[1 2 3] Homonymous bilateral field defects
- ☐ H53.47   Heteronymous bilateral field defects
- ☐ H55.00   Unspec nystagmus
  {1-RT 2-LT 3-Bilateral}

RETINAL DISORDERS
- ☐ E10.31[1 9]   T1 diab w unsp diab rtnop
- ☐ E10.321[1 2 3] T1 diab w mild nonprlf diab rtnop w mac edema
- ☐ E10.329[1 2 3] T1 diab w mild nonprlf diab rtnop wo mac edema
- ☐ E10.331[1 2 3] T1 diab w mod nonprlf diab rtnop w mac edema
- ☐ E10.339[1 2 3] T1 diab w mon nonprlf diab rtnop wo mac edema
- ☐ E10.341[1 2 3] T1 diab w severe nonprlf diab rtnop w mac edema
- ☐ E10.349[1 2 3] T1 diab w severe nonprlf diab rtnop wo mac edema
- ☐ E10.351[1 2 3] T1 diab w prlif diab rtnop w mac edema
- ☐ E10.355[1 2 3] T1 diab w stable prolif diab rtnop
- ☐ E10.359[1 2 3] T1 diab w prlif diab rtnop wo mac edema
- ☐ E11.31[1 9]   T2 diab w unsp diab rtnop
- ☐ E11.321[1 2 3] T2 diab w mild nonprlf diab rtnop w mac edema
- ☐ E11.329[1 2 3] T2 diab w mild nonprlf diab rtnop wo mac edema
- ☐ E11.331[1 2 3] T2 diab w mod nonprlf diab rtnop w mac edema
- ☐ E11.339[1 2 3] T2 diab w mod nonprlf diab rtnop wo mac edema
- ☐ E11.341[1 2 3] T2 diab w severe nonprlf diab rtnop w mac edema
- ☐ E11.349[1 2 3] T2 diab w severe nonprlf diab rtnop wo mac edema
- ☐ E11.351[1 2 3] T2 diab w prolif diab rtnop w mac edema
- ☐ E11.355[1 2 3] T2 diab w stable prolif diab rtnop
- ☐ E11.359[1 2 3] T2 diab w prolif diab rtnop wo mac edema
- ☐ H31.01[1 2 3] Macula scars
- ☐ H31.09[1 2 3] Other chorioretinal scars
- ☐ H32   Chorioretinal disorder
- ☐ H33.01[1 2 3] Retinal detachment w single break
- ☐ H33.31[1 2 3] Horseshoe tear of retina wo detachment
- ☐ H33.32[1 2 3] Round hole
- ☐ H33.8   Other retinal detachments
- ☐ H34.1[1 2 3]   Central retinal artery occlusion
- ☐ H34.21[1 2 3] Partial retinal artery occlusion
- ☐ H35.01[1 2 3] Vascular sheathing
- ☐ H35.03[1 2 3] Hypertensive retinopathy
- ☐ H35.04[1 2 3] Retinal micro-aneurysms
- ☐ H35.35[1 2 3] Cystoid macular degeneration
- ☐ H35.34[1 2 3] Macular cyst, hole or pseudohole
- ☐ H35.36[1 2 3] Drusen (degenerative) of macula
- ☐ H35.37[1 2 3] Puckering of macule, ERM
- ☐ H35.40   Unspec peripheral retinal degeneration
- ☐ H35.41[1 2 3] Lattice degeneration of retina
- ☐ H35.71[1 2 3] Central serous chorioretinopathy
- ☐ H35.82   Retinal ischemia
- ☐ H43.31[1 2 3] Vitreous membranes
- ☐ H43.81[1 2 3] Viterous degeneration
  RT LT BL   {RT-Right LT-Left BL-Bilateral}
- ☐ H34.81{10 20 30} Central retinal vein occlusion w mac edema
- ☐ H34.81[11 21 31] Central retinal vein occlusion w retinal neovascularization
- ☐ H34.81[12 22 32] Central retinal vein occlusion, stable
- ☐ H34.83[10 20 30] Tributary retinal vein occlusion w mac edema
- ☐ H34.83[11 21 31] Tributary retinal vein occlusion w retinal neovascularization
- ☐ H34.83[12 22 32] Tributary retinal vein occlusion, stable
- ☐ H35.31[11 21 31] Nonexudative ARMD, early dry stage
- ☐ H35.31[12 22 32] Nonexudative ARMD, intermediate dry stage
- ☐ H35.31[13 23 33] Nonexudative ARMD, advanced atropic wo subfoveal inv
- ☐ H35.31[14 24 34] Nonexudative ARMD, advanced atropic w subfoveal inv
- ☐ H35.32[11 21 31] Exudative ARMD, active chorodial neovascularization
- ☐ H35.32[12 22 32] Exudative ARMD, inactive chorodial neovascularization
- ☐ H35.32[13 23 33] Exudative ARMD, inactive scar
  {1-RT 2-LT 3-Bilateral}
  {1-With Edema 9-Without Edema}

LACRIMAL SYSTEM
- ☐ H04.01[1 2 3] Acute dacryoadenitis
- ☐ H04.12[1 2 3] Dry eye syndrome
- ☐ H04.21[1 2 3] Epiphora due to excess lacrimation
  {1-RT 2-LT 3-Bilateral}

GLAUCOMA
- ☐ H40.01[1 2 3] Open angle w borderline findings low risk
- ☐ H40.02[1 2 3] Open angle w borderline findings high risk
- ☐ H40.05[1 2 3] Ocular hypertension
- ☐ H40.06[1 2 3] Primary angle closure wo glaucoma damage
- ☐ H40.21[1 2 3] Acute angle-closure glaucoma
  RT LT BL   {RT-Right LT-Left BL-Bilateral}
- ☐ H40.11[11 21 31] Primary open-angle glaucoma, mild
- ☐ H40.11[12 22 32] Primary open-angle glaucoma, mod
- ☐ H40.11[13 23 33] Primary open-angle glaucoma, severe
- ☐ H40.11[14 24 34] Primary open-angle glaucoma, indeterminate
- ☐ H40.12[11 21 31] Low-tens glaucoma, mild stage
- ☐ H40.12[12 22 32] Low-tens glaucoma, mod stage
- ☐ H40.12[13 23 33] Low-tens glaucoma, severe stage
- ☐ H40.13[11 21 31] Pigmentary glaucoma, mild stage
- ☐ H40.13[12 22 32] Pigmentary glaucoma, mod stage
- ☐ H40.13[13 23 33] Pigmentary glaucoma, severe stage
- ☐ H40.22[11 21 31] Chronic angle-closure glaucoma, mild stage
- ☐ H40.22[12 22 32] Chronic angle-closure glaucoma, mod stage
- ☐ H40.22[13 23 33] Chronic angle-closure glaucoma, severe stage
  {1-RT 2-LT 3-Bilateral}

NEURO-OPHTHALMOLOGY
- ☐ H46.1[1 2 3]   Retrobulbar neuritis
- ☐ H47.01[1 2 3] Ischemic optic neuropathy
- ☐ H47.1[1 2 3]   Papilledema assoc. w increased intracranial pressure
- ☐ H47.21[1 2 3] Primary optic atrophy
- ☐ H47.32[1 2 3] Drusen of optic disc
  {1-RT 2-LT 3-Bilateral}

CONJUNCTIVA
- ☐ B30.0   Viral conjunctivitis
- ☐ H10.3[1 2 3]   Acute conjunctivitis
- ☐ H10.41[1 2 3] Chronic giant papillary conjunctivitis
- ☐ H10.43[1 2 3] Chronic follicular conjunctivitis
- ☐ H11.05[1 2 3] Peripheral pterygium, progressive
- ☐ H11.12[1 2 3] Conjunctival concretions
- ☐ H11.15[1 2 3] Pinguecula
- ☐ H11.3[1 2 3]   Conjunctival hemorrhage
- ☐ S05.01X[A D S] Inj conjunctiva & corneal abrasion wo fb, RT, init
- ☐ S05.02X[A D S] Inj conjunctiva & corneal abrasion wo fb, LT, init
- ☐ T15.11X[A D S] Foreign body in conjunctival sac, RT, init
- ☐ T15.12X[A D S] Foreign body in conjunctival sac, LT init
  {1-RT 2-LT 3-Bilateral}
  {A-Initial D-Subsequent S-Sequela}

CORNEA
- ☐ H16.00[1 2 3] Unspec corneal ulcer
- ☐ H16.01[1 2 3] Central corneal ulcer
- ☐ H16.04[1 2 3] Marginal corneal ulcer
- ☐ H16.12[1 2 3] Filamentary keratitis
- ☐ H16.14[1 2 3] Punctate keratitis
- ☐ H16.42[1 2 3] Pannus (corneal)
- ☐ H18.22[1 2 3] Idiopathic corneal edema
- ☐ H18.41[1 2 3] Arcus senilis
- ☐ H18.51   Endothelial corneal dystrophies
- ☐ H18.59   Other hereditary corneal dystrophies
- ☐ H18.82[1 2 3] Corneal edema due to contact lens
- ☐ H18.83[1 2 3] Recurrent erosion of cornea
- ☐ T15.01X[A D S] Foreign body in cornea, RT, initial
- ☐ T15.02X[A D S] Foreign body in cornea, LT, initial
  {1-RT 2-LT 3-Bilateral}
  {A- Initial D-Subsequent S-Sequela}

STRABISMUS
- ☐ H50.00   Unspec esotropia
- ☐ H50.10   Unspec exotropia

RT-Right LT-Left

Fee
☐ S0620	_____
☐ S0621	_____
☐ 65210	_____ ♦
☐ 65222	_____ ♦
☐ 65430	_____
☐ 65435	_____
☐ 67820	_____
☐ 67938	_____ ♦
☐ 68761	_____
☐ 68801	_____ ♦
☐ 76510	_____
☐ 76514	_____
☐ 83516QW	_____
☐ 83861QW	_____
☐ 87809QW	_____
☐ 92002	_____
☐ 92004	_____
☐ 92012	_____
☐ 92014	_____
☐ 92015	_____ +
☐ 92020	_____
☐ 92025	_____
☐ 92060	_____
☐ 92071	_____
☐ 92072	_____
☐ 92082	_____
☐ 92083	_____
☐ 92100	_____
☐ 92132	_____
☐ 92133	_____
☐ 92134	_____
☐ 92225	_____ ♦
☐ 92226	_____ ♦
☐ 92250	_____
☐ 92274	_____
☐ 92285	_____
☐ 92286	_____
☐ 92310	_____ +
☐ 95930	_____
☐ 99201	_____
☐ 99202	_____
☐ 99203	_____
☐ 99204	_____
☐ 99205	_____
☐ 99212	_____
☐ 99213	_____
☐ 99214	_____
☐ 99215	_____

♦ May require modifier
+ Not paid by MC

☐ 5010F	☐ G8428
☐ G8397	☐ 4004F
☐ G8398	☐ 1036F
☐ 2022F	☐ G8783
☐ 2024F	☐ G8950
☐ 2026F	☐ G8784
☐ 3072F	☐ G8785
☐ 2019F	☐ G8951
☐ 4177F	☐ G8952
☐ 2027F	☐ G8730
☐ 3284F	☐ G8731
☐ 3285F	☐ G8442
☐ 0517F	☐ G8939
☐ G8427	☐ G8732
☐ G8430	☐ G8509

Revised 08/16

Supplementary Tests

15

Patient_____ Date_____
- ☐ **Visual Fields** (92081, 92082, 92083)
- ☐ **Sensorimotor Examination** (92060)
- ☐ **Scanning Computerized Ophthalmic Diagnostic Imaging** (92132, 92133, 92134) ☐ HRT ☐ OCT ☐ GDX
- ☐ **Serial Tonometry** (92100)
- ☐ **Visual Evoked Potential** (95930)
- ☐ **Gonioscopy** (92020)
- ☐ **Fundus Photography** (92250)
- ☐ **External Ocular Photography** (92285)
- ☐ **Corneal Topography** (92025)
- ☐ **Pattern Electroretinography** (92275)
- ☐ **Specular Microscopy** (92286)

OD OS

Findings_____ _____
_____ _____
_____ _____

Diagnosis_____ _____
_____ _____
_____ _____

Plan_____ _____
_____ _____
_____ _____
_____ _____

Signature_____ _____

Extended Ophthalmoscopy (92225, 92226)

☐ 78D Lens ☐ 90D Lens ☐ 20D Lens ☐ 2.2D Lens ☐ 3-Mirror ☐ Scleral depression

OD OS

Findings_____ _____
Diagnosis_____ _____
Plan_____ _____
_____ _____

Signature_____ _____

Rev. 4/14

GLAUCOMA FLOW SHEET

Name _____ DOB _____

Pharmacy _____ Phone Number _____

Type _____ CCT: Thick/Avg/Thin c/d _____

Risk Factors _____

Target IOP _____

Date	IOP	VF	DFE	GON	Pho	CCT	Scan Laser	VEP	Comments / Results	Referral	**MEDS**/Start/ Δ

A Pt advised to notify family members of risk. Date _____

Rev. 1/15

Confirmation of Post-operative Co-Management Arrangement

Patient Confirmation

It is my desire to have my own optometrist, Dr._____ perform my post-operative follow-up care after my cataract surgery. I understand that my optometrist will contact my ophthalmologist immediately if I experience any complications related to my eye surgery.

_____   _____
Patient   Date

_____   _____
Witness   Date

Optometrist Confirmation

I have agreed to provide follow-up care for _____. I will see the patient after surgery when Dr._____ notifies me that he/she is releasing the patient to my care. I agree to notify Dr._____ immediately should complication arise and to provide written progress reports regularly during my portion of the post-operative period.

_____   _____
Optometrist   Date

Rev. 11/11

Example #1
Diabetic Retinopathy

• DIABETIC RETINOPATHY •
PAGE 1

EXAMINATION

Example #1

Patient: Jan Doe Date: 10-03-10 Sex: M/(F) DOB: 04-19-33 Age: ___ Last Exam: 1 year
Chief Complaint: Referred by doctor for diabetic eye exam

History
HPI: NID diabetes x 9 year
Tx by Dr. Jones, M.D.
Symptoms: Blood sugar well controlled
Location
Quality: Taking Metformin
Severity: Last A1C - 7.2
Duration
Timing
Context
Modifiers

Allergies
Medications
Ocular ROS
Medical History & ROS from ___/___/___ reviewed: ☐ no changes
Dr. Initials ___

Examination
Head/Face ☑ nl   Psych: Mood/Affect (anxiety/depression) ☑ nl   Neuro: Oriented (person/time/place) ☑ y ☐ n

VA: sc<   cc< 30/40   ph<   near<

K: OD ___ OS ___
OLD RX: OD ___ OS ___
R-scopy: OD ___ OS ___
REF: OD +2.25 -1.75 X 180 20/20 add +2.50
       OS +2.00 -1.25 X 175 20/25 add ___

Perimetry: ☑ nl CF ☐ nl   Color ☐ nl ☐ RG defect   **ADNEXA** ☑ nl
Motility: ☑ Full   Stereo Animals /3 WD /9   **EYELIDS:** ☐ Blepharitis OD OS OU
Cover Test: ☐ Eso ___   ☐ Exo ___   ☑ Ortho   ☐ Meibomianitis OD OS OU

Pupils: ☑ no afferent defect   ☑ round OU   Size: OD 4 OS 4   ☐ 20D
☐ 90D/78D
☐ 3 Mirror
☐ ___

- macular edema (OD)   - macular edema (OS)

SLE: OD
☑ nl
☑ nl ☐ arcus
☑ nl ☐ pterygium
☑ nl ☐ infiltrate
☑ nl ☐ spk
☑ nl ☐
☑ nl ☐ injection
☑ nl ☐ pinguecula
☑ D&Q ☐
☑ nl ☐ rubeosis
☐ clear ☑ cat ☐ ns

TEAR FILM / CORNEA / SCLERA / CONJ. / AC / IRIS / LENS

OS
☑ nl ☐ FBUT:____
☑ nl ☐ arcus
☑ nl ☐ pterygium
☑ nl ☐ infiltrate
☑ nl ☐ spk
☑ nl
☑ nl ☐ injection
☑ nl ☐ pinguecula
☑ D&Q ☐
☑ nl ☐ rubeosis
☐ clear ☑ cat ☐ ns

RETINA: OD
☑ nl ☐ drusen   MACULA
☑ nl ☐ RPE chgs
☑ nl ☐ cotton wool POST POLE
☐ nl ☑ hemes
☑ nl ☐ DME
☑ nl ☐   VESSELS
☑ nl ☐ PVD   VITREOUS
☑ nl ☐ strands
☑ nl ☐   PERIPHERY

OS
☑ nl ☐ drusen
☑ nl ☐ RPE chgs
☑ nl ☐ cotton wool
☐ nl ☑ hemes
☑ nl ☐ DME
☑ nl ☐
☑ nl ☐ PVD
☑ nl ☐ strands
☑ nl ☐

OPTIC DISCS: OD
☑ nl
☐ .4/.4 C/D
SIZE/APPEARANCE/NFL
OS
☑ nl
☐ .4/.4

NCT / @   **Pachymetry:** OD ___
TAG 16/16 @ 9:43 am   OS ___
Dilated: M .5% 1% (PA 1%/0.25%) C 1% 2% Ph 2.5% 10% OU @ 9:51 am

Diagnosis/Plan MDM 1 2 (3) 4

NID diabetes
Mild non proliferative diabetic retinopathy
Cataracts OU

Letter sent to Dr. Jones
Order VF, photos, Full Field ERG, gonioscopy today
Order OCT mac cube, 5 line raster 1 week

(Order:) ☑ HRT/GDX/OCT   RTO: ___ day
☑ Photo   1 week
☐ VF   ___ month
☐ Consult   ___ year

Dr. E. Botts

Rev.11/11 ©2007 - E. Botts, O.D.

• DIABETIC RETINOPATHY •
PAGE 2
EXAMINATION
Supplementary Tests

Patient: Jan Doe Date: 10-03-10

Fundus Photography (92250)

OD
- Findings: Dot blot hemes
- Diagnosis: neg macular edema
- Plan: Mild non proliferative diabetic retinopathy - Monitor 6 months
- Signature: E. Botts

OS
- Findings: Dot blot hemes
- Diagnosis: neg macular edema
- Plan: Mild non proliferative diabetic retinopathy - Monitor 6 months

Gonioscopy (92020)

OD
- Findings: Neg neovascularization
- Diagnosis: in angles/iris
- Plan: Mild non proliferative diabetic retinopathy - Monitor 6 months
- Signature: E. Botts

OS
- Findings: Neg neovascularization
- Diagnosis: in angles/iris
- Plan: Mild non proliferative diabetic retinopathy - Monitor 6 months

Visual Fields (92081, 92082, (92083))

OD
- Findings: No defect
- Diagnosis: Good responder
- Plan: Mild non proliferative diabetic retinopathy
- Signature: E. Botts

OS
- Findings: No defect
- Diagnosis: Good responder
- Plan: Mild non proliferative diabetic retinopathy

Electroretinography ((92273) Full Field, 92274 Multifocal, 0509T Pattern)

OD
- Findings: Reduced retinal receptor cell response
- Diagnosis: Mild non proliferative diabetic retinopathy
- Plan: Monitor 6 months
- Signature: E. Botts

OS
- Findings: Reduced retinal receptor cell response
- Diagnosis: Mild non proliferative diabetic retinopathy
- Plan: Monitor 6 months

Rev. 8/15 ©2007 - E. Botts, O.D.

BILLING STATEMENT

• DIABETIC RETINOPATHY •
PAGE 3

Dr. Eric Botts
Phone 309/836-3373

Date of Service **10 / 03 / 10**
Patient's Name **Jan Doe**   DOB **04 / 19 / 33**   ☐ Male ☑ Female
Address **2100 RedBud St.**   City **Smithville**   State **IL**   Zip **69321**
Telephone (___) ___-____   Insured's Name _____   Insured's DOB ___/___/___
ID Number **349 27 8567A**   Secondary Ins **BCBS**   Total **457.08**
Special Instructions _____
                    Refraction Paid **18.00**
                    Co-Pay/Deductible Paid _____
                    Ins/Mcaid/Mcare Paid _____
                    Secondary Paid _____
                    Write Off _____
                    Balance Due _____

MODIFIERS 24 25 26 50 55 59 79 RT LT E1 E2 E3 E4 1P 2P 8P TC GW QW

MISCELLANEOUS
- ☐ E10.65   Type 1 Diabetes w complications
- ☐ E10.9   Type 1 Diabetes wo complications
- ☐ E11.65   Type 2 Diabetes w complications
- ☐ E11.9   Type 2 Diabetes wo complications
- ☐ H27.0 [1 2 3] Aphakia
- ☐ H53.8   Blurred Vision
- ☐ H57.1 [1 2 3] Ocular Pain
- ☐ M06.9   Rheumatoid Arthritis
- ☐ Z79.4   Insulin Dependent
- ☑ Z79.84 Non-Insulin Dependent
- ☐ Z79.899 High Risk meds

(1-RT 2-LT 3-Bilateral)

UVEAL DISORDERS
- ☐ H20.01 [1 2 3] Primary iridocyclitis
- ☐ H21.0 [1 2 3] Hyphema
- ☐ H21.23 [1 2 3] Degeneration of Iris
- ☐ H21.26 [1 2 3] Iris Atrophy
- ☐ H21.4 [1 2 3] Pupillary membranes
- ☐ H57.05 [1 2 3] Tonic Pupil

(1-RT 2-LT 3-Bilateral)

EYELIDS
- ☐ H00.023 Hordeolum internum RT eye
- ☐ H00.026 Hordeolum internum LT eye
- ☐ H00.13   Chalazion RT eye
- ☐ H00.16   Chalazion LT eye
- ☐ H01.023 Squamous blepharitis RT eye
- ☐ H01.026 Squamous blepharitis LT eye
- ☐ H01.113 Allergic dermatitis RT eye
- ☐ H01.116 Allergic dermatitis LT eye
- ☐ H02.033 Senile entropion RT eye
- ☐ H02.036 Senile entropion LT eye
- ☐ H02.053 Trichiasis wo entropion RT eye
- ☐ H05.056 Trichiasis wo entropion LT eye
- ☐ H02.133 Senile ectropion RT eye
- ☐ H02.136 Senile ectropion LT eye
- ☐ H02.40 [1 2 3] Unspec ptosis of eyelid
- ☐ H02.833 Dermatochalasis RT eye
- ☐ H02.836 Dermatochalasis LT eye

(1-RT 2-LT 3-Bilateral)

CATARACT/LENS
- ☐ H25.01 [1 2 3] Cortical age-related cat
- ☑ H25.04 [1 ② 3] Post subcap polar age-related cat
- ☐ H25.1 [1 2 3] Age-related nuclear cat
- ☐ H25.89 Other age-related cat
- ☐ Z96.1   Presence of intraocular lens

(1-RT 2-LT 3-Bilateral)

DISORDER OF REFRACTION
- ☐ H52.0 [1 2 3] Hypermetropia
- ☐ H52.1 [1 2 3] Myopia
- ☐ H52.22 [1 2 3] Regular Astigmatism
- ☐ H52.4   Presbyopia

(1-RT 2-LT 3-Bilateral)

VISUAL DISORDERS
- ☐ H51.11 Convergence insufficiency
- ☐ H51.12 Convergence excess
- ☐ H52.53 [1 2 3] Spasm of accommodation
- ☐ H53.02 [1 2 3] Refractive amblyopia
- ☐ H53.03 [1 2 3] Strabismic amblyopia
- ☐ H53.14 [1 2 3] Visual discomfort
- ☐ H53.41 [1 2 3] Scotoma involving central area
- ☐ H53.42 [1 2 3] Scotoma of blind spot area
- ☐ H53.43 [1 2 3] Sector or arcuate defects
- ☐ H53.46 [1 2 3] Homonymous bilateral field defects
- ☐ H53.47 Heteronymous bilateral field defects
- ☐ H55.00 Unspec nystagmus

(1-RT 2-LT 3-Bilateral)

©2017 - E. Botts, O.D.

RETINAL DISORDERS
- ☐ E10.31 [1 9]   T1 diab w unsp diab rtnop
- ☐ E10.321 [1 2 3] T1 diab w mild nonprlf diab rtnop w mac edema
- ☐ E10.329 [1 2 3] T1 diab w mild nonprlf diab rtnop wo mac edema
- ☐ E10.331 [1 2 3] T1 diab w mod nonprlf diab rtnop w mac edema
- ☐ E10.339 [1 2 3] T1 diab w mon nonprlf diab rtnop wo mac edema
- ☐ E10.341 [1 2 3] T1 diab w severe nonprlf diab rtnop w mac edema
- ☐ E10.349 [1 2 3] T1 diab w severe nonprlf diab rtnop wo mac edema
- ☐ E10.351 [1 2 3] T1 diab w prlif diab rtnop w mac edema
- ☐ E10.355 [1 2 3] T1 diab w stable prolif diab rtnop
- ☐ E10.359 [1 2 3] T1 diab w prlif diab rtnop wo mac edema
- ☐ E11.31 [1 9]   T2 diab w unsp diab rtnop
- ☐ E11.321 [1 2 3] T2 diab w mild nonprlf diab rtnop w mac edema
- ☑ E11.329 [1 ② 3] T2 diab w mild nonprlf diab rtnop wo mac edema
- ☐ E11.331 [1 2 3] T2 diab w mod nonprlf diab rtnop w mac edema
- ☐ E11.339 [1 2 3] T2 diab w mod nonprlf diab rtnop wo mac edema
- ☐ E11.341 [1 2 3] T2 diab w severe nonprlf diab rtnop w mac edema
- ☐ E11.349 [1 2 3] T2 diab w severe nonprlf diab rtnop wo mac edema
- ☐ E11.351 [1 2 3] T2 diab w prlif diab rtnop w mac edema
- ☐ E11.355 [1 2 3] T2 diab w stable prolif diab rtnop
- ☐ E11.359 [1 2 3] T2 diab w prlif diab rtnop wo mac edema
- ☐ H31.01 [1 9]   Macula scars
- ☐ H31.09 [1 2 3] Other chorioretinal scars
- ☐ H32   Chorioretinal disorder
- ☐ H33.01 [1 2 3] Retinal detachment w single break
- ☐ H33.31 [1 2 3] Horseshoe tear of retina wo detachment
- ☐ H33.32 [1 2 3] Round hole
- ☐ H33.8 Other retinal detachments
- ☐ H34.1 [1 2 3] Central retinal artery occlusion
- ☐ H34.21 [1 2 3] Partial retinal artery occlusion
- ☐ H35.01 [1 2 3] Vascular sheathing
- ☐ H35.03 [1 2 3] Hypertensive retinopathy
- ☐ H35.04 [1 2 3] Retinal micro-aneurysms
- ☐ H35.34 [1 2 3] Macular cyst, hole or pseudohole
- ☐ H35.35 [1 2 3] Cystoid macular degeneration
- ☐ H35.36 [1 2 3] Drusen (degenerative) of macula
- ☐ H35.37 [1 2 3] Puckering of macule, ERM
- ☐ H35.40 Unspec peripheral retinal degeneration
- ☐ H35.41 [1 2 3] Lattice degeneration of retina
- ☐ H35.71 [1 2 3] Central serous chorioretinopathy
- ☐ H35.82 Retinal ischemia
- ☐ H43.31 [1 2 3] Viterous membranes
- ☐ H43.81 [1 2 3] Viterous degeneration

RT LT BI (RT-Right LT-Left BI-Bilateral)

- ☐ H34.81 [10 20 30] Central retinal vein occlusion w mac edema
- ☐ H34.81 [11 21 31] Central retinal vein occlusion w retinal neovascularization
- ☐ H34.81 [12 22 32] Central retinal vein occlusion, stable
- ☐ H34.83 [10 20 30] Tributary retinal vein occlusion w mac edema
- ☐ H34.83 [11 21 31] Tributary retinal vein occlusion w retinal neovascularization
- ☐ H34.83 [12 22 32] Tributary retinal vein occlusion, stable
- ☐ H35.31 [11 21 31] Nonexudative ARMD, early dry stage
- ☐ H35.31 [12 22 32] Nonexudative ARMD, intermediate dry stage
- ☐ H35.31 [13 23 33] Nonexudative ARMD, advanced atropic wo subfoveal inv
- ☐ H35.31 [14 24 34] Nonexudative ARMD, advanced atropic w subfoveal inv
- ☐ H35.32 [11 21 31] Exudative ARMD, active chorodial neovascularization
- ☐ H35.32 [12 22 32] Exudative ARMD, inactive chorodial neovascularization
- ☐ H35.32 [13 23 33] Exudative ARMD, inactive scar

(1-RT 2-LT 3-Bilateral)
(1-With Edema 9-Without Edema)

LACRIMAL SYSTEM
- ☐ H04.01 [1 2 3] Acute dacryoadenitis
- ☐ H04.12 [1 2 3] Dry eye syndrome
- ☐ H04.21 [1 2 3] Epiphora due to excess lacrimation

(1-RT 2-LT 3-Bilateral)

GLAUCOMA
- ☐ H40.01 [1 2 3] Open angle w borderline findings low risk
- ☐ H40.02 [1 2 3] Open angle w borderline findings high risk
- ☐ H40.05 [1 2 3] Ocular hypertension
- ☐ H40.06 [1 2 3] Primary angle closure wo glaucoma damage
- ☐ H40.21 [1 2 3] Acute angle-closure glaucoma

RT LT BI (RT-Right LT-Left BI-Bilateral)

- ☐ H40.11 [11 21 31] Primary open-angle glaucoma, mild
- ☐ H40.11 [12 22 32] Primary open-angle glaucoma, mod
- ☐ H40.11 [13 23 33] Primary open-angle glaucoma, severe
- ☐ H40.11 [14 24 34] Primary open-angle glaucoma, indeterminate
- ☐ H40.12 [11 21 31] Low-tens glaucoma, mild stage
- ☐ H40.12 [12 22 32] Low-tens glaucoma, mod stage
- ☐ H40.12 [13 23 33] Low-tens glaucoma, severe stage
- ☐ H40.13 [11 21 31] Pigmentary glaucoma, mild stage
- ☐ H40.13 [12 22 32] Pigmentary glaucoma, mod stage
- ☐ H40.13 [13 23 33] Pigmentary glaucoma, severe stage
- ☐ H40.22 [11 21 31] Chronic angle-closure glaucoma, mild stage
- ☐ H40.22 [12 22 32] Chronic angle-closure glaucoma, mod stage
- ☐ H40.22 [13 23 33] Chronic angle-closure glaucoma, severe stage

(1-RT 2-LT 3-Bilateral)

NEURO-OPHTHALMOLOGY
- ☐ H46.1 [1 2 3] Retrobulbar neuritis
- ☐ H47.01 [1 2 3] Ischemic optic neuropathy
- ☐ H47.1 [1 2 3] Papilledema assc w increased intracranial pressure
- ☐ H47.21 [1 2 3] Primary optic atrophy
- ☐ H47.32 [1 2 3] Drusen of optic disc

(1-RT 2-LT 3-Bilateral)

CONJUNCTIVA
- ☐ B30.0   Viral conjunctivitis
- ☐ H10.3 [1 2 3] Acute conjunctivitis
- ☐ H10.41 [1 2 3] Chronic giant papillary conjunctivitis
- ☐ H10.43 [1 2 3] Chronic follicular conjunctivitis
- ☐ H11.05 [1 2 3] Peripheral pterygium, progressive
- ☐ H11.12 [1 2 3] Conjunctival concretions
- ☐ H11.15 [1 2 3] Pinguecula
- ☐ H11.3   Conjunctival hemorrhage
- ☐ S05.01X [A D S] Inj conjunctiva & corneal abrasion wo fb, RT, init
- ☐ S05.02X [A D S] Inj conjunctiva & corneal abrasion wo fb, LT, init
- ☐ T15.11X [A D S] Foreign body in conjunctival sac, RT, init
- ☐ T15.12X [A D S] Foreign body in conjunctival sac, LT init

(1-RT 2-LT 3-Bilateral)
(A-Initial D-Subsequent S-Sequela)

CORNEA
- ☐ H16.00 [1 2 3] Unspec corneal ulcer
- ☐ H16.01 [1 2 3] Central corneal ulcer
- ☐ H16.04 [1 2 3] Marginal corneal ulcer
- ☐ H16.12 [1 2 3] Filamentary keratitis
- ☐ H16.14 [1 2 3] Punctate keratitis
- ☐ H16.42 [1 2 3] Pannus (corneal)
- ☐ H18.22 [1 2 3] Idiopathic corneal edema
- ☐ H18.41 [1 2 3] Arcus senilis
- ☐ H18.51 Endothelial corneal dystrophie
- ☐ H18.59 Other hereditary corneal dystrophies
- ☐ H18.82 [1 2 3] Corneal edema due to contact lens
- ☐ H18.83 [1 2 3] Recurrent erosion of cornea
- ☐ T15.01X [A D S] Foreign body in cornea, RT, initial
- ☐ T15.02X [A D S] Foreign body in cornea, LT, initial

(1-RT 2-LT 3-Bilateral)
(A-Initial D-Subsequent S-Sequela)

STRABISMUS
- ☐ H50.00 Unspec esotropia
- ☐ H50.10 Unspec exotropia

(RT-Right LT-Left)

FEE
- ☐ S0620 _____
- ☐ S0621 _____
- ☐ 65210 _____ *
- ☐ 65222 _____ *
- ☐ 65430 _____ *
- ☐ 65435 _____ *
- ☐ 65778 _____ *
- ☐ 67820 _____ *
- ☐ 67938 _____ *
- ☐ 68761 _____ *
- ☐ 68801 _____ *
- ☐ 76510 _____
- ☐ 76514 _____
- ☐ 83516QW _____
- ☐ 83861QW _____
- ☐ 87809QW _____
- ☐ 92002 _____
- ☐ 92004 _____
- ☐ 92012 _____
- ☐ 92014 _____
- ☑ 92015 **18 00** +
- ☑ 92020 **24 40**
- ☐ 92025 _____ *
- ☐ 92060 _____
- ☐ 92071 _____
- ☐ 92072 _____
- ☐ 92082 _____
- ☑ 92083 **72 94**
- ☐ 92100 _____
- ☐ 92132 _____
- ☐ 92133 _____
- ☐ 92134 _____
- ☐ 92225 _____ *
- ☐ 92226 _____ *
- ☑ 92250 **64 57**
- ☑ 92273 **127 42**
- ☐ 92284 _____
- ☐ 92285 _____
- ☐ 92286 _____
- ☐ 92310 _____ +
- ☐ 95930 _____
- ☐ 99201 _____
- ☐ 99202 _____
- ☐ 99203 _____
- ☑ 99204 **149 75**
- ☐ 99205 _____
- ☐ 99212 _____
- ☐ 99213 _____
- ☐ 99214 _____
- ☐ 99215 _____

* May Require Modifier
+ Not Paid by MC

☐ 5010F	☐ G8428
☐ G8397	☐ 4004F
☐ G8398	☐ 1036F
☐ 2022F	☐ G8783
☐ 2024F	☐ G8950
☐ 2026F	☐ G8784
☐ 3072F	☐ G8785
☐ 2019F	☐ G8951
☐ 4177F	☐ G8952
☐ 2027F	☐ G8730
☐ 3284F	☐ G8731
☐ 3285F	☐ G8442
☐ 0517F	☐ G8939
☐ G8427	☐ G8732
☐ G8430	☐ G8509

v2.1 Revised 3/6/17

• DIABETIC RETINOPATHY •
PAGE 4

ICD-10

HEALTH INSURANCE CLAIM FORM
APPROVED BY NATIONAL UNIFORM CLAIM COMMITTEE (NUCC) 02/12

PICA		PICA
1. MEDICARE ☐ MEDICAID ☐ TRICARE ☐ CHAMPVA ☐ GROUP HEALTH PLAN ☐ FECA BLK LUNG ☐ OTHER ☐	1a. INSURED'S I.D. NUMBER (For Program in Item 1)	349 27 8567A
2. PATIENT'S NAME: Doe, Jan	3. PATIENT'S BIRTH DATE: 04 / 19 / 33 SEX: F ✓	4. INSURED'S NAME
5. PATIENT'S ADDRESS: 2100 Red Bud St.	6. PATIENT RELATIONSHIP TO INSURED: Self ✓	7. INSURED'S ADDRESS
CITY: Smithville STATE: IL	8. RESERVED FOR NUCC USE	CITY STATE
ZIP CODE: 69321 TELEPHONE: ( )		ZIP CODE TELEPHONE: ( )
9. OTHER INSURED'S NAME	10. IS PATIENT'S CONDITION RELATED TO:	11. INSURED'S POLICY GROUP OR FECA NUMBER: None
a. OTHER INSURED'S POLICY OR GROUP NUMBER	a. EMPLOYMENT? ☐ YES ☐ NO	a. INSURED'S DATE OF BIRTH SEX M ☐ F ☐
b. RESERVED FOR NUCC USE	b. AUTO ACCIDENT? ☐ YES ☐ NO PLACE (State)	b. OTHER CLAIM ID
c. RESERVED FOR NUCC USE	c. OTHER ACCIDENT? ☐ YES ☐ NO	c. INSURANCE PLAN NAME OR PROGRAM NAME
d. INSURANCE PLAN NAME OR PROGRAM NAME	10d. CLAIM CODES	d. IS THERE ANOTHER HEALTH BENEFIT PLAN? ☐ YES ☐ NO

READ BACK OF FORM BEFORE COMPLETING & SIGNING THIS FORM.

12. PATIENT'S OR AUTHORIZED PERSON'S SIGNATURE SIGNED: SOF DATE: 10-03-10

13. INSURED'S OR AUTHORIZED PERSON'S SIGNATURE SIGNED: _____

14. DATE OF CURRENT ILLNESS, INJURY, or PREGNANCY (LMP) QUAL.
15. OTHER DATE QUAL. MM DD YY
16. DATES PATIENT UNABLE TO WORK FROM _ TO _
17. NAME OF REFERRING PROVIDER OR OTHER SOURCE: DK | Eric Botts
17b. NPI: Individual NPI#
18. HOSPITALIZATION DATES: FROM _ TO _
19. ADDITIONAL CLAIM INFORMATION
20. OUTSIDE LAB? ☐ YES ☐ NO $ CHARGES

21. DIAGNOSIS OR NATURE OF ILLNESS OR INJURY ICD Ind. 10
A. Z79.84 B. E11.3293 C. H25.043 D. _
E. _ F. _ G. _ H. _
I. _ J. _ K. _ L. _

22. RESUBMISSION CODE ORIGINAL REF. NO.
23. PRIOR AUTHORIZATION NUMBER

#	DATE(S) OF SERVICE From — To	PLACE OF SERVICE	EMG	CPT/HCPCS	MODIFIER	DIAGNOSIS POINTER	$ CHARGES	DAYS/UNITS	EPSDT	ID QUAL	RENDERING PROVIDER ID. #
1	10 03 10 — 10 03 10	11		99204		ABC	149 75	1		NPI	Individual NPI #
2	10 03 10 — 10 03 10	11		92250		B	64 57	1		NPI	Individual NPI #
3	10 03 10 — 10 03 10	11		92020		B	24 40	1		NPI	Individual NPI #
4	10 03 10 — 10 03 10	11		92083		B	72 94	1		NPI	Individual NPI #
5	10 03 10 — 10 03 10	11		92015		C	18 00	1		NPI	Individual NPI #
6	10 03 10 — 10 03 10	11		99273		B	127 42	1		NPI	Individual NPI #

25. FEDERAL TAX I.D. NUMBER: 411743621 EIN ✓
26. PATIENT'S ACCOUNT NO.
27. ACCEPT ASSIGNMENT? YES ✓
28. TOTAL CHARGE: $ 457.08
29. AMOUNT PAID: $ 0
30. Rsvd for NUCC Use: 457.08

31. SIGNATURE OF PHYSICIAN OR SUPPLIER: E. Botts 10-03-10
32. SERVICE FACILITY LOCATION INFORMATION:
Eric K. Botts, O.D.
1730 East Jackson Street
Macomb, IL 61455
309-836-3373

33. BILLING PROVIDER INFO & PH #:
Eric K. Botts, O.D.
1730 East Jackson Street
Macomb, IL 61455
309-836-3373

NUCC Instruction Manual available at: www.nucc.org
PLEASE PRINT OR TYPE
APPROVED OMB-0938-1197 FORM 1500 (02-12)

©2014 - E. Botts, O.D. Group NPI # if available, otherwise individual NPI #

• DIABETIC RETINOPATHY •
PAGE 5

Medicare
Remittance
Notice

Eric K. Botts, OD
1730 East Jackson Street
Macomb, IL 61455-2531

NPI #: 47932761
Page #: 1 of 2
Date: 10-22-10
Check/Eft #: 115449098

PERF PROV	SERV DATE	POS	NOS	PROC	MODS	BILLED	ALLOWED	DEDUCT	COINS	GRP/RC-AMT	PROV PD
NAME DOE, JAN			HIC 36030715A		ACNT 111036P			ICN 0206222466720	ASG Y	MOA MAO 1	MA 18
47932761	1003 100310	11	1	99204		149.75	135.00	0.00	27.00	14.75	108.00
47932761	1003 100310	11	1	92250		64.57	62.00	0.00	12.40	2.57	49.60
47932761	1003 100310	11	1	92083		72.94	56.42	0.00	11.28	16.52	45.14
47932761	1003 100310	11	1	92020		24.40	20.00	0.00	4.00	4.40	16.00
47932761	1003 100310	11	1	92015		18.00	0.00	0.00	0.00	PR-96	0.00
47932761	1003 100310	11	1	99273		127.42	127.42	0.00	25.48	5.09	96.85
PT RESP	80.16		1	CLAIM TOTALS		457.08	400.84	0.00	80.16	43.33	315.59

CLAIM INFORMATION FORWARDED TO: HCSC-BCBS OF IL (STD A & B)   218.74 NET

PR   Patient Responsibility. Amount that may be billed to a patient or another payer.

96   Non-covered charge(s).

DIABETIC RETINOPATHY
PAGE 6
EXAMINATION
Supplementary Tests

Patient **Jan Doe**   Date **10-03-10**

External Ocular Photography (92285, 92286)

OD

Findings _____

Diagnosis _____

Plan _____

_____

Signature _____

OS

_____

_____

_____

_____

Scanning Computerized Ophthalmic Diagnostic Imaging (92132, 92133, 92134)

☐ HRT   ☑ OCT   ☐ GDX

OD

Findings: Small heme near macular

Diagnosis: neg edema

Plan: Mild non proliferative diabetic retinopathy - Monitor 6 months

Signature: E. Botts

OS

Findings: Small heme near macular

Diagnosis: neg edema

Plan: Mild non proliferative diabetic retinopathy - Monitor 6 months

Extended Ophthalmoscopy (92225, 92226)

☐ 78D Lens   ☐ 90D Lens   ☐ 20D Lens   ☐ 2.2D Lens   ☐ 3-Mirror   ☐ Scleral depression

OD   **OS**

Findings _____

Diagnosis _____

Plan _____

_____

Signature _____

©2007 - E. Botts, O.D.

BILLING STATEMENT

DIABETIC RETINOPATHY
PAGE 7

Dr. Eric Botts
Phone 309/836-3373

Date of Service: 10/03/10
Patient's Name: Jan Doe
DOB: 04/19/33 ☐ Male ☑ Female
Address: 2100 RedBud St.
City: Smithville
State: IL Zip: 69321
Telephone: ( ) -
Insured's Name:
Insured's DOB: / /
ID Number: 349 27 8567A
Secondary Ins: BCBS
Total: 43.34
Special Instructions:

Refraction Paid: _____
Co-Pay/Deductible Paid: _____
Ins/Mcaid/Mcare Paid: _____
Secondary Paid: _____
Write Off: _____
Balance Due: _____

MODIFIERS 24 25 26 50 55 59 79 RT LT E1 E2 E3 E4 1P 2P 8P TC GW QW

MISCELLANEOUS
- E10.65 — Type 1 Diabetes w complications
- E10.9 — Type 1 Diabetes wo complications
- E11.65 — Type 2 Diabetes w complications
- E11.9 — Type 2 Diabetes wo complications
- H27.0 [1 2 3] — Aphakia
- H53.8 — Blurred Vision
- H57.1 [1 2 3] — Ocular Pain
- M06.9 — Rheumatoid Arthritis
- Z79.4 — Insulin Dependent
- Z79.84 — Non-Insulin Dependent
- Z79.899 — High Risk meds
  (1-RT 2-LT 3-Bilateral)

UVEAL DISORDERS
- H20.01 [1 2 3] — Primary iridocyclitis
- H21.0 [1 2 3] — Hyphema
- H21.23 [1 2 3] — Degeneration of Iris
- H21.26 [1 2 3] — Iris Atrophy
- H21.4 [1 2 3] — Pupillary membranes
- H57.05 [1 2 3] — Tonic Pupil
  (1-RT 2-LT 3-Bilateral)

EYELIDS
- H00.023 — Hordeolum internum RT eye
- H00.026 — Hordeolum internum LT eye
- H00.13 — Chalazion RT eye
- H00.16 — Chalazion LT eye
- H01.023 — Squamous blepharitis RT eye
- H01.026 — Squamous blepharitis LT eye
- H01.113 — Allergic dermatitis RT eye
- H01.116 — Allergic dermatitis LT eye
- H02.033 — Senile entropion RT eye
- H02.036 — Senile entropion LT eye
- H02.053 — Trichiasis wo entropion RT eye
- H05.056 — Trichiasis wo entropion LT eye
- H02.133 — Senile ectropion RT eye
- H02.136 — Senile ectropion LT eye
- H02.40 [1 2 3] — Unspec ptosis of eyelid
- H02.833 — Dermatochalasis RT eye
- H02.836 — Dermatochalasis LT eye
  (1-RT 2-LT 3-Bilateral)

CATARACT/LENS
- H25.01 [1 2 3] — Cortical age-related cat
- H25.04 [1 2 3] — Post subcap polar age-related cat
- H25.1 [1 2 3] — Age-related nuclear cat
- H25.89 — Other age-related cat
- Z96.1 — Presence of intraocular lens
  (1-RT 2-LT 3-Bilateral)

DISORDER OF REFRACTION
- H52.0 [1 2 3] — Hypermetropia
- H52.1 [1 2 3] — Myopia
- H52.22 [1 2 3] — Regular Astigmatism
- H52.4 — Presbyopia
  (1-RT 2-LT 3-Bilateral)

VISUAL DISORDERS
- H51.11 — Convergence insufficiency
- H51.12 — Convergence excess
- H52.53 [1 2 3] — Spasm of accommodation
- H53.02 [1 2 3] — Refractive amblyopia
- H53.03 [1 2 3] — Strabismic amblyopia
- H53.14 [1 2 3] — Visual discomfort
- H53.41 [1 2 3] — Scotoma involving central area
- H53.42 [1 2 3] — Scotoma of blind spot area
- H53.43 [1 2 3] — Sector or arcuate defects
- H53.46 [1 2 3] — Homonymous bilateral field defects
- H53.47 [1 2 3] — Heteronymous bilateral field defects
- H55.00 — Unspec nystagmus
  (1-RT 2-LT 3-Bilateral)

RETINAL DISORDERS
- E10.31 [1 9] — T1 diab w unsp diab rtnop
- E10.321 [1 2 3] — T1 diab w mild nonprlf diab rtnop w mac edema
- E10.329 [1 2 3] — T1 diab w mild nonprlf diab rtnop wo mac edema
- E10.331 [1 2 3] — T1 diab w mod nonprlf diab rtnop w mac edema
- E10.339 [1 2 3] — T1 diab w mod nonprlf diab rtnop wo mac edema
- E10.341 [1 2 3] — T1 diab w severe nonprlf diab rtnop w mac edema
- E10.349 [1 2 3] — T1 diab w severe nonprlf diab rtnop wo mac edema
- E10.351 [1 2 3] — T1 diab w prlif diab rtnop w mac edema
- E10.355 [1 2 3] — T1 diab w stable prolif diab rtnop
- E10.359 [1 2 3] — T1 diab w prlif diab rtnop wo mac edema
- E11.31 [1 9] — T2 diab w unsp diab rtnop
- E11.321 [1 2 3] — T2 diab w mild nonprlf diab rtnop w mac edema
- ☑ E11.329 [1 2 ③] — T2 diab w mild nonprlf diab rtnop wo mac edema
- E11.331 [1 2 3] — T2 diab w mod nonprlf diab rtnop w mac edema
- E11.339 [1 2 3] — T2 diab w mod nonprlf diab rtnop wo mac edema
- E11.341 [1 2 3] — T2 diab w severe nonprlf diab rtnop w mac edema
- E11.349 [1 2 3] — T2 diab w severe nonprlf diab rtnop wo mac edema
- E11.351 [1 2 3] — T2 diab w prolif diab rtnop w mac edema
- E11.355 [1 2 3] — T2 diab w stable prolif diab rtnop
- E11.359 [1 2 3] — T2 diab w prolif diab rtnop wo mac edema
- H31.01 [1 2 3] — Macula scars
- H31.09 [1 2 3] — Other chorioretinal scars
- H32 — Chorioretinal disorder
- H33.01 [1 2 3] — Retinal detachment w single break
- H33.31 [1 2 3] — Horseshoe tear of retina wo detachment
- H33.32 [1 2 3] — Round hole
- H33.8 — Other retinal detachments
- H34.1 [1 2 3] — Central retinal artery occlusion
- H34.21 [1 2 3] — Partial retinal artery occlusion
- H35.01 [1 2 3] — Vascular sheathing
- H35.03 [1 2 3] — Hypertensive retinopathy
- H35.04 [1 2 3] — Retinal micro-aneurysms
- H35.34 [1 2 3] — Macular cyst, hole or pseudohole
- H35.35 [1 2 3] — Cystoid macular degeneration
- H35.36 [1 2 3] — Drusen (degenerative) of macula
- H35.37 [1 2 3] — Puckering of macule, ERM
- H35.40 — Unspec peripheral retinal degeneration
- H35.41 [1 2 3] — Lattice degeneration of retina
- H35.71 [1 2 3] — Central serous chorioretinopathy
- H35.82 — Retinal ischemia
- H43.31 [1 2 3] — Viterous membranes
- H43.81 [1 2 3] — Viterous degeneration

RT LT BI (RT-Right LT-Left BI-Bilateral)
- H34.81 [10 20 30] — Central retinal vein occlusion w mac edema
- H34.81 [11 21 31] — Central retinal vein occlusion w retinal neovascularization
- H34.81 [12 22 32] — Central retinal vein occlusion, stable
- H34.83 [10 20 30] — Tributary retinal vein occlusion w mac edema
- H34.83 [11 21 31] — Tributary retinal vein occlusion w retinal neovascularization
- H34.83 [12 22 32] — Tributary retinal vein occlusion, stable
- H35.31 [11 21 31] — Nonexudative ARMD, early dry stage
- H35.31 [12 22 32] — Nonexudative ARMD, intermediate dry stage
- H35.31 [13 23 33] — Nonexudative ARMD, advanced wo subfoveal inv
- H35.31 [14 24 34] — Nonexudative ARMD, advanced w subfoveal inv
- H35.32 [11 21 31] — Exudative ARMD, active choroidal neovascularization
- H35.32 [12 22 32] — Exudative ARMD, inactive choroidal neovascularization
- H35.32 [13 23 33] — Exudative ARMD, inactive scar
  (1-RT 2-LT 3-Bilateral)
  (1-With Edema 9-Without Edema)

LACRIMAL SYSTEM
- H04.01 [1 2 3] — Acute dacryoadenitis
- H04.12 [1 2 3] — Dry eye syndrome
- H04.21 [1 2 3] — Epiphora due to excess lacrimation
  (1-RT 2-LT 3-Bilateral)

GLAUCOMA
- H40.01 [1 2 3] — Open angle w borderline findings low risk
- H40.02 [1 2 3] — Open angle w borderline findings high risk
- H40.05 [1 2 3] — Ocular hypertension
- H40.06 [1 2 3] — Primary angle closure wo glaucoma damage
- H40.21 [1 2 3] — Acute angle-closure glaucoma

RT LT BI (RT-Right LT-Left BI-Bilateral)
- H40.11 [11 21 31] — Primary open-angle glaucoma, mild
- H40.11 [12 22 32] — Primary open-angle glaucoma, mod
- H40.11 [13 23 33] — Primary open-angle glaucoma, severe
- H40.11 [14 24 34] — Primary open-angle glaucoma, indeterminate
- H40.12 [11 21 31] — Low-tens glaucoma, mild stage
- H40.12 [12 22 32] — Low-tens glaucoma, mod stage
- H40.12 [13 23 33] — Low-tens glaucoma, severe stage
- H40.13 [11 21 31] — Pigmentary glaucoma, mild stage
- H40.13 [12 22 32] — Pigmentary glaucoma, mod stage
- H40.13 [13 23 33] — Pigmentary glaucoma, severe stage
- H40.22 [11 21 31] — Chronic angle-closure glaucoma, mild stage
- H40.22 [12 22 32] — Chronic angle-closure glaucoma, mod stage
- H40.22 [13 23 33] — Chronic angle-closure glaucoma, severe stage
  (1-RT 2-LT 3-Bilateral)

NEURO-OPHTHALMOLOGY
- H46.1 [1 2 3] — Retrobulbar neuritis
- H47.01 [1 2 3] — Ischemic optic neuropathy
- H47.1 [1 2 3] — Papilledema assoc. w increased intracranial pressure
- H47.21 [1 2 3] — Primary optic atrophy
- H47.32 [1 2 3] — Drusen of optic disc
  (1-RT 2-LT 3-Bilateral)

CONJUNCTIVA
- B30.0 — Viral conjunctivitis
- H10.3 [1 2 3] — Acute conjunctivitis
- H10.41 [1 2 3] — Chronic giant papillary conjunctivitis
- H10.43 [1 2 3] — Chronic follicular conjunctivitis
- H11.05 [1 2 3] — Peripheral pterygium, progressive
- H11.12 [1 2 3] — Conjunctival concretions
- H11.15 [1 2 3] — Pinguecula
- H11.3 [1 2 3] — Conjunctival hemorrhage
- S05.01X [A D S] — Inj conjunctiva & corneal abrasion wo fb, RT, init
- S05.02X [A D S] — Inj conjunctiva & corneal abrasion wo fb, LT, init
- T15.11X [A D S] — Foreign body in conjunctival sac, RT, init
- T15.12X [A D S] — Foreign body in conjunctival sac, LT init
  (1-RT 2-LT 3-Bilateral)
  A-Initial D-Subsequent S-Sequela

CORNEA
- H16.00 [1 2 3] — Unspec corneal ulcer
- H16.01 [1 2 3] — Central corneal ulcer
- H16.04 [1 2 3] — Marginal corneal ulcer
- H16.12 [1 2 3] — Filamentary keratitis
- H16.14 [1 2 3] — Punctate keratitis
- H16.42 [1 2 3] — Pannus (corneal)
- H18.22 [1 2 3] — Idiopathic corneal edema
- H18.41 [1 2 3] — Arcus senilis
- H18.51 — Endothelial corneal dystrophy
- H18.59 — Other hereditary corneal dystrophies
- H18.82 [1 2 3] — Corneal edema due to contact lens
- H18.83 [1 2 3] — Recurrent erosion of cornea
- T15.01X [A D S] — Foreign body in cornea, RT, initial
- T15.02X [A D S] — Foreign body in cornea, LT, initial
  (1-RT 2-LT 3-Bilateral)
  (A-Initial D-Subsequent S-Sequela)

STRABISMUS
- H50.00 — Unspec esotropia
- H50.10 — Unspec exotropia
  (RT-Right LT-Left)

FEE
- S0620 _____
- S0621 _____
- 65210 _____ *
- 65222 _____ *
- 65430 _____ *
- 65435 _____ *
- 65778 _____
- 67820 _____ *
- 67938 _____ *
- 68761 _____ *
- 68801 _____ *
- 76510 _____
- 76514 _____
- 83516QW _____
- 83861QW _____
- 87809QW _____
- 92002 _____
- 92004 _____
- 92012 _____
- 92014 _____
- 92015 _____ +
- 92020 _____
- 92025 _____ *
- 92060 _____
- 92071 _____
- 92072 _____
- 92082 _____
- 92083 _____
- 92100 _____
- 92132 _____
- 92133 _____
- ☑ 92134 43.34
- 92225 _____ *
- 92226 _____ *
- 92250 _____
- 92274 _____
- 92284 _____
- 92285 _____
- 92286 _____
- 92310 _____ +
- 95930 _____
- 99201 _____
- 99202 _____
- 99203 _____
- 99204 _____
- 99205 _____
- 99212 _____
- 99213 _____
- 99214 _____
- 99215 _____

* May Require Modifier
+ Not Paid by MC

- 5010F G8428
- G8397 4004F
- G8398 1036F
- 2022F G8783
- 2024F G8950
- 2026F G8784
- 3072F G8785
- 2019F G8951
- 4177F G8952
- 2027F G8730
- 3284F G8731
- 3285F G8442
- 0517F G8939
- G8427 G8732
- G8430 G8509

v2.1 Revised 3/6/17

©2017 - E. Botts, O.D.

• DIABETIC RETINOPATHY •
PAGE 8

ICD-10

HEALTH INSURANCE CLAIM FORM
APPROVED BY NATIONAL UNIFORM CLAIM COMMITTEE (NUCC) 02/12

PICA		PICA

1. MEDICARE ☐ (Medicare#) MEDICAID ☐ (Medicaid#) TRICARE ☐ (ID#/DoD#) CHAMPVA ☐ (Member ID#) GROUP HEALTH PLAN ☐ (ID#) FECA BLK LUNG ☐ (ID#) OTHER ☐ (ID#)
1a. INSURED'S I.D. NUMBER (For Program in Item 1): 349 27 8567A

2. PATIENT'S NAME (Last Name, First Name, Middle Initial): Doe, Jan
3. PATIENT'S BIRTH DATE: 04 | 19 | 33 **SEX**: F ✔
4. INSURED'S NAME (Last Name, First Name, Middle Initial):

5. PATIENT'S ADDRESS (No., Street): 2100 Red Bud St.
6. PATIENT RELATIONSHIP TO INSURED: Self ✔ Spouse ☐ Child ☐ Other ☐
7. INSURED'S ADDRESS (No., Street):

CITY: Smithville **STATE**: IL
8. RESERVED FOR NUCC USE
CITY: **STATE**:

ZIP CODE: 69321 **TELEPHONE**: ( )
ZIP CODE: **TELEPHONE**: ( )

9. OTHER INSURED'S NAME:
10. IS PATIENT'S CONDITION RELATED TO:
11. INSURED'S POLICY GROUP OR FECA NUMBER: None

a. OTHER INSURED'S POLICY OR GROUP NUMBER:
a. EMPLOYMENT? (Current or Previous) ☐ YES ☐ NO
a. INSURED'S DATE OF BIRTH **SEX**: M ☐ F ☐

b. RESERVED FOR NUCC USE:
b. AUTO ACCIDENT? ☐ YES ☐ NO PLACE (State):
b. OTHER CLAIM ID (Designated by NUCC):

c. RESERVED FOR NUCC USE:
c. OTHER ACCIDENT? ☐ YES ☐ NO
c. INSURANCE PLAN NAME OR PROGRAM NAME:

d. INSURANCE PLAN NAME OR PROGRAM NAME:
10d. CLAIM CODES (Designated by NUCC):
d. IS THERE ANOTHER HEALTH BENEFIT PLAN? ☐ YES ☐ NO *If yes, complete items 9, 9a, and 9d.*

READ BACK OF FORM BEFORE COMPLETING & SIGNING THIS FORM.
12. PATIENT'S OR AUTHORIZED PERSON'S SIGNATURE
SIGNED: SOF   DATE: 10-03-10
13. INSURED'S OR AUTHORIZED PERSON'S SIGNATURE
SIGNED:

14. DATE OF CURRENT ILLNESS, INJURY, or PREGNANCY (LMP): QUAL.
15. OTHER DATE: QUAL.
16. DATES PATIENT UNABLE TO WORK IN CURRENT OCCUPATION FROM | TO

17. NAME OF REFERRING PROVIDER OR OTHER SOURCE: DK | Eric Botts
17a. **17b. NPI**: Individual NPI#
18. HOSPITALIZATION DATES RELATED TO CURRENT SERVICES FROM | TO

19. ADDITIONAL CLAIM INFORMATION (Designated by NUCC):
20. OUTSIDE LAB? ☐ YES ☐ NO **$ CHARGES**:

21. DIAGNOSIS OR NATURE OF ILLNESS OR INJURY ICD Ind. 10
A. E11.3293 B. C. D.
E. F. G. H.
I. J. K. L.
22. RESUBMISSION CODE: **ORIGINAL REF. NO.**:
23. PRIOR AUTHORIZATION NUMBER:

24. A. DATE(S) OF SERVICE From–To	B. PLACE OF SERVICE	C. EMG	D. PROCEDURES, SERVICES, OR SUPPLIES CPT/HCPCS MODIFIER	E. DIAGNOSIS POINTER	F. $ CHARGES	G. DAYS OR UNITS	H. EPSDT	I. ID. QUAL.	J. RENDERING PROVIDER ID. #
1 10 13 10 10 13 10	11		92134	A	43 34	1		NPI	Individual NPI #
2								NPI	
3								NPI	
4								NPI	
5								NPI	
6								NPI	

25. FEDERAL TAX I.D. NUMBER: 411743621 SSN ☐ EIN ✔
26. PATIENT'S ACCOUNT NO.:
27. ACCEPT ASSIGNMENT? ✔ YES ☐ NO
28. TOTAL CHARGE: $ 43 34
29. AMOUNT PAID: $ 0
30. Rsvd for NUCC Use: 43 34

31. SIGNATURE OF PHYSICIAN OR SUPPLIER INCLUDING DEGREES OR CREDENTIALS
E. Botts   10-13-10
32. SERVICE FACILITY LOCATION INFORMATION
Eric K. Botts, O.D.
1730 East Jackson Street
Macomb, IL 61455
309-836-3373
33. BILLING PROVIDER INFO & PH #: ( )
Eric K. Botts, O.D.
1730 East Jackson Street
Macomb, IL 61455
309-836-3373

DIABETIC RETINOPATHY
PAGE 9

Medicare
Remittance
Notice

Eric K. Botts, OD
1730 East Jackson Street
Macomb, IL 61455-2531

NPI #: 47932761
Page #: 1 of 2
Date: 10-22-10
Check/Eft #: 115449098

PERF PROV	SERV DATE	POS	NOS	PROC	MODS	BILLED	ALLOWED	DEDUCT	COINS	GRP/RC-AMT	PROV PD
NAME DOE, JAN			HIC 36030715A		ACNT 111036P			ICN 0206222466720	ASG Y	MOA MAO 1	MA 18
47932761	1013 101310	11	1	92134		43.34	38.37	0.00	7.67	4.97	30.70

| PT RESP | 7.67 | | 1 | CLAIM TOTALS | | 43.34 | 38.37 | 0.00 | 7.67 | 4.97 | 30.70 |

CLAIM INFORMATION FORWARDED TO: HCSC-BCBS OF IL (STD A & B)   30.70 NET

© 2018 - E. Botts, O.D.

Example #2
Glaucoma Patient

· GLAUCOMA PATIENT ·
PAGE 1

EXAMINATION

Example #2

Patient: Jim Doe Date: 08-08-10 Sex: (M)/F DOB: 01-01-11 Age: ___ Last Exam: ___
Chief Complaint: Blurry Vision

History
HPI: Can't read fine print up close
Symptoms: Glare bothers on bright sunny
Location: days all the time
Quality: Diagnosed with glaucoma 2 years
Severity: ago. Using prostaglandin at bed
Duration: time, both eyes
Timing:
Context:
Modifiers:

Allergies
Medications
Ocular ROS

Medical History & ROS from ___/___/___ reviewed: ☐ no changes
Dr. Initials ___

Examination
Head/Face ☑ nl   Psych: Mood/Affect (anxiety/depression) ☑ nl   Neuro: Oriented (person/time/place) ☑ y ☐ n

VA: sc<   cc< 40/30   ph<   near<

K: OD ___   OLD RX: OD +3.75 - 0.25 x 084   add +2.75
      OS ___   OS +3.75 - 0.25 x 085   add ___
R-scopy: OD ___   REF: OD +4.50 - 0.50 x 090   20/30   add +2.75
           OS ___   OS +4.50 - 0.50 x 075   20/25   add ___

Perimetry:	☑ nl CF ☐ nl	Color ☑ nl ☐ RG defect	**ADNEXA** ☑ nl		
Motility:	☑ Full	Stereo Animals /3 WD /9	**EYELIDS:**	☐ Blepharitis	OD OS OU
Cover Test:	☐ Eso ___	☐ Exo ___ ☑ Ortho		☐ Meibomianitis	OD OS OU

Pupils: ☑ no afferent defect   ☑ round OU   Size: OD 3 OS 3
☐ 20D
☐ 90D/78D
☐ 3 Mirror

SLE: OD / OS
OD			OS	
☑ nl ☐ FBUT:	TEAR FILM	☑ nl	☐ FBUT:	
☑ nl ☐ arcus	CORNEA	☑ nl	☐ arcus	
☑ nl ☐ pterygium		☑ nl	☐ pterygium	
☑ nl ☐ infiltrate		☑ nl	☐ infiltrate	
☑ nl ☐ spk		☑ nl	☐ spk	
☑ nl ☐	SCLERA	☑ nl		
☑ nl ☐ injection	CONJ.	☑ nl	☐ injection	
☑ nl ☐ pinguecula		☑ nl	☐ pinguecula	
☑ D&Q ☐	AC	☑ D&Q ☐		
☑ nl ☐ rubeosis	IRIS	☑ nl	☐ rubeosis	
☐ clear ☐ cat ☑ ns	LENS	☐ clear ☐ cat ☑ ns		

RETINA: OD / OS
OD			OS	
☑ nl ☐ drusen	MACULA	☑ nl	☐ drusen	
☑ nl ☐ RPE chgs		☑ nl	☐ RPE chgs	
☑ nl ☐ cotton wool	POST POLE	☑ nl	☐ cotton wool	
☑ nl ☐ hemes		☑ nl	☐ hemes	
☑ nl ☐ DME		☑ nl	☐ DME	
☑ nl ☐	VESSELS	☑ nl		
☑ nl ☐ PVD	VITREOUS	☑ nl	☐ PVD	
☑ nl ☐ strands		☑ nl	☐ strands	
☑ nl ☐	PERIPHERY	☑ nl		

OPTIC DISCS: OD / OS
☐ nl   SIZE/APPEARANCE/NFL   ☐ nl
☑ .6/.6   C/D   ☑ .6/.6

NCT / @ ___   Pachymetry: OD 577
TAG 16/17 @ 11:16 am   OS 568   Dilated: M .5% 1% (PA 1%/0.25%) C 1% 2% Ph 2.5% 10% OU @ 11:32am

Diagnosis/Plan   MDM 1 2 (3) 4
POAG Bilateral Stable
Nuclear Sclerosis

Monitor Cataract 1 year
Monitor IOP 3 months
Continue prostaglandin hs

Order: ☐ HRT/GDX/OCT   RTO: ___ day
☑ Photo   TVF gonioscopy   ___ week
☐ VF   Schedule   1 month
☐ Consult   OCT Sept. 7   ___ year

Dr. E. Botts

• GLAUCOMA PATIENT •
PAGE 2
EXAMINATION
Supplementary Tests

Patient: John Doe   Date: 08-08-10

Fundus Photography (92250)

OD
- Findings: CD .6/.6 good rim tissue superior & inferior
- Diagnosis: POAG
- Plan: Repeat 6 months
- Signature: E. Botts

OS
- Findings: CD .6/.6 good rim tissue superior & inferior
- Diagnosis: POAG
- Plan: Repeat 6 months

Gonioscopy (92020)

OD
- Findings: View Trabeular meshwork 360°
- Diagnosis: POAG
- Plan: Repeat 1 year
- Signature: E. Botts

OS
- Findings: View Trabeular meshwork 360°
- Diagnosis: POAG
- Plan: Repeat 1 year

Visual Fields (92081, 92082, (92083))

OD
- Findings: Patient responded well
- Diagnosis: No defect
- Plan:
- Repeat 6 months
- Signature: E. Botts

OS
- Findings: Patient responded well
- Diagnosis: No defect
- Repeat 6 months

Sensorimotor Examination (92060)

OD
- Findings:
- Diagnosis:
- Plan:
- Signature:

OS

BILLING STATEMENT

• GLAUCOMA PATIENT •
PAGE 3

Dr. Eric Botts
Phone 309/836-3373

Date of Service **08/08/10**
Patient's Name **John Doe** DOB **01/01/11** ☑ Male ☐ Female
Address **2100 RedBud St.** City **Smithville** State **IL** Zip **69321**
Telephone ( ) - Insured's Name Insured's DOB / /
ID Number **359 26 8567A** Secondary Ins **BCBS** Total **360.00**
Special Instructions Refraction Paid **18.00**
Co-Pay/Deductible Paid
Ins/Mcaid/Mcare Paid
Secondary Paid
Write Off
Balance Due

MODIFIERS 24 25 26 50 55 59 79 RT LT E1 E2 E3 E4 1P 2P 8P TC GW QW

MISCELLANEOUS
- E10.65 Type 1 Diabetes w complications
- E10.9 Type 1 Diabetes wo complications
- E11.65 Type 2 Diabetes w complications
- E11.9 Type 2 Diabetes wo complications
- H27.0 [1 2 3] Aphakia
- H53.8 Blurred Vision
- H57.1 [1 2 3] Ocular Pain
- M06.9 Rheumatoid Arthritis
- Z79.4 Insulin Dependent
- Z79.84 Non-Insulin Dependent
- Z79.899 High Risk meds

(1-RT 2-LT 3-Bilateral)

UVEAL DISORDERS
- H20.01 [1 2 3] Primary iridocyclitis
- H21.0 [1 2 3] Hyphema
- H21.23 [1 2 3] Degeneration of Iris
- H21.26 [1 2 3] Iris Atrophy
- H21.4 [1 2 3] Pupillary membranes
- H57.05 [1 2 3] Tonic Pupil

(1-RT 2-LT 3-Bilateral)

EYELIDS
- H00.023 Hordeolum internum RT eye
- H00.026 Hordeolum internum LT eye
- H00.13 Chalazion RT eye
- H00.16 Chalazion LT eye
- H01.023 Squamous blepharitis RT eye
- H01.026 Squamous blepharitis LT eye
- H01.113 Allergic dermatitis RT eye
- H01.116 Allergic dermatitis LT eye
- H02.033 Senile entropion RT eye
- H02.036 Senile entropion LT eye
- H02.053 Trichiasis wo entropion RT eye
- H05.056 Trichiasis wo entropion LT eye
- H02.133 Senile ectropion RT eye
- H02.136 Senile ectropion LT eye
- H02.40 [1 2 3] Unspec ptosis of eyelid
- H02.833 Dermatochalasis RT eye
- H02.836 Dermatochalasis LT eye

(1-RT 2-LT 3-Bilateral)

CATARACT/LENS
- ☐ H25.01 [1 2 3] Cortical age-related cat
- ☐ H25.04 [1 2 3] Post subcap polar age-related cat
- ☑ H25.1 [1 2 ③] Age-related nuclear cat
- H25.89 Other age-related cat
- Z96.1 Presence of intraocular lens

(1-RT 2-LT 3-Bilateral)

DISORDER OF REFRACTION
- H52.0 [1 2 3] Hypermetropia
- H52.1 [1 2 3] Myopia
- H52.22 [1 2 3] Regular Astigmatism
- H52.4 Presbyopia

(1-RT 2-LT 3-Bilateral)

VISUAL DISORDERS
- H51.11 Convergence insufficiency
- H51.12 Convergence excess
- H52.53 [1 2 3] Spasm of accommodation
- H53.02 [1 2 3] Refractive amblyopia
- H53.03 [1 2 3] Strabismic amblyopia
- H53.14 [1 2 3] Visual discomfort
- H53.41 [1 2 3] Scotoma involving central area
- H53.42 [1 2 3] Scotoma of blind spot area
- H53.43 [1 2 3] Sector or arcuate defects
- H53.46 [1 2 3] Homonymous bilateral field defects
- H53.47 Heteronymous bilateral field defects
- H55.00 Unspec nystagmus

(1-RT 2-LT 3-Bilateral)

RETINAL DISORDERS
- E10.31 [1 9] T1 diab w unsp diab rtnop
- E10.321 [1 2 3] T1 diab w mild nonprlf diab rtnop w mac edema
- E10.329 [1 2 3] T1 diab w mild nonprlf diab rtnop wo mac edema
- E10.331 [1 2 3] T1 diab w mod nonprlf diab rtnop w mac edema
- E10.339 [1 2 3] T1 diab w mon nonprlf diab rtnop wo mac edema
- E10.341 [1 2 3] T1 diab w severe nonprlf diab rtnop w mac edema
- E10.349 [1 2 3] T1 diab w severe nonprlf diab rtnop wo mac edema
- E10.351 [1 2 3] T1 diab w prlif diab rtnop w mac edema
- E10.355 [1 2 3] T1 diab w stable prolif diab rtnop
- E10.359 [1 2 3] T1 diab w prlif diab rtnop wo mac edema
- E11.31 [1 9] T2 diab w unsp diab rtnop
- E11.321 [1 2 3] T2 diab w mild nonprlf diab rtnop w mac edema
- E11.329 [1 2 3] T2 diab w mild nonprlf diab rtnop wo mac edema
- E11.331 [1 2 3] T2 diab w mod nonprlf diab rtnop w mac edema
- E11.339 [1 2 3] T2 diab w mod nonprlf diab rtnop wo mac edema
- E11.341 [1 2 3] T2 diab w severe nonprlf diab rtnop w mac edema
- E11.349 [1 2 3] T2 diab w severe nonprlf diab rtnop wo mac edema
- E11.351 [1 2 3] T2 diab w prolif diab rtnop w mac edema
- E11.355 [1 2 3] T2 diab w stable prolif diab rtnop
- E11.359 [1 2 3] T2 diab w prolif diab rtnop wo mac edema
- H31.01 [1 2 3] Macula scars
- H31.09 [1 2 3] Other chorioretinal scars
- H32 Chorioretinal disorder
- H33.01 [1 2 3] Retinal detachment w single break
- H33.31 [1 2 3] Horseshoe tear of retina wo detachment
- H33.32 [1 2 3] Round hole
- H33.8 Other retinal detachments
- H34.1 [1 2 3] Central retinal artery occlusion
- H34.21 [1 2 3] Partial retinal artery occlusion
- H35.01 [1 2 3] Vascular sheathing
- H35.03 [1 2 3] Hypertensive retinopathy
- H35.04 [1 2 3] Retinal micro-aneurysms
- H35.34 [1 2 3] Macular cyst, hole or pseudohole
- H35.35 [1 2 3] Cystoid macular degeneration
- H35.36 [1 2 3] Drusen (degenerative) of macula
- H35.37 [1 2 3] Puckering of macule, ERM
- H35.40 Unspec peripheral retinal degeneration
- H35.41 [1 2 3] Lattice degeneration of retina
- H35.71 [1 2 3] Central serous chorioretinopathy
- H35.82 Retinal ischemia
- H43.31 [1 2 3] Viterous membranes
- H43.81 [1 2 3] Viterous degeneration

RT LT BI (RT-Right LT-Left BI-Bilateral)
- H34.81 [10 20 30] Central retinal vein occlusion w mac edema
- H34.81 [11 21 31] Central retinal vein occlusion w retinal neovascularization
- H34.81 [12 22 32] Central retinal vein occlusion, stable
- H34.83 [10 20 30] Tributary retinal vein occlusion w mac edema
- H34.83 [11 21 31] Tributary retinal vein occlusion w retinal neovascularization
- H34.83 [12 22 32] Tributary retinal vein occlusion, stable
- H35.31 [11 21 31] Nonexudative ARMD, early dry stage
- H35.31 [12 22 32] Nonexudative ARMD, intermediate dry stage
- H35.31 [13 23 33] Nonexudative ARMD, advanced atropic wo subfoveal inv
- H35.31 [14 24 34] Nonexudative ARMD, advanced atropic w subfoveal inv
- H35.32 [11 21 31] Exudative ARMD, active choroidal neovascularization
- H35.32 [12 22 32] Exudative ARMD, inactive choroidal neovascularization
- H35.32 [13 23 33] Exudative ARMD, inactive scar

(1-RT 2-LT 3-Bilateral)
(1-With Edema 9-Without Edema)

LACRIMAL SYSTEM
- H04.01 [1 2 3] Acute dacryoadenitis
- H04.12 [1 2 3] Dry eye syndrome
- H04.21 [1 2 3] Epiphora due to excess lacrimation

(1-RT 2-LT 3-Bilateral)

GLAUCOMA
- H40.01 [1 2 3] Open angle w borderline findings low risk
- H40.02 [1 2 3] Open angle w borderline findings high risk
- H40.05 [1 2 3] Ocular hypertension
- H40.06 [1 2 3] Primary angle closure w glaucoma damage
- H40.21 [1 2 3] Acute angle-closure glaucoma

RT LT BI (RT-Right LT-Left BI-Bilateral)
- H40.11 [11 21 31] Primary open-angle glaucoma, mild
- ☑ H40.11 [12 22 32] Primary open-angle glaucoma, mod
- H40.11 [13 23 33] Primary open-angle glaucoma, severe
- H40.11 [14 24 34] Primary open-angle glaucoma, indeterminate
- H40.12 [11 21 31] Low-tens glaucoma, mild stage
- H40.12 [12 22 32] Low-tens glaucoma, mod stage
- H40.12 [13 23 33] Low-tens glaucoma, severe stage
- H40.13 [11 21 31] Pigmentary glaucoma, mild stage
- H40.13 [12 22 32] Pigmentary glaucoma, mod stage
- H40.13 [13 23 33] Pigmentary glaucoma, severe stage
- H40.22 [11 21 31] Chronic angle-closure glaucoma, mild stage
- H40.22 [12 22 32] Chronic angle-closure glaucoma, mod stage
- H40.22 [13 23 33] Chronic angle-closure glaucoma, severe stage

(1-RT 2-LT 3-Bilateral)

NEURO-OPHTHALMOLOGY
- H46.1 [1 2 3] Retrobulbar neuritis
- H47.01 [1 2 3] Ischemic optic neuropathy
- H47.1 [1 2 3] Papilledema assoc. w increased intracranial pressure
- H47.21 [1 2 3] Primary optic atrophy
- H47.32 [1 2 3] Drusen of optic disc

(1-RT 2-LT 3-Bilateral)

CONJUNCTIVA
- B30.0 Viral conjunctivitis
- H10.3 [1 2 3] Acute conjunctivitis
- H10.41 [1 2 3] Chronic giant papillary conjunctivitis
- H10.43 [1 2 3] Chronic follicular conjunctivitis
- H11.05 [1 2 3] Peripheral pterygium, progressive
- H11.12 [1 2 3] Conjunctival concretions
- H11.15 [1 2 3] Pinguecula
- H11.3 [1 2 3] Conjunctival hemorrhage
- S05.01X [A D S] Inj conjunctiva & corneal abrasion wo fb, RT, init
- S05.02X [A D S] Inj conjunctiva & corneal abrasion wo fb, LT, init
- T15.11X [A D S] Foreign body in conjunctival sac, RT, init
- T15.12X [A D S] Foreign body in conjunctival sac, LT, init

(1-RT 2-LT 3-Bilateral)
(A-Initial D-Subsequent S-Sequela)

CORNEA
- H16.00 [1 2 3] Unspec corneal ulcer
- H16.01 [1 2 3] Central corneal ulcer
- H16.04 [1 2 3] Marginal corneal ulcer
- H16.12 [1 2 3] Filamentary keratitis
- H16.14 [1 2 3] Punctate keratitis
- H16.42 [1 2 3] Pannus (corneal)
- H18.22 [1 2 3] Idiopathic corneal edema
- H18.41 [1 2 3] Arcus senilis
- H18.51 Endothelial corneal dystrophie
- H18.59 Other hereditary corneal dystrophies
- H18.82 [1 2 3] Corneal edema due to contact lens
- H18.83 [1 2 3] Recurrent erosion of cornea
- T15.01X [A D S] Foreign body in cornea, RT, initial
- T15.02X [A D S] Foreign body in cornea, LT, initial

(1-RT 2-LT 3-Bilateral)
(A-Initial D-Subsequent S-Sequela)

STRABISMUS
- H50.00 Unspec esotropia
- H50.10 Unspec exotropia

(RT-Right LT-Left)

FEE
- S0620
- S0621
- 65210 *
- 65222 *
- 65430 *
- 65435 *
- 65778 *
- 67820 *
- 67938 *
- 68761 *
- 68801 *
- 76510
- ☑ 76514 **1400**
- 83516QW
- 83861QW
- 87809QW
- 92002
- 92004
- 92012
- 92014
- ☑ 92015 **1800** +
- ☑ 92020 **2600**
- 92025 *
- 92060
- 92071
- 92072
- 92082
- ☑ 92083 **7500**
- 92100
- 92132
- 92133
- 92134
- 92225 *
- 92226 *
- ☑ 92250 **7200** *
- 92274
- 92284
- 92285
- 92286
- 92310 +
- 95930
- 99201
- 99202
- 99203
- ☑ 99204 **15500**
- 99205
- 99212
- 99213
- 99214
- 99215

* May Require Modifier
\+ Not Paid by MC

- 5010F ☐ G8428
- G8397 ☐ 4004F
- G8398 ☐ 1036F
- 2022F ☐ G8783
- 2024F ☐ G8950
- 2026F ☐ G8784
- 3072F ☐ G8785
- 2019F ☐ G8951
- 4177F ☐ G8952
- 2027F ☐ G8730
- 3284F ☐ G8731
- 3285F ☐ G8442
- 0517F ☐ G8939
- G8427 ☐ G8732
- G8430 ☐ G8509

v2.1 Revised 3/6/17

©2017 - E. Botts, O.D.

• GLAUCOMA PATIENT •
PAGE 4

ICD-10

HEALTH INSURANCE CLAIM FORM
APPROVED BY NATIONAL UNIFORM CLAIM COMMITTEE (NUCC) 02/12

PICA	PICA

1. MEDICARE ☐ MEDICAID ☐ TRICARE ☐ CHAMPVA ☐ GROUP HEALTH PLAN ☐ FECA BLK LUNG ☐ OTHER ☐
1a. INSURED'S I.D. NUMBER (For Program in Item 1): 359 26 8567A

2. PATIENT'S NAME: Doe, John
3. PATIENT'S BIRTH DATE: 01 01 1911 SEX: M ✓
4. INSURED'S NAME:

5. PATIENT'S ADDRESS: 2100 Red Bud St.
6. PATIENT RELATIONSHIP TO INSURED: Self ✓
7. INSURED'S ADDRESS:

CITY: Smithville   STATE: IL
8. RESERVED FOR NUCC USE
CITY: STATE:

ZIP CODE: 69321   TELEPHONE: (000) 000-0000
ZIP CODE: TELEPHONE: ( )

9. OTHER INSURED'S NAME:
10. IS PATIENT'S CONDITION RELATED TO:
11. INSURED'S POLICY GROUP OR FECA NUMBER: None

a. OTHER INSURED'S POLICY OR GROUP NUMBER:
a. EMPLOYMENT? ☐ YES ☐ NO
a. INSURED'S DATE OF BIRTH: SEX: M ☐ F ☐

b. RESERVED FOR NUCC USE
b. AUTO ACCIDENT? ☐ YES ☐ NO   PLACE (State):
b. OTHER CLAIM ID (Designated by NUCC):

c. RESERVED FOR NUCC USE
c. OTHER ACCIDENT? ☐ YES ☐ NO
c. INSURANCE PLAN NAME OR PROGRAM NAME:

d. INSURANCE PLAN NAME OR PROGRAM NAME:
10d. CLAIM CODES (Designated by NUCC):
d. IS THERE ANOTHER HEALTH BENEFIT PLAN? ☐ YES ☐ NO

12. PATIENT'S OR AUTHORIZED PERSON'S SIGNATURE
SIGNED: John Doe   DATE: 08-08-10
13. INSURED'S OR AUTHORIZED PERSON'S SIGNATURE
SIGNED:

14. DATE OF CURRENT ILLNESS, INJURY, or PREGNANCY (LMP):   QUAL.:
15. OTHER DATE   QUAL.:
16. DATES PATIENT UNABLE TO WORK IN CURRENT OCCUPATION: FROM   TO

17. NAME OF REFERRING PROVIDER OR OTHER SOURCE: DK Eric Botts
17b. NPI: Individual NPI#
18. HOSPITALIZATION DATES RELATED TO CURRENT SERVICES: FROM   TO

19. ADDITIONAL CLAIM INFORMATION (Designated by NUCC):
20. OUTSIDE LAB? ☐ YES ☐ NO $ CHARGES:

21. DIAGNOSIS OR NATURE OF ILLNESS OR INJURY   ICD Ind. 10
A. H40.1132   B. H25.13   C.   D.
E.   F.   G.   H.
I.   J.   K.   L.

22. RESUBMISSION CODE: ORIGINAL REF. NO.:
23. PRIOR AUTHORIZATION NUMBER:

#	24.A. DATE(S) OF SERVICE From / To	B. PLACE OF SERVICE	C. EMG	D. PROCEDURES CPT/HCPCS	MODIFIER	E. DIAGNOSIS POINTER	F. $ CHARGES	G. DAYS/UNITS	H. EPSDT	I. ID QUAL	J. RENDERING PROVIDER ID. #
1	08 08 10 / 08 08 10	11		99204		A	155 00	1		NPI	Individual NPI #
2	08 08 10 / 08 08 10	11		92250		A	72 00	1		NPI	Individual NPI #
3	08 08 10 / 08 08 10	11		92083		A	75 00	1		NPI	Individual NPI #
4	08 08 10 / 08 08 10	11		92020		A	26 00	1		NPI	Individual NPI #
5	08 08 10 / 08 08 10	11		92015		B	18 00	1		NPI	Individual NPI #
6	08 08 10 / 08 08 10	11		76514		A	14 00	1		NPI	Individual NPI #

25. FEDERAL TAX I.D. NUMBER: 411329761   EIN ✓
26. PATIENT'S ACCOUNT NO.:
27. ACCEPT ASSIGNMENT? YES ✓
28. TOTAL CHARGE: $ 360 00
29. AMOUNT PAID: $ 0
30. Rsvd for NUCC Use: 360 00

31. SIGNATURE OF PHYSICIAN OR SUPPLIER: E. Botts 08-08-10
32. SERVICE FACILITY LOCATION INFORMATION:
Eric K. Botts, O.D.
1730 East Jackson Street
Macomb, IL 61455
309-836-3373

33. BILLING PROVIDER INFO & PH #:
Eric K. Botts, O.D.
1730 East Jackson Street
Macomb, IL 61455
309-836-3373

NUCC Instruction Manual available at: www.nucc.org   APPROVED OMB-0938-1197 FORM 1500 (02-12)

©2014 - E. Botts, O.D.   Group NPI # if available, otherwise individual NPI #

• GLAUCOMA PATIENT •
PAGE 5

Medicare
Remittance
Notice

Eric K. Botts, OD
1730 East Jackson Street
Macomb, IL 61455-2531

NPI #: 47932761
Page #: 1 of 2
Date: 08-22-10
Check/Eft #: 115449098

PERF PROV	SERV DATE	POS	NOS	PROC	MODS	BILLED	ALLOWED	DEDUCT	COINS	GRP/RC-AMT	PROV PD
NAME DOE, JOHN			HIC 36030715A		ACNT 111036P			ICN 0206222466720	ASG Y	MOA MAO 1	MA 18
47932761	0808 080810	11	1	99204	25	155.00	149.75	35.00	22.95	5.25	91.80
47932761	0808 080810	11	1	92250		72.00	64.57	0.00	12.91	7.43	51.66
47932761	0808 080810	11	1	92083		75.00	72.94	0.00	14.58	2.06	58.36
47932761	0808 080810	11	1	92020		26.00	24.40	0.00	4.88	1.60	19.52
47932761	0808 080810	11	1	92015		18.00	0.00	0.00	0.00	PR-96	0.00
47932761	0808 080810	11	1	76514		14.00	13.12	0.00	2.62	0.88	10.50
PT RESP	110.94		1	CLAIM TOTALS		360.00	324.78	35.00	57.94	17.22	231.84

CLAIM INFORMATION FORWARDED TO: HCSC-BCBS OF IL (STD A & B)

231.84 NET

PR Patient Responsibility. Amount that may be billed to a patient or another payer.

96 Non-covered charge(s).

• GLAUCOMA •
PAGE 6
Supplementary Tests

Patient **Jan Doe** Date **11-03-14**

- ☐ **Visual Fields** (92081, 92082, 92083)
- ☐ **Fundus Photography** (92250)
- ☐ **Sensorimotor Examination** (92060)
- ☐ **External Ocular Photography** (92285)
- ☐ **Scanning Computerized Ophthalmic Diagnostic Imaging** (92132, 92133, 92134) ☐ HRT ☐ OCT ☐ GDX
- ☐ **Serial Tonometry** (92100)
- ☐ **Corneal Topography** (92025)
- ☒ **Gonioscopy** (92020)
- ☐ **Pattern Electroretinography** (92275)
- ☐ **Specular Microscopy** (92286)

Scanning Computerized Ophthalmic Diagnostic Imaging (92132, (92133), 92134) ☐ HRT ☒ OCT ☐ GDX

	OD	OS
Findings	Thinning Retinal Nerve Fiber, Avg Thickness 50	Thinning Retinal Nerve Fiber, Avg Thickness 54
Diagnosis	Primary Open Angle Glaucoma	Primary Open Angle Glaucoma
Plan	Repeat 1 year	Repeat 1 year

Signature _E. Bolt_

BILLING STATEMENT

• GLAUCOMA PATIENT •
PAGE 7

Dr. Eric Botts
Phone 309/836-3373

41

Date of Service **08/08/10**
Patient's Name **John Doe** DOB **01/01/11** ☑ Male ☐ Female
Address **2100 RedBud St.** City **Smithville** State **IL** Zip **69321**
Telephone ( ) -   Insured's Name _____ Insured's DOB __/__/__
ID Number **359 26 8567A** Secondary Ins **BCBS** Total **107.33**
Special Instructions _____

Refraction Paid _____
Co-Pay/Deductible Paid _____
Ins/Mcaid/Mcare Paid _____
Secondary Paid _____
Write Off _____
Balance Due _____

MODIFIERS 24 25 26 50 55 59 79 RT LT E1 E2 E3 E4 1P 2P 8P TC GW QW

MISCELLANEOUS
- ☐ E10.65 Type 1 Diabetes w complications
- ☐ E10.9 Type 1 Diabetes wo complications
- ☐ E11.65 Type 2 Diabetes w complications
- ☐ E11.9 Type 2 Diabetes wo complications
- ☐ H27.0 [1 2 3] Aphakia
- ☐ H53.8 Blurred Vision
- ☐ H57.1 [1 2 3] Ocular Pain
- ☐ M06.9 Rheumatoid Arthritis
- ☐ Z79.4 Insulin Dependent
- ☐ Z79.84 Non-Insulin Dependent
- ☐ Z79.899 High Risk meds

(1-RT 2-LT 3-Bilateral)

UVEAL DISORDERS
- ☐ H20.01 [1 2 3] Primary iridocyclitis
- ☐ H21.0 [1 2 3] Hyphema
- ☐ H21.23 [1 2 3] Degeneration of Iris
- ☐ H21.26 [1 2 3] Iris Atrophy
- ☐ H21.4 [1 2 3] Pupillary membranes
- ☐ H57.05 [1 2 3] Tonic Pupil

(1-RT 2-LT 3-Bilateral)

EYELIDS
- ☐ H00.023 Hordeolum internum RT eye
- ☐ H00.026 Hordeolum internum LT eye
- ☐ H00.13 Chalazion RT eye
- ☐ H00.16 Chalazion LT eye
- ☐ H01.023 Squamous blepharitis RT eye
- ☐ H01.026 Squamous blepharitis LT eye
- ☐ H01.113 Allergic dermatitis RT eye
- ☐ H01.116 Allergic dermatitis LT eye
- ☐ H02.033 Senile entropion RT eye
- ☐ H02.036 Senile entropion LT eye
- ☐ H02.053 Trichiasis wo entropion RT eye
- ☐ H05.056 Trichiasis wo entropion LT eye
- ☐ H02.133 Senile ectropion RT eye
- ☐ H02.136 Senile ectropion LT eye
- ☐ H02.40 [1 2 3] Unspec ptosis of eyelid
- ☐ H02.833 Dermatochalasis RT eye
- ☐ H02.836 Dermatochalasis LT eye

(1-RT 2-LT 3-Bilateral)

CATARACT/LENS
- ☐ H25.01 [1 2 3] Cortical age-related cat
- ☐ H25.04 [1 2 3] Post subcap polar age-related cat
- ☐ H25.1 [1 2 3] Age-related nuclear cat
- ☐ H25.89 Other age-related cat
- ☐ Z96.1 Presence of intraocular lens

(1-RT 2-LT 3-Bilateral)

DISORDER OF REFRACTION
- ☐ H52.0 [1 2 3] Hypermetropia
- ☐ H52.1 [1 2 3] Myopia
- ☐ H52.22 [1 2 3] Regular Astigmatism
- ☐ H52.4 Presbyopia

(1-RT 2-LT 3-Bilateral)

VISUAL DISORDERS
- ☐ H51.11 Convergence insufficiency
- ☐ H51.12 Convergence excess
- ☐ H52.53 [1 2 3] Spasm of accommodation
- ☐ H53.02 [1 2 3] Refractive amblyopia
- ☐ H53.03 [1 2 3] Strabismic amblyopia
- ☐ H53.14 [1 2 3] Visual discomfort
- ☐ H53.41 [1 2 3] Scotoma involving central area
- ☐ H53.42 [1 2 3] Scotoma of blind spot area
- ☐ H53.43 [1 2 3] Sector or arcuate defects
- ☐ H53.46 [1 2 3] Homonymous bilateral field defects
- ☐ H53.47 Heteronymous bilateral field defects
- ☐ H55.00 Unspec nystagmus

(1-RT 2-LT 3-Bilateral)

©2017 - E. Botts, O.D.

RETINAL DISORDERS
- ☐ E10.31 [1 9] T1 diab w unsp diab rtnop
- ☐ E10.321 [1 2 3] T1 diab w mild nonprlf diab rtnop w mac edema
- ☐ E10.329 [1 2 3] T1 diab w mild nonprlf diab rtnop wo mac edema
- ☐ E10.331 [1 2 3] T1 diab w mod nonprlf diab rtnop w mac edema
- ☐ E10.339 [1 2 3] T1 diab w mon nonprlf diab rtnop wo mac edema
- ☐ E10.341 [1 2 3] T1 diab w severe nonprlf diab rtnop w mac edema
- ☐ E10.349 [1 2 3] T1 diab w severe nonprlf diab rtnop wo mac edema
- ☐ E10.351 [1 2 3] T1 diab w prlif diab rtnop w mac edema
- ☐ E10.355 [1 2 3] T1 diab w stable prolif diab rtnop
- ☐ E10.359 [1 2 3] T1 diab w prlif diab rtnop wo mac edema
- ☐ E11.31 [1 9] T2 diab w unsp diab rtnop
- ☐ E11.321 [1 2 3] T2 diab w mild nonprlf diab rtnop w mac edema
- ☐ E11.329 [1 2 3] T2 diab w mild nonprlf diab rtnop wo mac edema
- ☐ E11.331 [1 2 3] T2 diab w mod nonprlf diab rtnop w mac edema
- ☐ E11.339 [1 2 3] T2 diab w mod nonprlf diab rtnop wo mac edema
- ☐ E11.341 [1 2 3] T2 diab w severe nonprlf diab rtnop w mac edema
- ☐ E11.349 [1 2 3] T2 diab w severe nonprlf diab rtnop wo mac edema
- ☐ E11.351 [1 2 3] T2 diab w prolif diab rtnop w mac edema
- ☐ E11.355 [1 2 3] T2 diab w stable prolif diab rtnop
- ☐ E11.359 [1 2 3] T2 diab w prolif diab rtnop wo mac edema
- ☐ H31.01 [1 2 3] Macula scars
- ☐ H31.09 [1 2 3] Other chorioretinal scars
- ☐ H32 Chorioretinal disorder
- ☐ H33.01 [1 2 3] Retinal detachment w single break
- ☐ H33.31 [1 2 3] Horseshoe tear of retina wo detachment
- ☐ H33.32 [1 2 3] Round hole
- ☐ H33.8 Other retinal detachments
- ☐ H34.1 [1 2 3] Central retinal artery occlusion
- ☐ H34.21 [1 2 3] Partial retinal artery occlusion
- ☐ H35.01 [1 2 3] Vascular sheathing
- ☐ H35.03 [1 2 3] Hypertensive retinopathy
- ☐ H35.04 [1 2 3] Retinal micro-aneurysms
- ☐ H35.34 [1 2 3] Macular cyst, hole or pseudohole
- ☐ H35.35 [1 2 3] Cystoid macular degeneration
- ☐ H35.36 [1 2 3] Drusen (degenerative) of macula
- ☐ H35.37 [1 2 3] Puckering of macule, ERM
- ☐ H35.40 Unspec peripheral retinal degeneration
- ☐ H35.41 [1 2 3] Lattice degeneration of retina
- ☐ H35.71 [1 2 3] Central serous chorioretinopathy
- ☐ H35.82 Retinal ischemia
- ☐ H43.31 [1 2 3] Viterous membranes
- ☐ H43.81 [1 2 3] Viterous degeneration

RT LT BI *(RT-Right LT-Left BI-Bilateral)*
- ☐ H34.81 [10 20 30] Central retinal vein occlusion w mac edema
- ☐ H34.81 [11 21 31] Central retinal vein occlusion w retinal neovascularization
- ☐ H34.81 [12 22 32] Central retinal vein occlusion, stable
- ☐ H34.83 [10 20 30] Tributary retinal vein occlusion w mac edema
- ☐ H34.83 [11 21 31] Tributary retinal vein occlusion w retinal neovascularization
- ☐ H34.83 [12 22 32] Tributary retinal vein occlusion, stable
- ☐ H35.31 [11 21 31] Nonexudative ARMD, early dry stage
- ☐ H35.31 [12 22 32] Nonexudative ARMD, intermediate dry stage
- ☐ H35.31 [13 23 33] Nonexudative ARMD, advanced atropic wo subfoveal inv
- ☐ H35.31 [14 24 34] Nonexudative ARMD, advanced atropic w subfoveal inv
- ☐ H35.32 [11 21 31] Exudative ARMD, active chorodial neovascularization
- ☐ H35.32 [12 22 32] Exudative ARMD, inactive chorodial neovascularization
- ☐ H35.32 [13 23 33] Exudative ARMD, inactive scar

(1-RT 2-LT 3-Bilateral)
(1-With Edema 9-Without Edema)

LACRIMAL SYSTEM
- ☐ H04.01 [1 2 3] Acute dacryoadenitis
- ☐ H04.12 [1 2 3] Dry eye syndrome
- ☐ H04.21 [1 2 3] Epiphora due to excess lacrimation

(1-RT 2-LT 3-Bilateral)

GLAUCOMA
- ☐ H40.01 [1 2 3] Open angle w borderline findings low risk
- ☐ H40.02 [1 2 3] Open angle w borderline findings high risk
- ☐ H40.05 [1 2 3] Ocular hypertension
- ☐ H40.06 [1 2 3] Primary angle closure wo glaucoma damage
- ☐ H40.21 [1 2 3] Acute angle-closure glaucoma

RT LT BI *(RT-Right LT-Left BI-Bilateral)*
- ☐ H40.11 [11 21 31] Primary open-angle glaucoma, mild
- ☑ H40.11 [12 22 32] Primary open-angle glaucoma, mod
- ☐ H40.11 [13 23 33] Primary open-angle glaucoma, severe
- ☐ H40.11 [14 24 34] Primary open-angle glaucoma, indeterminate
- ☐ H40.12 [11 21 31] Low-tens glaucoma, mild stage
- ☐ H40.12 [12 22 32] Low-tens glaucoma, mod stage
- ☐ H40.12 [13 23 33] Low-tens glaucoma, severe stage
- ☐ H40.13 [11 21 31] Pigmentary glaucoma, mild stage
- ☐ H40.13 [12 22 32] Pigmentary glaucoma, mod stage
- ☐ H40.13 [13 23 33] Pigmentary glaucoma, severe stage
- ☐ H40.22 [11 21 31] Chronic angle-closure glaucoma, mild stage
- ☐ H40.22 [12 22 32] Chronic angle-closure glaucoma, mod stage
- ☐ H40.22 [13 23 33] Chronic angle-closure glaucoma, severe stage

(1-RT 2-LT 3-Bilateral)

NEURO-OPHTHALMOLOGY
- ☐ H46.1 [1 2 3] Retrobulbar neuritis
- ☐ H47.01 [1 2 3] Ischemic optic neuropathy
- ☐ H47.1 [1 2 3] Papilledema assoc. w increased intracranial pressure
- ☐ H47.21 [1 2 3] Primary optic atrophy
- ☐ H47.32 [1 2 3] Drusen of optic disc

(1-RT 2-LT 3-Bilateral)

CONJUNCTIVA
- ☐ B30.0 Viral conjunctivitis
- ☐ H10.3 [1 2 3] Acute conjunctivitis
- ☐ H10.41 [1 2 3] Chronic giant papillary conjunctivitis
- ☐ H10.43 [1 2 3] Chronic follicular conjunctivitis
- ☐ H11.05 [1 2 3] Peripheral pterygium, progressive
- ☐ H11.12 [1 2 3] Conjunctival concretions
- ☐ H11.15 [1 2 3] Pinguecula
- ☐ H11.3 [1 2 3] Conjunctival hemorrhage
- ☐ S05.01X [A D S] Inj conjunctiva & corneal abrasion wo fb, RT, init
- ☐ S05.02X [A D S] Inj conjunctiva & corneal abrasion wo fb, LT, init
- ☐ T15.11X [A D S] Foreign body in conjunctival sac, RT, init
- ☐ T15.12X [A D S] Foreign body in conjunctival sac, LT init

(1-RT 2-LT 3-Bilateral)
(A-Initial D-Subsequent S-Sequela)

CORNEA
- ☐ H16.00 [1 2 3] Unspec corneal ulcer
- ☐ H16.01 [1 2 3] Central corneal ulcer
- ☐ H16.04 [1 2 3] Marginal corneal ulcer
- ☐ H16.12 [1 2 3] Filamentary keratitis
- ☐ H16.14 [1 2 3] Punctate keratitis
- ☐ H16.42 [1 2 3] Pannus (corneal)
- ☐ H18.22 [1 2 3] Idiopathic corneal edema
- ☐ H18.41 [1 2 3] Arcus senilis
- ☐ H18.51 Endothelial corneal dystrophy
- ☐ H18.59 Other hereditary corneal dystrophies
- ☐ H18.82 [1 2 3] Corneal edema due to contact lens
- ☐ H18.83 [1 2 3] Recurrent erosion of cornea
- ☐ T15.01X [A D S] Foreign body in cornea, RT, initial
- ☐ T15.02X [A D S] Foreign body in cornea, LT, initial

(1-RT 2-LT 3-Bilateral)
(A-Initial D-Subsequent S-Sequela)

STRABISMUS
- ☐ H50.00 Unspec esotropia
- ☐ H50.10 Unspec exotropia

(RT-Right LT-Left)

FEE
- ☐ S0620
- ☐ S0621
- ☐ 65210 *
- ☐ 65222 *
- ☐ 65430 *
- ☐ 65435 *
- ☐ 65778 *
- ☐ 67820 *
- ☐ 67938 *
- ☐ 68761 *
- ☐ 68801 *
- ☐ 76510
- ☐ 76514
- ☐ 83516QW
- ☐ 83861QW
- ☐ 87809QW
- ☐ 92002
- ☐ 92004
- ☐ 92012
- ☐ 92014
- ☐ 92015 +
- ☐ 92020
- ☐ 92025 *
- ☐ 92060
- ☐ 92071
- ☐ 92072
- ☐ 92082
- ☐ 92083
- ☐ 92100
- ☐ 92132
- ☑ 92133 **43.34**
- ☐ 92134
- ☐ 92225 *
- ☐ 92226 *
- ☐ 92250
- ☐ 92274
- ☐ 92284
- ☐ 92285
- ☐ 92286
- ☐ 92310 +
- ☐ 95930
- ☐ 99201
- ☐ 99202
- ☐ 99203
- ☐ 99204
- ☐ 99205
- ☐ 99212
- ☑ 99213 **63.99**
- ☐ 99214
- ☐ 99215

* May Require Modifier
+ Not Paid by MC

- ☐ 5010F ☐ G8428
- ☐ G8397 ☐ 4004F
- ☐ G8398 ☐ 1036F
- ☐ 2022F ☐ G8783
- ☐ 2024F ☐ G8950
- ☐ 2026F ☐ G8784
- ☐ 3072F ☐ G8785
- ☐ 2019F ☐ G8951
- ☐ 4177F ☐ G8952
- ☐ 2027F ☐ G8730
- ☐ 3284F ☐ G8731
- ☐ 3285F ☐ G8442
- ☐ 0517F ☐ G8939
- ☐ G8427 ☐ G8732
- ☐ G8430 ☐ G8509

v2.1 Revised 3/6/17

• GLAUCOMA PATIENT •
PAGE 8

ICD-10

HEALTH INSURANCE CLAIM FORM
APPROVED BY NATIONAL UNIFORM CLAIM COMMITTEE (NUCC) 02/12

PICA	PICA

1. MEDICARE ☐ MEDICAID ☐ TRICARE ☐ CHAMPVA ☐ GROUP HEALTH PLAN ☐ FECA BLK LUNG ☐ OTHER ☐
1a. INSURED'S I.D. NUMBER (For Program in Item 1): 359 26 8567A

2. PATIENT'S NAME (Last Name, First Name, Middle Initial): Doe, John
3. PATIENT'S BIRTH DATE: 01 | 01 | 1911 SEX: M ✔
4. INSURED'S NAME (Last Name, First Name, Middle Initial):

5. PATIENT'S ADDRESS (No., Street): 2100 Red Bud St.
6. PATIENT RELATIONSHIP TO INSURED: Self ✔
7. INSURED'S ADDRESS (No., Street):

CITY: Smithville STATE: IL
8. RESERVED FOR NUCC USE
CITY: STATE:

ZIP CODE: 69321 TELEPHONE: (000) 000-0000
ZIP CODE: TELEPHONE: ( )

9. OTHER INSURED'S NAME:
10. IS PATIENT'S CONDITION RELATED TO:
11. INSURED'S POLICY GROUP OR FECA NUMBER: None

a. OTHER INSURED'S POLICY OR GROUP NUMBER:
a. EMPLOYMENT? ☐ YES ☐ NO
a. INSURED'S DATE OF BIRTH: SEX: M ☐ F ☐

b. RESERVED FOR NUCC USE:
b. AUTO ACCIDENT? ☐ YES ☐ NO PLACE (State):
b. OTHER CLAIM ID (Designated by NUCC):

c. RESERVED FOR NUCC USE:
c. OTHER ACCIDENT? ☐ YES ☐ NO
c. INSURANCE PLAN NAME OR PROGRAM NAME:

d. INSURANCE PLAN NAME OR PROGRAM NAME:
10d. CLAIM CODES (Designated by NUCC):
d. IS THERE ANOTHER HEALTH BENEFIT PLAN? ☐ YES ☐ NO

READ BACK OF FORM BEFORE COMPLETING & SIGNING THIS FORM.
12. PATIENT'S OR AUTHORIZED PERSON'S SIGNATURE
SIGNED: *John Doe* DATE: 08-08-10
13. INSURED'S OR AUTHORIZED PERSON'S SIGNATURE
SIGNED:

14. DATE OF CURRENT ILLNESS, INJURY, or PREGNANCY (LMP): QUAL.
15. OTHER DATE QUAL. MM DD YY
16. DATES PATIENT UNABLE TO WORK IN CURRENT OCCUPATION: FROM TO

17. NAME OF REFERRING PROVIDER OR OTHER SOURCE: DK | Eric Botts
17a.
17b. NPI: Individual NPI#
18. HOSPITALIZATION DATES RELATED TO CURRENT SERVICES: FROM TO

19. ADDITIONAL CLAIM INFORMATION (Designated by NUCC):
20. OUTSIDE LAB? ☐ YES ☐ NO $ CHARGES:

21. DIAGNOSIS OR NATURE OF ILLNESS OR INJURY ICD Ind. 10
A. H40.1132 B. C. D.
E. F. G. H.
I. J. K. L.

22. RESUBMISSION CODE: ORIGINAL REF. NO.:
23. PRIOR AUTHORIZATION NUMBER:

24.	A. DATE(S) OF SERVICE From – To	B. PLACE OF SERVICE	C. EMG	D. PROCEDURES, SERVICES, OR SUPPLIES CPT/HCPCS	MODIFIER	E. DIAGNOSIS POINTER	F. $ CHARGES	G. DAYS OR UNITS	H. EPSDT	I. ID. QUAL.	J. RENDERING PROVIDER ID. #
1	09 07 10 – 09 07 10	11		92133		A	43 34	1		NPI	Individual NPI #
2	09 07 10 – 09 07 10	11		99213		A	63 99	1		NPI	Individual NPI #
3										NPI	
4										NPI	
5										NPI	
6										NPI	

25. FEDERAL TAX I.D. NUMBER: 4117743621 SSN ☐ EIN ✔
26. PATIENT'S ACCOUNT NO.:
27. ACCEPT ASSIGNMENT? ✔ YES ☐ NO
28. TOTAL CHARGE: $ 107 33
29. AMOUNT PAID: $ 0
30. Rsvd for NUCC Use: 107 33

31. SIGNATURE OF PHYSICIAN OR SUPPLIER INCLUDING DEGREES OR CREDENTIALS
SIGNED: *E. Botts* DATE: 09-07-10

32. SERVICE FACILITY LOCATION INFORMATION:
Eric K. Botts, O.D.
1730 East Jackson Street
Macomb, IL 61455
309-836-3373

33. BILLING PROVIDER INFO & PH #:
Eric K. Botts, O.D.
1730 East Jackson Street
Macomb, IL 61455
309-836-3373

NUCC Instruction Manual available at: www.nucc.org PLEASE PRINT OR TYPE APPROVED OMB-0938-1197 FORM 1500 (02-12)

©2014 - E. Botts, O.D. Group NPI # if available, otherwise individual NPI #

• GLAUCOMA PATIENT •
PAGE 9

Medicare
Remittance
Notice

Eric K. Botts, OD
1730 East Jackson Street
Macomb, IL 61455-2531

NPI #: 47932761
Page #: 1 of 2
Date: 09-22-10
Check/Eft #: 115449098

PERF PROV	SERV DATE	POS	NOS	PROC	MODS	BILLED	ALLOWED	DEDUCT	COINS	GRP/RC-AMT	PROV PD
NAME DOE, JOHN			HIC 36030715A		ACNT 111036P			ICN 0206222466720	ASG Y	MOA MAO 1	MA 18
47932761	0907 090710	11	1	92133		43.34	39.75	0.00	7.95	3.59	31.80
47932761	0907 090710	11	1	99213		63.99	54.57	0.00	10.91	9.42	43.66
PT RESP	18.86		1	CLAIM TOTALS		107.33	94.32	0.00	18.86	13.01	75.46

CLAIM INFORMATION FORWARDED TO: HCSC-BCBS OF IL (STD A & B)

75.46 NET

GLAUCOMA PATIENT
PAGE 10

GLAUCOMA FLOW SHEET

Name **John Doe**   DOB **01-01-11**

Pharmacy _____ Phone Number _____

Type **POAG OS**   CCT: Thick / (Avg) / Thin   c/d **OD .4/.4   OS .6/.6**

Risk Factors **None**

Target IOP **14 OU**

Date	IOP	VF	DFE	GON	Pho	CCT	Scan Laser	VEP	Comments / Results	Referral	MEDS/Start/Δ
8-8-10	16/17	X	X	X	X	X					∅
9-7-10	15/15						X		Anterior OCT – open angles OU ON OCT – thin RNFL OU		∅
11-10-10	15/15								IOP stable		
2-9-11	15/15	X	X		X						
5-7-11	15/18								IOP elevated, monitor 1 month		
6-7-11	15/20							X	Delated Peak Time OU		Begin Travatan 2 OS
8-6-11	14/14	X	X		X				Lower IOP, cup stable		Continue Travatan 2 OS
9-10-11	14/14						X		Thin but stable RNFL, no progression		Continue Travatan 2 OS

A   Pt advised to notify family members of risk.   Date _____

Example #3
AMD

EXAMINATION

• AMD •
PAGE 1

Example #3

Patient: *Jane Doe* Date: *11-03-14* Sex: M/(F) DOB: *04-22-37* Age: *37* Last Exam: ____
Chief Complaint: *Blurry Vision*

History
HPI: *Blurry both eyes, consistent since it started.*
- Symptoms: *First noticed 3 days ago*
- Location: *Faces look washed out.*
- Quality
- Severity
- Duration
- Timing
- Context
- Modifiers

Allergies: ____
Medications: ____
Ocular ROS: ____
Medical History & ROS from ___/___/___ reviewed: ☐ no changes
Dr. Initials: ____

Examination
Head/Face ☑ nl   Psych: Mood/Affect (anxiety/depression) ☑ nl   Neuro: Oriented (person/time/place) ☑ y ☐ n

VA: sc<   cc< 80/40   ph<   near<

K: OD____ OS____   **OLD RX:** OD____ add____ OS____ add____ △
R-scopy: OD____ OS____   **REF:** OD____ 20/__ add____ OS____ 20/__ add____

Perimetry:	☑ nl CF ☐ nl	Color ☐ nl ☐ RG defect		**ADNEXA** ☑ nl	
Motility:	☑ Full	Stereo __ Animals /3 WD /9		**EYELIDS:** ☐ Blepharitis	OD OS OU
Cover Test:	☐ Eso____	☐ Exo____ ☐ Ortho		☐ Meibomianitis	OD OS OU

Pupils: ☑ no afferent defect   ☑ round OU   Size: OD____ OS____
☐ 20D
☑ 90D/78D
☐ 3 Mirror

Drusen macula heme (OD)   *Drusen* (OS)

SLE: OD / OS
OD			OS		
☑ nl	☐ FBUT:__	TEAR FILM	☑ nl	☐ FBUT:__	
☑ nl	☑ arcus	CORNEA	☑ nl	☑ arcus	
☑ nl	☐ pterygium		☑ nl	☐ pterygium	
☑ nl	☐ infiltrate		☑ nl	☐ infiltrate	
☑ nl	☐ spk		☑ nl	☐ spk	
☑ nl	☐	SCLERA	☑ nl	☐	
☑ nl	☐ injection	CONJ.	☑ nl	☐ injection	
☑ nl	☐ pinguecula		☑ nl	☐ pinguecula	
☑ D&Q	☐	AC	☑ D&Q	☐	
☑ nl	☐ rubeosis	IRIS	☑ nl	☐ rubeosis	
☐ clear	☑ cat ☐ ns	LENS	☐ clear	☑ cat ☐ ns	

RETINA: OD / OS
OD			OS		
☐ nl	☑ drusen	MACULA	☐ nl	☑ drusen
☐ nl	☑ RPE chgs		☐ nl	☑ RPE chgs
☑ nl	☐ cotton wool	POST POLE	☑ nl	☐ cotton wool
☐ nl	☑ hemes		☑ nl	☐ hemes
☑ nl	☐ DME		☑ nl	☐ DME
☑ nl	☐	VESSELS	☑ nl	☐
☑ nl	☐ PVD	VITREOUS	☑ nl	☐ PVD
☑ nl	☐ strands		☑ nl	☐ strands
☑ nl	☐	PERIPHERY	☑ nl	☐

OPTIC DISCS: OD ☑ nl   OS ☑ nl
SIZE/APPEARANCE/NFL
☐ .35/.35 C/D ☐ .4/.4

NCT: __/__ @ ____   Pachymetry: OD____ OS____
TAG: 14/16 @ 9:32 am   Dilated: M .5% 1% (PA 1%/0.25%) C 1% 2% Ph 2.5% 10% OU@____

Diagnosis/Plan   MDM 1 2 ③ 4

Wet AMD OD
Dry AMD OS
CATS ou

Immediate consult retinal MD
Order TVF OCT to monitor AMD
Order Dark Adaptation
Discuss Areds/Nutrition/Omega 3
Monitor CATS 1 year

Order: ☑ HRT/GDX/OCT   RTO: ___ day
☐ Photo   ___ week
☑ VF   *2* month
☑ Consult   ___ year

Dr. *E. Botts*

Rev.11/11 ©2007 - E. Botts, O.D.

• AMD •
PAGE 2
Supplementary Tests

Patient: **Jan Doe** Date: **11-03-14**

- ☐ **Visual Fields** (92081, 92082, 92083)
- ☐ **Sensorimotor Examination** (92060)
- ☐ **Scanning Computerized Ophthalmic Diagnostic Imaging** (92132, 92133, 92134) ☐ HRT ☐ OCT ☐ GDX
- ☐ **Serial Tonometry** (92100)
- ☐ **Visual Evoked Potential** (95930)
- ☐ **Gonioscopy** (92020)
- ☐ **Fundus Photography** (92250)
- ☐ **External Ocular Photography** (92285)
- ☐ **Corneal Topography** (92025)
- ☐ **Pattern Electroretinography** (92275)
- ☐ **Specular Microscopy** (92286)

Scanning Computerized Ophthalmic Diagnostic Imaging (92132, 92133, (92134)) ☐ HRT ☒ OCT ☐ GDX

	OD	OS
Findings	Macular hemes and drusen with RPE Changes	Macular drusen with RPE Changes
Diagnosis	Wet AMD	Dry AMD
Plan	Order Retinal Consult	Order Retinal Consult
Signature	E. Bold	

Visual Fields (92081, (92082), 92083)

	OD	OS
Findings	Small Central defect	No Defect
Diagnosis	Wet AMD	Dry AMD
Plan	Order Retinal Consult	Monitor 3 months
Signature	E. Bold	

Dark Adaptometry (92284)

	OD	OS
Findings	Rod Intercept 16.37 min	Rod Intercept 12.18 min
Diagnosis	Wet AMD	Dry AMD
Plan	Repeat 3 months	Repeat 6 months
Signature	E. Bold	

	OD	OS
Findings		
Diagnosis		
Plan		
Signature		

BILLING STATEMENT

• AMD •
PAGE 3

Dr. Eric Botts
Phone 309/836-3373

Date of Service **11/03/14**
Patient's Name **Jane Doe** DOB **04/22/37** ☐ Male ☑ Female
Address **2100 RedBud St.** City **Smithville** State **IL** Zip **69321**
Telephone ( ) - Insured's Name Insured's DOB / /
ID Number **359 26 8567A** Secondary Ins **BCBS** Total **299.32**
Special Instructions
Refraction Paid
Co-Pay/Deductible Paid
Ins/Mcaid/Mcare Paid
Secondary Paid

MODIFIERS 24 25 26 50 55 59 79 RT LT E1 E2 E3 E4 1P 2P 8P TC GW QW
Write Off
Balance Due

MISCELLANEOUS
- E10.65 Type 1 Diabetes w complications
- E10.9 Type 1 Diabetes wo complications
- E11.65 Type 2 Diabetes w complications
- E11.9 Type 2 Diabetes wo complications
- H27.0 [1 2 3] Aphakia
- H53.8 Blurred Vision
- H57.1 [1 2 3] Ocular Pain
- M06.9 Rheumatoid Arthritis
- Z79.4 Insulin Dependent
- Z79.84 Non-Insulin Dependent
- Z79.899 High Risk meds

(1-RT 2-LT 3-Bilateral)

UVEAL DISORDERS
- H20.01 [1 2 3] Primary iridocyclitis
- H21.0 [1 2 3] Hyphema
- H21.23 [1 2 3] Degeneration of Iris
- H21.26 [1 2 3] Iris Atrophy
- H21.4 [1 2 3] Pupillary membranes
- H57.05 [1 2 3] Tonic Pupil

(1-RT 2-LT 3-Bilateral)

EYELIDS
- H00.023 Hordeolum internum RT eye
- H00.026 Hordeolum internum LT eye
- H00.13 Chalazion RT eye
- H00.16 Chalazion LT eye
- H01.023 Squamous blepharitis RT eye
- H01.026 Squamous blepharitis LT eye
- H01.113 Allergic dermatitis RT eye
- H01.116 Allergic dermatitis LT eye
- H02.033 Senile entropion RT eye
- H02.036 Senile entropion LT eye
- H02.053 Trichiasis wo entropion RT eye
- H05.056 Trichiasis wo entropion LT eye
- H02.133 Senile ectropion RT eye
- H02.136 Senile ectropion LT eye
- H02.40 [1 2 3] Unspec ptosis of eyelid
- H02.833 Dermatochalasis RT eye
- H02.836 Dermatochalasis LT eye

(1-RT 2-LT 3-Bilateral)

CATARACT/LENS
- H25.01 [1 2 3] Cortical age-related cat
- H25.04 [1 2 3] Post subcap polar age-related cat
- H25.1 [1 2 3] Age-related nuclear cat
- H25.89 Other age-related cat
- Z96.1 Presence of intraocular lens

(1-RT 2-LT 3-Bilateral)

DISORDER OF REFRACTION
- H52.0 [1 2 3] Hypermetropia
- H52.1 [1 2 3] Myopia
- H52.22 [1 2 3] Regular Astigmatism
- H52.4 Presbyopia

(1-RT 2-LT 3-Bilateral)

VISUAL DISORDERS
- H51.11 Convergence insufficiency
- H51.12 Convergence excess
- H52.53 [1 2 3] Spasm of accommodation
- H53.02 [1 2 3] Refractive amblyopia
- H53.03 [1 2 3] Strabismic amblyopia
- H53.14 [1 2 3] Visual discomfort
- H53.41 [1 2 3] Scotoma involving central area
- H53.42 [1 2 3] Scotoma of blind spot area
- H53.43 [1 2 3] Sector or arcuate defects
- H53.46 [1 2 3] Homonymous bilateral field defects
- H53.47 Heteronymous bilateral field defects
- H55.00 Unspec nystagmus

(1-RT 2-LT 3-Bilateral)

RETINAL DISORDERS
- E10.31 [1 9] T1 diab w unsp diab rtnop
- E10.321 [1 2 3] T1 diab w mild nonprlf diab rtnop w mac edema
- E10.329 [1 2 3] T1 diab w mild nonprlf diab rtnop wo mac edema
- E10.331 [1 2 3] T1 diab w mod nonprlf diab rtnop w mac edema
- E10.339 [1 2 3] T1 diab w mon nonprlf diab rtnop wo mac edema
- E10.341 [1 2 3] T1 diab w severe nonprlf diab rtnop w mac edema
- E10.349 [1 2 3] T1 diab w severe nonprlf diab rtnop wo mac edema
- E10.351 [1 2 3] T1 diab w prlif diab rtnop w mac edema
- E10.355 [1 2 3] T1 diab w stable prolif diab rtnop
- E10.359 [1 2 3] T1 diab w prlif diab rtnop wo mac edema
- E11.31 [1 9] T2 diab w unsp diab rtnop
- E11.321 [1 2 3] T2 diab w mild nonprlf diab rtnop w mac edema
- E11.329 [1 2 3] T2 diab w mild nonprlf diab rtnop wo mac edema
- E11.331 [1 2 3] T2 diab w mod nonprlf diab rtnop w mac edema
- E11.339 [1 2 3] T2 diab w mod nonprlf diab rtnop wo mac edema
- E11.341 [1 2 3] T2 diab w severe nonprlf diab rtnop w mac edema
- E11.349 [1 2 3] T2 diab w severe nonprlf diab rtnop wo mac edema
- E11.351 [1 2 3] T2 diab w prolif diab rtnop w mac edema
- E11.355 [1 2 3] T2 diab w stable prolif diab rtnop
- E11.359 [1 2 3] T2 diab w prolif diab rtnop wo mac edema
- H31.01 [1 2 3] Macula scars
- H31.09 [1 2 3] Other chorioretinal scars
- H32 Chorioretinal disorder
- H33.01 [1 2 3] Retinal detachment w single break
- H33.31 [1 2 3] Horseshoe tear of retina wo detachment
- H33.32 [1 2 3] Round hole
- H33.8 Other retinal detachments
- H34.1 [1 2 3] Central retinal artery occlusion
- H34.21 [1 2 3] Partial retinal artery occlusion
- H35.01 [1 2 3] Vascular sheathing
- H35.03 [1 2 3] Hypertensive retinopathy
- H35.04 [1 2 3] Retinal micro-aneurysms
- H35.34 [1 2 3] Macular cyst, hole or pseudohole
- H35.35 [1 2 3] Cystoid macular degeneration
- H35.36 [1 2 3] Drusen (degenerative) of macula
- H35.37 [1 2 3] Puckering of macule, ERM
- H35.40 Unspec peripheral retinal degeneration
- H35.41 [1 2 3] Lattice degeneration of retina
- H35.71 [1 2 3] Central serous chorioretinopathy
- H35.82 Retinal ischemia
- H43.31 [1 2 3] Viterous membranes
- H43.81 [1 2 3] Viterous degeneration

RT LT BI (RT-Right LT-Left BI-Bilateral)
- H34.81 [10 20 30] Central retinal vein occlusion w mac edema
- H34.81 [11 21 31] Central retinal vein occlusion w retinal neovascularization
- H34.81 [12 22 32] Central retinal vein occlusion, stable
- H34.83 [10 20 30] Tributary retinal vein occlusion w mac edema
- H34.83 [11 21 31] Tributary retinal vein occlusion w retinal neovascularization
- H34.83 [12 22 32] Tributary retinal vein occlusion, stable
- ☑ H35.31 [11 21 31] Nonexudative ARMD, early dry stage
- H35.31 [12 22 32] Nonexudative ARMD, intermediate dry stage
- H35.31 [13 23 33] Nonexudative ARMD, advanced atropic wo subfoveal inv
- H35.31 [14 24 34] Nonexudative ARMD, advanced atropic w subfoveal inv
- ☑ H35.32 [11 21 31] Exudative ARMD, active chorodial neovascularization
- H35.32 [12 22 32] Exudative ARMD, inactive chorodial neovascularization
- H35.32 [13 23 33] Exudative ARMD, inactive scar

(1-RT 2-LT 3-Bilateral)
(1-With Edema 9-Without Edema)

LACRIMAL SYSTEM
- H04.01 [1 2 3] Acute dacryoadenitis
- H04.12 [1 2 3] Dry eye syndrome
- H04.21 [1 2 3] Epiphora due to excess lacrimation

(1-RT 2-LT 3-Bilateral)

GLAUCOMA
- H40.01 [1 2 3] Open angle w borderline findings low risk
- H40.02 [1 2 3] Open angle w borderline findings high risk
- H40.05 [1 2 3] Ocular hypertension
- H40.06 [1 2 3] Primary angle closure wo glaucoma damage
- H40.21 [1 2 3] Acute angle-closure glaucoma

RT LT BI (RT-Right LT-Left BI-Bilateral)
- H40.11 [11 21 31] Primary open-angle glaucoma, mild
- H40.11 [12 22 32] Primary open-angle glaucoma, mod
- H40.11 [13 23 33] Primary open-angle glaucoma, severe
- H40.11 [14 24 34] Primary open-angle glaucoma, indeterminate
- H40.12 [11 21 31] Low-tens glaucoma, mild stage
- H40.12 [12 22 32] Low-tens glaucoma, mod stage
- H40.12 [13 23 33] Low-tens glaucoma, severe stage
- H40.13 [11 21 31] Pigmentary glaucoma, mild stage
- H40.13 [12 22 32] Pigmentary glaucoma, mod stage
- H40.13 [13 23 33] Pigmentary glaucoma, severe stage
- H40.22 [11 21 31] Chronic angle-closure glaucoma, mild stage
- H40.22 [12 22 32] Chronic angle-closure glaucoma, mod stage
- H40.22 [13 23 33] Chronic angle-closure glaucoma, severe stage

(1-RT 2-LT 3-Bilateral)

NEURO-OPHTHALMOLOGY
- H46.1 [1 2 3] Retrobulbar neuritis
- H47.01 [1 2 3] Ischemic optic neuropathy
- H47.1 [1 2 3] Papilledema assoc. w increased intracranial pressure
- H47.21 [1 2 3] Primary optic atrophy
- H47.32 [1 2 3] Drusen of optic disc

(1-RT 2-LT 3-Bilateral)

CONJUNCTIVA
- B30.0 Viral conjunctivitis
- H10.3 [1 2 3] Acute conjunctivitis
- H10.41 [1 2 3] Chronic giant papillary conjunctivitis
- H10.43 [1 2 3] Chronic follicular conjunctivitis
- H11.05 [1 2 3] Peripheral pterygium, progressive
- H11.12 [1 2 3] Conjunctival concretions
- H11.15 [1 2 3] Pinguecula
- H11.3 [1 2 3] Conjunctival hemorrhage
- S05.01X [A D S] Inj conjunctiva & corneal abrasion wo fb, RT, init
- S05.02X [A D S] Inj conjunctiva & corneal abrasion wo fb, LT, init
- T15.11X [A D S] Foreign body in conjunctival sac, RT, init
- T15.12X [A D S] Foreign body in conjunctival sac, LT, init

(1-RT 2-LT 3-Bilateral)
(A-Initial D-Subsequent S-Sequela)

CORNEA
- H16.00 [1 2 3] Unspec corneal ulcer
- H16.01 [1 2 3] Central corneal ulcer
- H16.04 [1 2 3] Marginal corneal ulcer
- H16.12 [1 2 3] Filamentary keratitis
- H16.14 [1 2 3] Punctate keratitis
- H16.42 [1 2 3] Pannus (corneal)
- H18.22 [1 2 3] Idiopathic corneal edema
- H18.41 [1 2 3] Arcus senilis
- H18.51 Endothelial corneal dystrophie
- H18.59 Other hereditary corneal dystrophies
- H18.82 [1 2 3] Corneal edema due to contact lens
- H18.83 [1 2 3] Recurrent erosion of cornea
- T15.01X [A D S] Foreign body in cornea, RT, initial
- T15.02X [A D S] Foreign body in cornea, LT, initial

(1-RT 2-LT 3-Bilateral)
(A-Initial D-Subsequent S-Sequela)

STRABISMUS
- H50.00 Unspec esotropia
- H50.10 Unspec exotropia

(RT-Right LT-Left)

FEE
- S0620
- S0621
- 65210 *
- 65222 *
- 65430 *
- 65435 *
- 65778 *
- 67820 *
- 67938 *
- 68761 *
- 68801 *
- 76510
- 76514
- 83516QW
- 83861QW
- 87809QW
- 92002
- 92004
- 92012
- 92014
- 92015 +
- 92020
- 92025 *
- 92060
- 92071
- 92072
- ☑ 92082 **47 20**
- 92083
- 92100
- 92132
- 92133
- ☑ 92134 **43 34**
- 92225 *
- 92226 *
- 92250
- 92275
- ☑ 92284 **59 03**
- 92285
- 92286
- 92310 +
- 92530
- 99201
- 99202
- 99203
- ☑ 99204 **149 75**
- 99205
- 99212
- 99213
- 99214
- 99215

* May Require Modifier
+ Not Paid by MC

- 5010F / G8428
- G8397 / 4004F
- G8398 / 1036F
- 2022F / G8783
- 2024F / G8950
- 2026F / G8784
- 3072F / G8785
- 2019F / G8951
- 4177F / G8952
- 2027F / G8730
- 3284F / G8731
- 3285F / G8442
- 0517F / G8939
- G8427 / G8732
- G8430 / G8509

v2.1 Revised 3/6/17

©2017 - E. Botts, O.D.

HEALTH INSURANCE CLAIM FORM

• AMD • PAGE 4

ICD-10

APPROVED BY NATIONAL UNIFORM CLAIM COMMITTEE (NUCC) 02/12

PICA		PICA

1. MEDICARE / MEDICAID / TRICARE / CHAMPVA / GROUP HEALTH PLAN / FECA BLK LUNG / OTHER

1a. INSURED'S I.D. NUMBER (For Program in Item 1): 479 99 1234A

2. PATIENT'S NAME (Last Name, First Name, Middle Initial): Doe, Jane

3. PATIENT'S BIRTH DATE: 04 | 22 | 37 **SEX**: M ✓

4. INSURED'S NAME:

5. PATIENT'S ADDRESS (No., Street): 322 North St

6. PATIENT RELATIONSHIP TO INSURED: Self ✓

7. INSURED'S ADDRESS:

CITY: Bowen **STATE**: IL

8. RESERVED FOR NUCC USE

ZIP CODE: 62314 **TELEPHONE**: ( )

9. OTHER INSURED'S NAME:

10. IS PATIENT'S CONDITION RELATED TO:
- a. EMPLOYMENT?
- b. AUTO ACCIDENT?
- c. OTHER ACCIDENT?

11. INSURED'S POLICY GROUP OR FECA NUMBER

10d. CLAIM CODES:

d. IS THERE ANOTHER HEALTH BENEFIT PLAN?

12. PATIENT'S OR AUTHORIZED PERSON'S SIGNATURE
SIGNED: SOF DATE: 11-03-14

13. INSURED'S OR AUTHORIZED PERSON'S SIGNATURE

14. DATE OF CURRENT ILLNESS, INJURY, or PREGNANCY (LMP)

15. OTHER DATE

16. DATES PATIENT UNABLE TO WORK IN CURRENT OCCUPATION

17. NAME OF REFERRING PROVIDER OR OTHER SOURCE: DK | Eric Botts
17b. NPI: Individual NPI#

18. HOSPITALIZATION DATES RELATED TO CURRENT SERVICES

19. ADDITIONAL CLAIM INFORMATION

20. OUTSIDE LAB?

21. DIAGNOSIS OR NATURE OF ILLNESS OR INJURY ICD Ind. 10
A. H35.3121 B. H35.3211

22. RESUBMISSION CODE

23. PRIOR AUTHORIZATION NUMBER

24. Services:

#	From	To	POS	EMG	CPT/HCPCS	MOD	DX Pointer	$ Charges	Days	ID	Rendering Provider ID
1	01 03 14	11 03 14	11		99204		AB	149 75	1	NPI	Individual NPI #
2	11 03 14	11 03 14	11		92134		A	43 34	1	NPI	Individual NPI #
3	11 03 14	11 03 14	11		92082		A	47 20	1	NPI	Individual NPI #
4	11 03 14	11 03 14	11		92284		A	59 03	1	NPI	Individual NPI #

25. FEDERAL TAX I.D. NUMBER: 4117743621 EIN ✓

26. PATIENT'S ACCOUNT NO.

27. ACCEPT ASSIGNMENT?: YES ✓

28. TOTAL CHARGE: $ 299 32

29. AMOUNT PAID: $ 00

30. Rsvd for NUCC Use: 299 32

31. SIGNATURE OF PHYSICIAN OR SUPPLIER: E. Botts 11-03-14

32. SERVICE FACILITY LOCATION INFORMATION:
Eric K. Botts, O.D.
1730 East Jackson Street
Macomb, IL 61455
309-836-3373

33. BILLING PROVIDER INFO & PH #:
Eric K. Botts, O.D.
1730 East Jackson Street
Macomb, IL 61455
309-836-3373

NUCC Instruction Manual available at: www.nucc.org PLEASE PRINT OR TYPE APPROVED OMB-0938-1197 FORM 1500 (02-12)

©2014 - E. Botts, O.D. Group NPI # if available, otherwise individual NPI #

AMD
PAGE 5

Medicare
Remittance
Notice

Eric K. Botts, OD
1730 East Jackson Street
Macomb, IL 61455-2531

NPI #: 47932761
Page #: 1 of 2
Date: 11-22-14
Check/Eft #: 115449098

PERF PROV	SERV DATE	POS	NOS	PROC	MODS	BILLED	ALLOWED	DEDUCT	COINS	GRP/RC-AMT	PROV PD
NAME DOE, JANE			HIC 36030715A		ACNT 111036P			ICN 0206222466720	ASG Y	MOA MAO 1	MA 18
47932761	1103 110314	11	1	99204		149.75	132.75	0.00	26.55	17.00	106.20
47932761	1103 110314	11	1	92134		43.34	32.94	0.00	6.59	10.40	26.35
47932761	1103 110314	11	1	92082		47.20	34.40	0.00	4.88	12.80	37.76
47932761	1103 110314	11	1	92284		59.03	50.01	0.00	10.00	9.02	40.01
PT RESP	48.02		1	CLAIM TOTALS		299.32	250.10	0.00	48.02	49.22	210.32

CLAIM INFORMATION FORWARDED TO: HCSC-BCBS OF IL (STD A & B)   290.78 NET

Example #4
Epiretinal Membrane

• EPIRETINAL MEMBRANE •
PAGE 1
EXAMINATION

Example #4

Patient: Jan Doe Date: 10-03-15 Sex: M (F) DOB: 05-21-37 Age: ___ Last Exam: 1 year
Chief Complaint: Blurry vision

History
HPI: Loss of sharpness right only x 2 months. Worse last two weeks.
Symptoms
Location
Quality
Severity
Duration
Timing
Context
Modifiers

Allergies
Medications
Ocular ROS

Medical History & ROS from 03/07/12 reviewed: ☑ no changes
Dr. Initials: EKB

Examination
Head/Face ☑ nl   Psych: Mood/Affect (anxiety/depression) ☑ nl   Neuro: Oriented (person/time/place) ☑ y ☐ n

VA: sc<   cc< 50/25   ph<   near<

K: OD ___ OS ___
OLD RX: OD ___ add ___ OS ___ add ___
R-scopy: OD ___ OS ___
REF: OD +2.25 -1.75 X 180 20/20 add +2.50
         OS +2.00 -1.25 X 175 20/25 add ___

Perimetry:	☑ nl	CF ☐ nl	Color ☐ nl ☐ RG defect	**ADNEXA**	☑ nl
Motility:	☑ Full		Stereo Animals /3 WD /9	**EYELIDS:**	☐ Blepharitis OD OS OU
Cover Test:	☐ Eso___		☐ Exo___ ☑ Ortho		☐ Meibomianitis OD OS OU

Pupils: ☑ no afferent defect   ☑ round OU   Size: OD 4 OS 4

☐ 20D
☐ 90D/78D
☐ 3 Mirror
☐ ___

- macular puckering

SLE: OD
☑ nl ☐ FBUT:____ TEAR FILM
☑ nl ☐ arcus   CORNEA
☑ nl ☐ pterygium
☑ nl ☐ infiltrate
☑ nl ☐ spk
☑ nl ☐   SCLERA
☑ nl ☐ injection   CONJ.
☑ nl ☐ pinguecula
☑ D&Q ☐   AC
☑ nl ☐ rubeosis   IRIS
☐ clear ☑ cat ☐ ns LENS

OS
☑ nl ☐ FBUT:____
☑ nl ☐ arcus
☑ nl ☐ pterygium
☑ nl ☐ infiltrate
☑ nl ☐ spk
☑ nl
☑ nl ☐ injection
☑ nl ☐ pinguecula
☑ D&Q ☐
☑ nl ☐ rubeosis
☐ clear ☑ cat ☐ ns

RETINA: OD
☑ nl ☐ drusen   MACULA
☑ nl ☐ RPE chgs
☑ nl ☐ cotton wool   POST POLE
☑ nl ☐ hemes
☑ nl ☐ DME
☑ nl ☐   VESSELS
☑ nl ☐ PVD   VITREOUS
☑ nl ☐ strands
☑ nl ☐   PERIPHERY
OPTIC DISCS: OD
☑ nl   SIZE/APPEARANCE/NFL
☐ .4/.4 C/D

OS
☑ nl ☐ drusen
☑ nl ☐ RPE chgs
☑ nl ☐ cotton wool
☑ nl ☐ hemes
☑ nl ☐ DME
☑ nl
☑ nl ☐ PVD
☑ nl ☐ strands
☑ nl

OS
☑ nl
☐ .4/.4

NCT: __/__ @ ___   Pachymetry: OD ___ OS ___
TAG: 16/16 @ 10:15 am
Dilated: M .5% 1% (PA 1%/0.25%) C 1% 2% Ph 2.5% 10% OU @ 10:28 am

Diagnosis/Plan   MDM 1 2 (3) 4
Epiretinal Membrane OD
Cataracts OU

Order VF photos and ERG today
RTC 1 week SL Raster OCT

Order: ☑ HRT/GDX/OCT RTO: ___ day
       ☑ Photo   1 week
       ☐ VF   ___ month
       ☐ Consult   ___ year

Dr. E. Botts

Rev.11/11 ©2007 - E. Botts, O.D.

• EPIRETINAL MEMBRANE •
PAGE 2
EXAMINATION
Supplementary Tests

Patient: Jan Doe Date: 10-03-15

Fundus Photography (92250)

OD	OS
Findings: Macular puckering	Normal
Diagnosis: Epiretinal membrane	
Plan: Monitor 6 months	Monitor 6 months

Signature: E. Botts

Visual Fields (92081, 92082, (92083))

OD	OS
Findings: Small central defect	No defect
Diagnosis: Epiretinal membrane	Good responder
Plan: Monitor 6 months	

Signature: E. Botts

Electroretinography (ERG) (92273, (92274), 0509T)

OD	OS
Findings: Low magnitude 1.12	Normal magnitude
Diagnosis: Epiretinal membrane	
Plan: Monitor 6 months	

Signature: E. Botts

BILLING STATEMENT

• EPIRETINAL MEMBRANE •
PAGE 3

Dr. Eric Botts
Phone 309/836-337

57

Date of Service **10 / 03 / 15**
Patient's Name **Jan Doe**   DOB **05 / 21 / 37**   ☐ Male ☑ Female
Address **21 Oak Drive**   City **Smithville**   State **IL** Zip **69321**
Telephone (___) ___-____   Insured's Name _____   Insured's DOB ___/___/___
ID Number **349 27 8567A**   Secondary Ins **BCBS**   Total **395.36**
Special Instructions _____   Refraction Paid **18.00**
Co-Pay/Deductible Paid _____
Ins/Mcaid/Mcare Paid _____
Secondary Paid _____
Write Off _____
Balance Due _____

MODIFIERS 24 25 26 50 55 59 79 RT LT E1 E2 E3 E4 1P 2P 8P TC GW QW

MISCELLANEOUS
- E10.65 — Type 1 Diabetes w complications
- E10.9 — Type 1 Diabetes wo complications
- E11.65 — Type 2 Diabetes w complications
- E11.9 — Type 2 Diabetes wo complications
- H27.0 [1 2 3] — Aphakia
- H53.8 — Blurred Vision
- H57.1 [1 2 3] — Ocular Pain
- M06.9 — Rheumatoid Arthritis
- Z79.4 — Insulin Dependent
- Z79.84 — Non-Insulin Dependent
- Z79.899 — High Risk meds

(1-RT 2-LT 3-Bilateral)

UVEAL DISORDERS
- H20.01 [1 2 3] — Primary iridocyclitis
- H21.0 — Hyphema
- H21.23 [1 2 3] — Degeneration of Iris
- H21.26 [1 2 3] — Iris Atrophy
- H21.4 [1 2 3] — Pupillary membranes
- H57.05 [1 2 3] — Tonic Pupil

(1-RT 2-LT 3-Bilateral)

EYELIDS
- H00.023 — Hordeolum internum RT eye
- H00.026 — Hordeolum internum LT eye
- H00.13 — Chalazion RT eye
- H00.16 — Chalazion LT eye
- H01.023 — Squamous blepharitis RT eye
- H01.026 — Squamous blepharitis LT eye
- H01.113 — Allergic dermatitis RT eye
- H01.116 — Allergic dermatitis LT eye
- H02.033 — Senile entropion RT eye
- H02.036 — Senile entropion LT eye
- H02.053 — Trichiasis wo entropion RT eye
- H05.056 — Trichiasis wo entropion LT eye
- H02.133 — Senile ectropion RT eye
- H02.136 — Senile ectropion LT eye
- H02.40 [1 2 3] — Unspec ptosis of eyelid
- H02.833 — Dermatochalasis RT eye
- H02.836 — Dermatochalasis LT eye

(1-RT 2-LT 3-Bilateral)

CATARACT/LENS
- ☑ H25.01 [1 2 3] — Cortical age-related cat
- H25.04 [1 2 ③] — Post subcap polar age-related cat
- H25.1 [1 2 3] — Age-related nuclear cat
- H25.89 — Other age-related cat
- Z96.1 — Presence of intraocular lens

(1-RT 2-LT 3-Bilateral)

DISORDER OF REFRACTION
- H52.0 [1 2 3] — Hypermetropia
- H52.1 [1 2 3] — Myopia
- H52.22 [1 2 3] — Regular Astigmatism
- H52.4 — Presbyopia

(1-RT 2-LT 3-Bilateral)

VISUAL DISORDERS
- H51.11 — Convergence insufficiency
- H51.12 — Convergence excess
- H52.53 [1 2 3] — Spasm of accommodation
- H53.02 [1 2 3] — Refractive amblyopia
- H53.03 [1 2 3] — Strabismic amblyopia
- H53.14 [1 2 3] — Visual discomfort
- H53.41 [1 2 3] — Scotoma involving central area
- H53.42 [1 2 3] — Scotoma of blind spot area
- H53.43 [1 2 3] — Sector or arcuate defects
- H53.46 [1 2 3] — Homonymous bilateral field defects
- H53.47 — Heteronymous bilateral field defects
- H55.00 — Unspec nystagmus

(1-RT 2-LT 3-Bilateral)

RETINAL DISORDERS
- E10.31 [1 9] — T1 diab w unsp diab rtnop
- E10.321 [1 2 3] — T1 diab w mild nonprlf diab rtnop w mac edema
- E10.329 [1 2 3] — T1 diab w mild nonprlf diab rtnop wo mac edema
- E10.331 [1 2 3] — T1 diab w mod nonprlf diab rtnop w mac edema
- E10.339 [1 2 3] — T1 diab w mon nonprlf diab rtnop wo mac edema
- E10.341 [1 2 3] — T1 diab w severe nonprlf diab rtnop w mac edema
- E10.349 [1 2 3] — T1 diab w severe nonprlf diab rtnop wo mac edema
- E10.351 [1 2 3] — T1 diab w prlif diab rtnop w mac edema
- E10.355 [1 2 3] — T1 diab w stable prolif diab rtnop
- E10.359 [1 2 3] — T1 diab w prlif diab rtnop wo mac edema
- E11.31 [1 9] — T2 diab w unsp diab rtnop
- E11.321 [1 2 3] — T2 diab w mild nonprlf diab rtnop w mac edema
- E11.329 [1 2 3] — T2 diab w mild nonprlf diab rtnop wo mac edema
- E11.331 [1 2 3] — T2 diab w mod nonprlf diab rtnop w mac edema
- E11.339 [1 2 3] — T2 diab w mod nonprlf diab rtnop wo mac edema
- E11.341 [1 2 3] — T2 diab w severe nonprlf diab rtnop w mac edema
- E11.349 [1 2 3] — T2 diab w severe nonprlf diab rtnop wo mac edema
- E11.351 [1 2 3] — T2 diab w prolif diab rtnop w mac edema
- E11.355 [1 2 3] — T2 diab w stable prolif diab rtnop
- E11.359 [1 2 3] — T2 diab w prolif diab rtnop wo mac edema
- H31.01 [1 2 3] — Macula scars
- H31.09 [1 2 3] — Other chorioretinal scars
- H32 — Chorioretinal disorder
- H33.01 [1 2 3] — Retinal detachment w single break
- H33.31 [1 2 3] — Horseshoe tear of retina wo detachment
- H33.32 [1 2 3] — Round hole
- H33.8 — Other retinal detachments
- H34.1 [1 2 3] — Central retinal artery occlusion
- H34.21 [1 2 3] — Partial retinal artery occlusion
- H35.01 [1 2 3] — Vascular sheathing
- H35.03 [1 2 3] — Hypertensive retinopathy
- H35.04 [1 2 3] — Retinal micro-aneurysms
- H35.34 [1 2 3] — Macular cyst, hole or pseudohole
- H35.35 [1 2 3] — Cystoid macular degeneration
- H35.36 [1 2 3] — Drusen (degenerative) of macula
- ☑ H35.37 [1 2 3] — Puckering of macula, ERM
- H35.40 — Unspec peripheral retinal degeneration
- H35.41 [1 2 3] — Lattice degeneration of retina
- H35.71 [1 2 3] — Central serous chorioretinopathy
- H35.82 — Retinal ischemia
- H43.31 [1 2 3] — Viterous membranes
- H43.81 [1 2 3] — Viterous degeneration

RT LT BI *(RT-Right LT-Left BI-Bilateral)*
- H34.81 [10 20 30] — Central retinal vein occlusion w mac edema
- H34.81 [11 21 31] — Central retinal vein occlusion w retinal neovascularization
- H34.81 [12 22 32] — Central retinal vein occlusion, stable
- H34.83 [10 20 30] — Tributary retinal vein occlusion w mac edema
- H34.83 [11 21 31] — Tributary retinal vein occlusion w retinal neovascularization
- H34.83 [12 22 32] — Tributary retinal vein occlusion, stable
- H35.31 [11 21 31] — Nonexudative ARMD, early dry stage
- H35.31 [12 22 32] — Nonexudative ARMD, intermediate dry stage
- H35.31 [13 23 33] — Nonexudative ARMD, advanced atropic wo subfoveal inv
- H35.31 [14 24 34] — Nonexudative ARMD, advanced atropic w subfoveal inv
- H35.32 [11 21 31] — Exudative ARMD, active chorodial neovascularization
- H35.32 [12 22 32] — Exudative ARMD, inactive chorodial neovascularization
- H35.32 [13 23 33] — Exudative ARMD, inactive scar

(1-RT 2-LT 3-Bilateral)
(1-With Edema 9-Without Edema)

LACRIMAL SYSTEM
- H04.01 [1 2 3] — Acute dacryoadenitis
- H04.12 [1 2 3] — Dry eye syndrome
- H04.21 [1 2 3] — Epiphora due to excess lacrimation

(1-RT 2-LT 3-Bilateral)

GLAUCOMA
- H40.01 [1 2 3] — Open angle w borderline findings low risk
- H40.02 [1 2 3] — Open angle w borderline findings high risk
- H40.05 [1 2 3] — Ocular hypertension
- H40.06 [1 2 3] — Primary angle closure wo glaucoma damage
- H40.21 [1 2 3] — Acute angle-closure glaucoma

RT LT BI *(RT-Right LT-Left BI-Bilateral)*
- H40.11 [11 21 31] — Primary open-angle glaucoma, mild
- H40.11 [12 22 32] — Primary open-angle glaucoma, mod
- H40.11 [13 23 33] — Primary open-angle glaucoma, severe
- H40.11 [14 24 34] — Primary open-angle glaucoma, indeterminate
- H40.12 [11 21 31] — Low-tens glaucoma, mild stage
- H40.12 [12 22 32] — Low-tens glaucoma, mod stage
- H40.12 [13 23 33] — Low-tens glaucoma, severe stage
- H40.13 [11 21 31] — Pigmentary glaucoma, mild stage
- H40.13 [12 22 32] — Pigmentary glaucoma, mod stage
- H40.13 [13 23 33] — Pigmentary glaucoma, severe stage
- H40.22 [11 21 31] — Chronic angle-closure glaucoma, mild stage
- H40.22 [12 22 32] — Chronic angle-closure glaucoma, mod stage
- H40.22 [13 23 33] — Chornic angle-closure glaucoma, severe stage

(1-RT 2-LT 3-Bilateral)

NEURO-OPHTHALMOLOGY
- H46.1 [1 2 3] — Retrobulbar neuritis
- H47.01 [1 2 3] — Ischemic optic neuropathy
- H47.1 [1 2 3] — Papilledema assoc. w increased intracranial pressure
- H47.21 [1 2 3] — Primary optic atrophy
- H47.32 [1 2 3] — Drusen of optic disc

(1-RT 2-LT 3-Bilateral)

CONJUNCTIVA
- B30.0 — Viral conjunctivitis
- H10.3 [1 2 3] — Acute conjunctivitis
- H10.41 [1 2 3] — Chronic giant papillary conjunctivitis
- H10.43 [1 2 3] — Chronic follicular conjunctivitis
- H11.05 [1 2 3] — Peripheral pterygium, progressive
- H11.12 [1 2 3] — Conjunctival concretions
- H11.15 [1 2 3] — Pinguecula
- H11.3 [1 2 3] — Conjunctival hemorrhage
- S05.01X [A D S] — Inj conjunctiva & corneal abrasion wo fb, RT, init
- S05.02X [A D S] — Inj conjunctiva & corneal abrasion wo fb, LT, init
- T15.11X [A D S] — Foreign body in conjunctival sac, RT, init
- T15.12X [A D S] — Foreign body in conjunctival sac, LT init

(1-RT 2-LT 3-Bilateral)
(A-Initial D-Subsequent S-Sequela)

CORNEA
- H16.00 [1 2 3] — Unspec corneal ulcer
- H16.01 [1 2 3] — Central corneal ulcer
- H16.04 [1 2 3] — Marginal corneal ulcer
- H16.12 [1 2 3] — Filamentary keratitis
- H16.14 [1 2 3] — Punctate keratitis
- H16.42 [1 2 3] — Pannus (degenerative)
- H18.22 [1 2 3] — Idiopathic corneal edema
- H18.41 [1 2 3] — Arcus senilis
- H18.51 — Endothelial corneal dystrophy
- H18.59 — Other hereditary corneal dystrophies
- H18.82 [1 2 3] — Corneal edema due to contact lens
- H18.83 [1 2 3] — Recurrent erosion of cornea
- T15.01X [A D S] — Foreign body in cornea, RT, initial
- T15.02X [A D S] — Foreign body in cornea, LT, initial

(1-RT 2-LT 3-Bilateral)
(A-Initial D-Subsequent S-Sequela)

STRABISMUS
- H50.00 — Unspec esotropia
- H50.10 — Unspec exotropia

(RT-Right LT-Left)

FEE
- S0620 _____
- S0621 _____
- 65210 _____ *
- 65222 _____ *
- 65430 _____ *
- 65435 _____ *
- 65778 _____ *
- 67820 _____ *
- 67938 _____ *
- 68761 _____ *
- 68801 _____ *
- 76510 _____
- 76514 _____
- 83516QW _____
- 83861QW _____
- 87809QW _____
- 92002 _____
- 92004 _____
- 92012 _____
- ☑ 92014 **116.23**
- ☑ 92015 **18.00** +
- 92020 _____
- 92025 _____ *
- 92060 _____
- 92071 _____
- 92072 _____
- 92082 _____
- ☑ 92083 **72.94**
- 92100 _____
- 92132 _____
- 92133 _____
- 92134 _____
- 92225 _____ *
- ☑ 92250 **64.57**
- ☑ 92274 **123.62**
- 92284 _____
- 92285 _____
- 92286 _____
- 92310 _____ +
- 95930 _____
- 99201 _____
- 99202 _____
- 99203 _____
- 99204 _____
- 99205 _____
- 99212 _____
- 99213 _____
- 99214 _____
- 99215 _____

* May Require Modifier
+ Not Paid by MC

5010F	G8428
G8397	4004F
G8398	1036F
2022F	G8783
2024F	G8950
2026F	G8784
3072F	G8785
2019F	G8951
4177F	G8952
2027F	G8730
3284F	G8731
3285F	G8442
0517F	G8939
G8427	G8732
G8430	G8509

v2.1 Revised 3/6/17

©2017 - E. Botts, O.D.

• EPIRETINAL MEMBRANE •
PAGE 4

HEALTH INSURANCE CLAIM FORM
APPROVED BY NATIONAL UNIFORM CLAIM COMMITTEE (NUCC) 02/12

ICD-10

PICA	PICA

1. MEDICARE ☐ MEDICAID ☐ TRICARE ☐ CHAMPVA ☐ GROUP HEALTH PLAN ☐ FECA BLK LUNG ☐ OTHER ☐
1a. INSURED'S I.D. NUMBER (For Program in Item 1): **349 27 8567A**

2. PATIENT'S NAME (Last Name, First Name, Middle Initial): **Doe, Jan**
3. PATIENT'S BIRTH DATE: **05 | 21 | 37** SEX: M ☐ F ☑
4. INSURED'S NAME (Last Name, First Name, Middle Initial):

5. PATIENT'S ADDRESS (No., Street): **21 Oak Drive**
6. PATIENT RELATIONSHIP TO INSURED: Self ☑ Spouse ☐ Child ☐ Other ☐
7. INSURED'S ADDRESS (No., Street):

CITY: **Smithville** STATE: **IL**
8. RESERVED FOR NUCC USE
CITY: STATE:

ZIP CODE: **69321** TELEPHONE: ( )
ZIP CODE: TELEPHONE: ( )

9. OTHER INSURED'S NAME (Last Name, First Name, Middle Initial):
10. IS PATIENT'S CONDITION RELATED TO:
11. INSURED'S POLICY GROUP OR FECA NUMBER: **None**

a. OTHER INSURED'S POLICY OR GROUP NUMBER:
a. EMPLOYMENT? (Current or Previous) YES ☐ NO ☐
a. INSURED'S DATE OF BIRTH: SEX M ☐ F ☐

b. RESERVED FOR NUCC USE:
b. AUTO ACCIDENT? YES ☐ NO ☐ PLACE (State):
b. OTHER CLAIM ID (Designated by NUCC):

c. RESERVED FOR NUCC USE:
c. OTHER ACCIDENT? YES ☐ NO ☐
c. INSURANCE PLAN NAME OR PROGRAM NAME:

d. INSURANCE PLAN NAME OR PROGRAM NAME:
10d. CLAIM CODES (Designated by NUCC):
d. IS THERE ANOTHER HEALTH BENEFIT PLAN? YES ☐ NO ☐ *If yes, complete items 9, 9a, and 9d.*

READ BACK OF FORM BEFORE COMPLETING & SIGNING THIS FORM.
12. PATIENT'S OR AUTHORIZED PERSON'S SIGNATURE — I authorize the release of any medical or other information necessary to process this claim. I also request payment of government benefits either to myself or to the party who accepts assignment below.
SIGNED: **SOF** DATE: **10-03-15**

13. INSURED'S OR AUTHORIZED PERSON'S SIGNATURE — I authorize payment of medical benefits to the undersigned physician or supplier for services described below.
SIGNED:

14. DATE OF CURRENT ILLNESS, INJURY, or PREGNANCY (LMP): QUAL.
15. OTHER DATE: QUAL. MM | DD | YY
16. DATES PATIENT UNABLE TO WORK IN CURRENT OCCUPATION: FROM | TO

17. NAME OF REFERRING PROVIDER OR OTHER SOURCE: **DK | Eric Botts**
17a.
17b. NPI: **Individual NPI#**
18. HOSPITALIZATION DATES RELATED TO CURRENT SERVICES: FROM | TO

19. ADDITIONAL CLAIM INFORMATION (Designated by NUCC):
20. OUTSIDE LAB? YES ☐ NO ☐ $ CHARGES

21. DIAGNOSIS OR NATURE OF ILLNESS OR INJURY Relate A-L to service line below (24E) ICD Ind. **10**
A. **H35.371** B. **H25.043** C. D.
E. F. G. H.
I. J. K. L.

22. RESUBMISSION CODE: ORIGINAL REF. NO.:
23. PRIOR AUTHORIZATION NUMBER:

#	A. DATE(S) OF SERVICE From MM DD YY	To MM DD YY	B. PLACE OF SERVICE	C. EMG	D. PROCEDURES, SERVICES, OR SUPPLIES CPT/HCPCS	MODIFIER	E. DIAGNOSIS POINTER	F. $ CHARGES	G. DAYS OR UNITS	H. EPSDT Family Plan	I. ID. QUAL.	J. RENDERING PROVIDER ID. #
1	10 03 15	10 03 15	11		92014		AB	116 23	1		NPI	Individual NPI #
2	10 03 15	10 03 15	11		92250		A	64 57	1		NPI	Individual NPI #
3	10 03 15	10 03 15	11		92274		A	123 62	1		NPI	Individual NPI #
4	10 03 15	10 03 15	11		92083		A	72 94	1		NPI	Individual NPI #
5	10 03 15	10 03 15	11		92015		B	18 00	1		NPI	Individual NPI #
6											NPI	

25. FEDERAL TAX I.D. NUMBER: **411743621** SSN ☐ EIN ☑
26. PATIENT'S ACCOUNT NO.:
27. ACCEPT ASSIGNMENT? YES ☑ NO ☐
28. TOTAL CHARGE: $ **395 36**
29. AMOUNT PAID: $ **0**
30. Rsvd for NUCC Use: **395 36**

31. SIGNATURE OF PHYSICIAN OR SUPPLIER INCLUDING DEGREES OR CREDENTIALS
E. Botts   **10-03-10**
SIGNED   DATE

32. SERVICE FACILITY LOCATION INFORMATION:
Eric K. Botts, O.D.
1730 East Jackson Street
Macomb, IL 61455
309-836-3373
a. NPI b.

33. BILLING PROVIDER INFO & PH # ( )
Eric K. Botts, O.D.
1730 East Jackson Street
Macomb, IL 61455
309-836-3373
a. NPI b.

NUCC Instruction Manual available at: www.nucc.org   PLEASE PRINT OR TYPE   APPROVED OMB-0938-1197 FORM 1500 (02-12)

©2014 - E. Botts, O.D.   Group NPI # if available, otherwise individual NPI #

• EPIRETINAL MEMBRANE •
PAGE 5

Medicare
Remittance
Notice

Eric K. Botts, OD
1730 East Jackson Street
Macomb, IL 61455-2531

NPI #: 47932761
Page #: 1 of 2
Date: 10-22-15
Check/Eft #: 115449098

PERF PROV	SERV DATE	POS	NOS	PROC	MODS	BILLED	ALLOWED	DEDUCT	COINS	GRP/RC-AMT	PROV PD
NAME DOE, JAN			HIC 36030715A		ACNT 111036P			ICN 0206222466720	ASG Y	MOA MAO 1	MA 18
47932761	1003	100315 11	1	92014		116.23	102.75	0.00	20.55	13.48	82.20
47932761	1003	100315 11	1	92250		64.57	60.57	0.00	12.11	4.00	48.46
47932761	1003	100315 11	1	92274		123.62	102.04	0.00	20.41	21.58	81.63
47932761	1003	100315 11	1	92083		72.94	54.40	0.00	10.88	18.54	43.52
47932761	1003	100315 11	1	92015		18.00	0.00	0.00	0.00	PR-96	0.00
PT RESP	81.95		1	CLAIM TOTALS		395.36	319.76	0.00	63.95	57.60	255.81

CLAIM INFORMATION FORWARDED TO: HCSC-BCBS OF IL (STD A & B)   255.81 NET

PR   Patient Responsibility. Amount that may be billed to a patient or another payer.

96   Non-covered charge(s).

EPIRETINAL MEMBRANE
PAGE 6

EXAMINATION
Supplementary Tests

Patient **Jan Doe** Date **10-03-15**

External Ocular Photography (92285, 92286)

OD | OS

Findings _____ | _____

Diagnosis _____ | _____

Plan _____ | _____

Signature _____

Scanning Computerized Ophthalmic Diagnostic Imaging (92132, 92133, (92134))

OD | OS

☐ HRT   ☑ OCT   ☐ GDX

Findings _Macular puckering w/ macular thickening_ | _Normal_

Diagnosis _ERM_ | _____

Plan _Monitor 6 months_ | _Monitor 6 months_

Signature _E. Botts_

Extended Ophthalmoscopy (92225, 92226)

☐ 78D Lens   ☐ 90D Lens   ☐ 20D Lens   ☐ 2.2D Lens   ☐ 3-Mirror   ☐ Scleral depression

OD | OS

Findings _____ | _____

Diagnosis _____ | _____

Plan _____ | _____

Signature _____

©2007 - E. Botts, O.D.

BILLING STATEMENT

• EPIRETINAL MEMBRANE •
PAGE 6

Dr. Eric Botts
Phone 309/836-3373

Date of Service **10 / 03 / 15**
Patient's Name **Jan Doe** DOB **05 / 21 / 37** ☐ Male ☑ Female
Address **21 Oak Drive** City **Smithville** State **IL** Zip **69321**
Telephone ( ) - Insured's Name Insured's DOB / /
ID Number **349 27 8567A** Secondary Ins **BCBS** Total **43.34**
Special Instructions

Refraction Paid
Co-Pay/Deductible Paid
Ins/Mcaid/Mcare Paid
Secondary Paid
Write Off
Balance Due

MODIFIERS 24 25 26 50 55 59 79 RT LT E1 E2 E3 E4 1P 2P 8P TC GW QW

MISCELLANEOUS
- E10.65 Type 1 Diabetes w complications
- E10.9 Type 1 Diabetes wo complications
- E11.65 Type 2 Diabetes w complications
- E11.9 Type 2 Diabetes wo complications
- H27.0 [1 2 3] Aphakia
- H53.8 Blurred Vision
- H57.1 [1 2 3] Ocular Pain
- M06.9 Rheumatoid Arthritis
- Z79.4 Insulin Dependent
- Z79.84 Non-Insulin Dependent
- Z79.899 High Risk meds
  (1-RT 2-LT 3-Bilateral)

UVEAL DISORDERS
- H20.01 [1 2 3] Primary iridocyclitis
- H21.0 [1 2 3] Hyphema
- H21.23 [1 2 3] Degeneration of Iris
- H21.26 [1 2 3] Iris Atrophy
- H21.4 [1 2 3] Pupillary membranes
- H57.05 [1 2 3] Tonic Pupil
  (1-RT 2-LT 3-Bilateral)

EYELIDS
- H00.023 Hordeolum internum RT eye
- H00.026 Hordeolum internum LT eye
- H00.13 Chalazion RT eye
- H00.16 Chalazion LT eye
- H01.023 Squamous blepharitis RT eye
- H01.026 Squamous blepharitis LT eye
- H01.113 Allergic dermatitis RT eye
- H01.116 Allergic dermatitis LT eye
- H02.033 Senile entropion RT eye
- H02.036 Senile entropion LT eye
- H02.053 Trichiasis w entropion RT eye
- H05.056 Trichiasis wo entropion LT eye
- H02.133 Senile ectropion RT eye
- H02.136 Senile ectropion LT eye
- H02.40 [1 2 3] Unspec ptosis of eyelid
- H02.833 Dermatochalasis RT eye
- H02.836 Dermatochalasis LT eye
  (1-RT 2-LT 3-Bilateral)

CATARACT/LENS
- H25.01 [1 2 3] Cortical age-related cat
- ☑ H25.04 [1 2 ③] Post subcap polar age-related cat
- H25.1 [1 2 3] Age-related nuclear cat
- H25.89 Other age-related cat
- Z96.1 Presence of intraocular lens
  (1-RT 2-LT 3-Bilateral)

DISORDER OF REFRACTION
- H52.0 [1 2 3] Hypermetropia
- H52.1 [1 2 3] Myopia
- H52.22 [1 2 3] Regular Astigmatism
- H52.4 Presbyopia
  (1-RT 2-LT 3-Bilateral)

VISUAL DISORDERS
- H51.11 Convergence insufficiency
- H51.12 Convergence excess
- H52.53 [1 2 3] Spasm of accommodation
- H53.02 [1 2 3] Refractive amblyopia
- H53.03 [1 2 3] Strabismic amblyopia
- H53.14 [1 2 3] Visual discomfort
- H53.41 [1 2 3] Scotoma involving central area
- H53.42 [1 2 3] Scotoma of blind spot area
- H53.43 [1 2 3] Sector or arcuate defects
- H53.46 [1 2 3] Homonymous bilateral field defects
- H53.47 Heteronymous bilateral field defects
- H55.00 Unspec nystagmus
  (1-RT 2-LT 3-Bilateral)

RETINAL DISORDERS
- E10.31 [1 9] T1 diab w unsp diab rtnop
- E10.321 [1 2 3] T1 diab w mild nonprlf diab rtnop w mac edema
- E10.329 [1 2 3] T1 diab w mild nonprlf diab rtnop wo mac edema
- E10.331 [1 2 3] T1 diab w mod nonprlf diab rtnop w mac edema
- E10.339 [1 2 3] T1 diab w mon nonprlf diab rtnop wo mac edema
- E10.341 [1 2 3] T1 diab w severe nonprlf diab rtnop w mac edema
- E10.349 [1 2 3] T1 diab w severe nonprlf diab rtnop wo mac edema
- E10.351 [1 2 3] T1 diab w prlif diab rtnop w mac edema
- E10.355 [1 2 3] T1 diab w stable prolif diab rtnop
- E10.359 [1 2 3] T1 diab w prlif diab rtnop wo mac edema
- E11.31 [1 9] T2 diab w unsp diab rtnop
- E11.321 [1 2 3] T2 diab w mild nonprlf diab rtnop w mac edema
- E11.329 [1 2 3] T2 diab w mild nonprlf diab rtnop wo mac edema
- E11.331 [1 2 3] T2 diab w mod nonprlf diab rtnop w mac edema
- E11.339 [1 2 3] T2 diab w mod nonprlf diab rtnop wo mac edema
- E11.341 [1 2 3] T2 diab w severe nonprlf diab rtnop w mac edema
- E11.349 [1 2 3] T2 diab w severe nonprlf diab rtnop wo mac edema
- E11.351 [1 2 3] T2 diab w prolif diab rtnop w mac edema
- E11.355 [1 2 3] T2 diab w stable prolif diab rtnop
- E11.359 [1 2 3] T2 diab w prolif diab rtnop wo mac edema
- H31.01 [1 2 3] Macula scars
- H31.09 [1 2 3] Other chorioretinal scars
- H32 Chorioretinal disorder
- H33.01 [1 2 3] Retinal detachment w single break
- H33.31 [1 2 3] Horseshoe tear of retina wo detachment
- H33.32 [1 2 3] Round hole
- H33.8 Other retinal detachments
- H34.1 [1 2 3] Central retinal artery occlusion
- H34.21 [1 2 3] Partial retinal artery occlusion
- H35.01 [1 2 3] Vascular sheathing
- H35.03 [1 2 3] Hypertensive retinopathy
- H35.04 [1 2 3] Retinal micro-aneurysms
- H35.34 [1 2 3] Macular cyst, hole or pseudohole
- H35.35 [1 2 3] Cystoid macular degeneration
- H35.36 [1 2 3] Drusen (degenerative) of macula
- ☑ H35.37 [① 2 3] Puckering of macule, ERM
- H35.40 Unspec peripheral retinal degeneration
- H35.41 [1 2 3] Lattice degeneration of retina
- H35.71 [1 2 3] Central serous chorioretinopathy
- H35.82 Retinal ischemia
- H43.31 [1 2 3] Viterous membranes
- H43.81 [1 2 3] Viterous degeneration

RT LT BI *(RT-Right LT-Left BI-Bilateral)*
- H34.81 [10 20 30] Central retinal vein occlusion w mac edema
- H34.81 [11 21 31] Central retinal vein occlusion w retinal neovascularization
- H34.81 [12 22 32] Central retinal vein occlusion, stable
- H34.83 [10 20 30] Tributary retinal vein occlusion w mac edema
- H34.83 [11 21 31] Tributary retinal vein occlusion w retinal neovascularization
- H34.83 [12 22 32] Tributary retinal vein occlusion, stable
- H35.31 [11 21 31] Nonexudative ARMD, early dry stage
- H35.31 [12 22 32] Nonexudative ARMD, intermediate dry stage
- H35.31 [13 23 33] Nonexudative ARMD, advanced atropic wo foveal inv
- H35.31 [14 24 34] Nonexudative ARMD, advanced atropic w subfoveal inv
- H35.32 [11 21 31] Exudative ARMD, active chorodial neovascularization
- H35.32 [12 22 32] Exudative ARMD, inactive chorodial neovascularization
- H35.32 [13 23 33] Exudative ARMD, inactive scar
  (1-RT 2-LT 3-Bilateral)
  (1-With Edema 9-Without Edema)

LACRIMAL SYSTEM
- H04.01 [1 2 3] Acute dacryoadenitis
- H04.12 [1 2 3] Dry eye syndrome
- H04.21 [1 2 3] Epiphora due to excess lacrimation
  (1-RT 2-LT 3-Bilateral)

GLAUCOMA
- H40.01 [1 2 3] Open angle w borderline findings low risk
- H40.02 [1 2 3] Open angle w borderline findings high risk
- H40.05 [1 2 3] Ocular hypertension
- H40.06 [1 2 3] Primary angle closure wo glaucoma damage
- H40.21 [1 2 3] Acute angle-closure glaucoma

RT LT BI *(RT-Right LT-Left BI-Bilateral)*
- H40.11 [11 21 31] Primary open-angle glaucoma, mild
- H40.11 [12 22 32] Primary open-angle glaucoma, mod
- H40.11 [13 23 33] Primary open-angle glaucoma, severe
- H40.11 [14 24 34] Primary open-angle glaucoma, indeterminate
- H40.12 [11 21 31] Low-tens glaucoma, mild stage
- H40.12 [12 22 32] Low-tens glaucoma, mod stage
- H40.12 [13 23 33] Low-tens glaucoma, severe stage
- H40.13 [11 21 31] Pigmentary glaucoma, mild stage
- H40.13 [12 22 32] Pigmentary glaucoma, mod stage
- H40.13 [13 23 33] Pigmentary glaucoma, severe stage
- H40.22 [11 21 31] Chronic angle-closure glaucoma, mild stage
- H40.22 [12 22 32] Chronic angle-closure glaucoma, mod stage
- H40.22 [13 23 33] Chronic angle-closure glaucoma, severe stage
  (1-RT 2-LT 3-Bilateral)

NEURO-OPHTHALMOLOGY
- H46.1 [1 2 3] Retrobulbar neuritis
- H47.01 [1 2 3] Ischemic optic neuropathy
- H47.1 [1 2 3] Papilledema assoc. w increased intracranial pressure
- H47.21 [1 2 3] Primary optic atrophy
- H47.32 [1 2 3] Drusen of optic disc
  (1-RT 2-LT 3-Bilateral)

CONJUNCTIVA
- B30.0 Viral conjunctivitis
- H10.3 [1 2 3] Acute conjunctivitis
- H10.41 [1 2 3] Chronic giant papillary conjunctivitis
- H10.43 [1 2 3] Chronic follicular conjunctivitis
- H11.05 [1 2 3] Peripheral pterygium, progressive
- H11.12 [1 2 3] Conjunctival concretions
- H11.15 [1 2 3] Pinguecula
- H11.3 [1 2 3] Conjunctival hemorrhage
- S05.01X [A D S] Inj conjunctiva & corneal abrasion wo fb, RT, init
- S05.02X [A D S] Inj conjunctiva & corneal abrasion wo fb, LT, init
- T15.11X [A D S] Foreign body in conjunctival sac, RT, init
- T15.12X [A D S] Foreign body in conjunctival sac, LT init
  (1-RT 2-LT 3-Bilateral)
  (A-Initial D-Subsequent S-Sequela)

CORNEA
- H16.00 [1 2 3] Unspec corneal ulcer
- H16.01 [1 2 3] Central corneal ulcer
- H16.04 [1 2 3] Marginal corneal ulcer
- H16.12 [1 2 3] Filamentary keratitis
- H16.14 [1 2 3] Punctate keratitis
- H16.42 [1 2 3] Pannus (corneal)
- H18.22 [1 2 3] Idiopathic corneal edema
- H18.41 [1 2 3] Arcus senilis
- H18.51 Endothelial corneal dystrophie
- H18.59 Other hereditary corneal dystrophies
- H18.82 [1 2 3] Corneal edema due to contact lens
- H18.83 [1 2 3] Recurrent erosion of cornea
- T15.01X [A D S] Foreign body in cornea, RT, initial
- T15.02X [A D S] Foreign body in cornea, LT, initial
  (1-RT 2-LT 3-Bilateral)
  (A-Initial D-Subsequent S-Sequela)

STRABISMUS
- H50.00 Unspec esotropia
- H50.10 Unspec exotropia
  (RT-Right LT-Left)

FEE
- S0620
- S0621
- 65210 *
- 65222 *
- 65430 *
- 65435 *
- 65778 *
- 67820
- 67938 *
- 68761 *
- 68801 *
- 76510
- 76514
- 83516QW
- 83861QW
- 87809QW
- 92002
- 92004
- 92012
- 92014
- 92015 +
- 92020
- 92025 *
- 92060
- 92071
- 92072
- 92082
- 92083
- 92100
- 92132
- 92133
- ☑ 92134 **43.34**
- 92225 *
- 92226 *
- 92250
- 92274
- 92284
- 92285
- 92286
- 92310 +
- 95930
- 99201
- 99202
- 99203
- 99204
- 99205
- 99212
- 99213
- 99214
- 99215

* May Require Modifier
\+ Not Paid by MC

- 5010F G8428
- G8397 4004F
- G8398 1036F
- 2022F G8783
- 2024F G8950
- 2026F G8784
- 3072F G8785
- 2019F G8951
- 4177F G8952
- 2027F G8730
- 3284F G8731
- 3285F G8442
- 0517F G8939
- G8427 G8732
- G8430 G8509

v2.1 Revised 3/6/17

©2017 - E. Botts, O.D.

· EPIRETINAL MEMBRANE ·
PAGE 8

HEALTH INSURANCE CLAIM FORM
APPROVED BY NATIONAL UNIFORM CLAIM COMMITTEE (NUCC) 02/12

ICD-10

PICA | | | | | | | | PICA

1. MEDICARE ☐ (Medicare#) MEDICAID ☐ (Medicaid#) TRICARE ☐ (ID#/DoD#) CHAMPVA ☐ (Member ID#) GROUP HEALTH PLAN ☐ (ID#) FECA BLK LUNG ☐ (ID#) OTHER ☐ (ID#) | 1a. INSURED'S I.D. NUMBER (For Program in Item 1): 349 27 8567A

2. PATIENT'S NAME (Last Name, First Name, Middle Initial): Doe, Jan
3. PATIENT'S BIRTH DATE: 05 21 37 SEX: F ☑
4. INSURED'S NAME (Last Name, First Name, Middle Initial)

5. PATIENT'S ADDRESS (No., Street): 21 Oak Drive
6. PATIENT RELATIONSHIP TO INSURED: Self ☑ Spouse ☐ Child ☐ Other ☐
7. INSURED'S ADDRESS (No., Street)

CITY: Smithville   STATE: IL
8. RESERVED FOR NUCC USE
CITY   STATE

ZIP CODE: 69321   TELEPHONE: (   )
ZIP CODE   TELEPHONE: (   )

9. OTHER INSURED'S NAME (Last Name, First Name, Middle Initial)
10. IS PATIENT'S CONDITION RELATED TO:
11. INSURED'S POLICY GROUP OR FECA NUMBER: None

a. OTHER INSURED'S POLICY OR GROUP NUMBER
a. EMPLOYMENT? (Current or Previous) ☐ YES ☐ NO
a. INSURED'S DATE OF BIRTH   SEX: M ☐ F ☐

b. RESERVED FOR NUCC USE
b. AUTO ACCIDENT? ☐ YES ☐ NO PLACE (State)
b. OTHER CLAIM ID (Designated by NUCC)

c. RESERVED FOR NUCC USE
c. OTHER ACCIDENT? ☐ YES ☐ NO
c. INSURANCE PLAN NAME OR PROGRAM NAME

d. INSURANCE PLAN NAME OR PROGRAM NAME
10d. CLAIM CODES (Designated by NUCC)
d. IS THERE ANOTHER HEALTH BENEFIT PLAN? ☐ YES ☐ NO

READ BACK OF FORM BEFORE COMPLETING & SIGNING THIS FORM.
12. PATIENT'S OR AUTHORIZED PERSON'S SIGNATURE I authorize the release of any medical or other information necessary to process this claim. I also request payment of government benefits either to myself or to the party who accepts assignment below.
SIGNED: SOF   DATE: 10-03-15
13. INSURED'S OR AUTHORIZED PERSON'S SIGNATURE I authorize payment of medical benefits to the undersigned physician or supplier for services described below.
SIGNED

14. DATE OF CURRENT ILLNESS, INJURY, or PREGNANCY (LMP) QUAL.
15. OTHER DATE QUAL. MM DD YY
16. DATES PATIENT UNABLE TO WORK IN CURRENT OCCUPATION FROM   TO

17. NAME OF REFERRING PROVIDER OR OTHER SOURCE: DK Eric Botts
17a.
17b. NPI Individual NPI#
18. HOSPITALIZATION DATES RELATED TO CURRENT SERVICES FROM   TO

19. ADDITIONAL CLAIM INFORMATION (Designated by NUCC)
20. OUTSIDE LAB? ☐ YES ☐ NO $ CHARGES

21. DIAGNOSIS OR NATURE OF ILLNESS OR INJURY Relate A-L to service line below (24E) ICD Ind. 10
A. H35.371 B. H25.043 C. D.
E. F. G. H.
I. J. K. L.
22. RESUBMISSION CODE   ORIGINAL REF. NO.
23. PRIOR AUTHORIZATION NUMBER

24. A. DATE(S) OF SERVICE From MM DD YY To MM DD YY	B. PLACE OF SERVICE	C. EMG	D. PROCEDURES, SERVICES, OR SUPPLIES CPT/HCPCS MODIFIER	E. DIAGNOSIS POINTER	F. $ CHARGES	G. DAYS OR UNITS	H. EPSDT Family Plan	I. ID. QUAL.	J. RENDERING PROVIDER ID. #
1 10 03 15 10 03 15	11		92134	A	43 34	1		NPI	Individual NPI #
2								NPI	
3								NPI	
4								NPI	
5								NPI	
6								NPI	

25. FEDERAL TAX I.D. NUMBER: 411743621   SSN ☐ EIN ☑
26. PATIENT'S ACCOUNT NO.
27. ACCEPT ASSIGNMENT? ☑ YES ☐ NO
28. TOTAL CHARGE: $ 43 34
29. AMOUNT PAID: $ 0
30. Rsvd for NUCC Use: 43 34

31. SIGNATURE OF PHYSICIAN OR SUPPLIER INCLUDING DEGREES OR CREDENTIALS (I certify that the statements on the reverse apply to this bill and are made a part thereof.)
SIGNED: E Botts   DATE: 10-03-10
32. SERVICE FACILITY LOCATION INFORMATION
Eric K. Botts, O.D.
1730 East Jackson Street
Macomb, IL 61455
309-836-3373
a. NPI   b.
33. BILLING PROVIDER INFO & PH # (   )
Eric K. Botts, O.D.
1730 East Jackson Street
Macomb, IL 61455
309-836-3373
a. NPI   b.

NUCC Instruction Manual available at: www.nucc.org   PLEASE PRINT OR TYPE   APPROVED OMB-0938-1197 FORM 1500 (02-12)

©2014 - E. Botts, O.D.   Group NPI # if available, otherwise individual NPI #

• EPIRETINAL MEMBRANE •
PAGE 9

Medicare
Remittance
Notice

Eric K. Botts, OD
1730 East Jackson Street
Macomb, IL 61455-2531

NPI #: 47932761
Page #: 1 of 2
Date: 10-22-15
Check/Eft #: 115449098

PERF PROV	SERV DATE	POS	NOS	PROC	MODS	BILLED	ALLOWED	DEDUCT	COINS	GRP/RC-AMT	PROV PD
NAME DOE, JAN			HIC 36030715A		ACNT 111036P			ICN 0206222466720	ASG Y	MOA MAO 1	MA 18
47932761	1003 100315	11	1	92134		43.34	37.75	0.00	7.55	5.59	30.20

| PT RESP | 7.55 | | 1 | CLAIM TOTALS | | 43.34 | 37.75 | 0.00 | 7.55 | 5.59 | 30.20 |

CLAIM INFORMATION FORWARDED TO: HCSC-BCBS OF IL (STD A & B)   30.20 NET

Example #5
High Risk Med

• HIGH RISK MED •
PAGE 1
EXAMINATION

Example #5

Patient: Jim Doe Date: 08-06-14 Sex: (M) F DOB: 06-7-47 Age: 67 Last Exam: ___
Chief Complaint: Advised by MD to have eyes examined

History
HPI: Taking Plaquenil x 4 years for Rheumatoid Arthritis 200 mg daily. Treated by Dr. Jones
Symptoms
Location
Quality — Allergies
Severity — Medications
Duration — Ocular ROS
Timing
Context — Medical History & ROS from ___/___/___ reviewed: ☐ no changes
Modifiers — Dr. Initials ___

Examination
Head/Face ☑ nl   Psych: Mood/Affect (anxiety/depression) ☑ nl   Neuro: Oriented (person/time/place) ☑ y ☐ n

VA: sc< ___ cc< ___   ph< ___   near< ___

K: OD ___ OLD RX: OD ___ add ___
     OS ___   OS ___ add ___
R-scopy: OD ___ REF: OD ___ 20/___ add ___
           OS ___   OS ___ 20/___ add ___

Perimetry: ☑ nl CF ☐ nl	Color ☐ nl ☐ RG defect	**ADNEXA** ☑ nl		
Motility: ☑ Full	Stereo Animals /3 WD /9	**EYELIDS:** ☐ Blepharitis	OD OS OU	
Cover Test: ☐ Eso___	☐ Exo___ ☑ Ortho	☐ Meibomianitis	OD OS OU	

Pupils: ☑ no afferent defect   ☑ round OU   Size: OD___ OS___

Neg Bullseye Retinopathy OU

☐ 20D
☐ 90D/78D
☐ 3 Mirror
☐

SLE: OD / **OS**   **RETINA: OD** / **OS**

SLE OD: ☑nl ☐FBUT:___ TEAR FILM; ☑nl ☐arcus CORNEA; ☑nl ☐pterygium; ☑nl ☐infiltrate; ☑nl ☐spk; ☑nl ☐ SCLERA; ☑nl ☐injection CONJ.; ☑nl ☐pinguecula; ☑D&Q ☐ AC; ☑nl ☐rubeosis IRIS; ☑clear ☐cat ☐ns LENS

SLE OS: ☑nl ☐FBUT:___; ☑nl ☐arcus; ☑nl ☐pterygium; ☑nl ☐infiltrate; ☑nl ☐spk; ☑nl ☐; ☑nl ☐injection; ☑nl ☐pinguecula; ☑D&Q ☐; ☑nl ☐rubeosis; ☑clear ☐cat ☐ns

RETINA OD: ☑nl ☐drusen MACULA; ☑nl ☐RPE chgs; ☑nl ☐cotton wool POST POLE; ☑nl ☐hemes; ☑nl ☐DME; ☑nl ☐ VESSELS; ☑nl ☐PVD VITREOUS; ☑nl ☐strands; ☑nl ☐ PERIPHERY

RETINA OS: ☑nl ☐drusen; ☑nl ☐RPE chgs; ☑nl ☐cotton wool; ☑nl ☐hemes; ☑nl ☐DME; ☑nl ☐; ☑nl ☐PVD; ☑nl ☐strands; ☑nl ☐

OPTIC DISCS: OD ☑nl ☐ .4/.4   SIZE/APPEARANCE/NFL   OS ☑nl ☐ .4/.4
C/D

NCT ___/___ @ ___   Pachymetry: OD ___
TAG 16/15 @ 10:43 am   OS ___ Dilated: M .5% 1% (PA 1%/0.25%) C 1% 2% Ph 2.5% 10% OU@ ___

Diagnosis/Plan   MDM   1 2 ③ 4
High Risk Med associated with Rheumatoid Arthritis

Order OCT, TVF,
Mf ERG (Multifocal electroretinogram)
Order photos 1 week
Monitor for retinopathy 6 month-
Send letter to MD

(Order:) ☑ HRT/GDX/OCT   RTO: ___ day
☑ Photo   ___ week
☐ VF   6 month
☐ Consult   ___ year

Dr. E. Botts

Rev. 11/11 ©2007 - E. Botts, O.D.

• HIGH RISK MED •
PAGE 2
Supplementary Tests

Patient _Jim Doe_ Date _08-06-14_

- ☐ **Visual Fields** (92081, 92082, 92083)
- ☐ **Sensorimotor Examination** (92060)
- ☐ **Scanning Computerized Ophthalmic Diagnostic Imaging** (92132, 92133, 92134) ☐ HRT ☐ OCT ☐ GDX
- ☐ **Serial Tonometry** (92100)
- ☐ **Visual Evoked Potential** (95930)
- ☐ **Gonioscopy** (92020)
- ☐ **Fundus Photography** (92250)
- ☐ **External Ocular Photography** (92285)
- ☐ **Corneal Topography** (92025)
- ☐ **Pattern Electroretinography** (92275)
- ☐ **Specular Microscopy** (92286)

Electroretinography (92273, (92274), 0509T)

	OD	OS
Findings	Normal Wave Pattern	Normal Wave Pattern
Diagnosis	Current Treatment with High Risk Med	Current Treatment with High Risk Med
Plan	Monitor 6 months for retinopathy associated with High Risk Med	Monitor 6 months for retinopathy associated with High Risk Med
Signature	E. Bolt	

Scanning Computerized Ophthalmic Diagnostic Imaging (92132, 92133, (92134)) ☐ HRT ☒ OCT ☐ GDX

	OD	OS
Findings	Normal Retina	Normal Retina
Diagnosis	Current Treatment with High Risk Med	Current Treatment with High Risk Med
Plan	Monitor 6 months for retinopathy associated with High Risk Med	Monitor 6 months for retinopathy associated with High Risk Med
Signature	E. Bolt	

Visual Fields (92081, (92082), 92083)

	OD	OS
Findings	No defect	No defect
Diagnosis	Current Treatment with High Risk Med	Current Treatment with High Risk Med
Plan	Monitor 6 months for Visual Field Loss associated with High Risk Med	Monitor 6 months for Visual Field Loss associated with High Risk Med
Signature	E. Bolt	

Rev. 4/14

BILLING STATEMENT

• HIGH RISK MED •
PAGE 3

Dr. Eric Botts
Phone 309/836-3373

69

Date of Service **08/06/14**
Patient's Name **Jim Doe** DOB **06/07/47** ☑ Male ☐ Female
Address **2100 RedBud St.** City **Smithville** State **IL** Zip **69321**
Telephone (___)___-_____ Insured's Name _____ Insured's DOB __/__/__
ID Number **359 26 8567A** Secondary Ins **BCBS** Total **363.55**
Special Instructions **T37.2XSA Anti-malarial drug**

Refraction Paid _____
Co-Pay/Deductible Paid _____
Ins/Mcaid/Mcare Paid _____
Secondary Paid _____
Write Off _____
Balance Due _____

MODIFIERS 24 25 26 50 55 59 79 RT LT E1 E2 E3 E4 1P 2P 8P TC GW QW

MISCELLANEOUS
- ☐ E10.65 Type 1 Diabetes w complications
- ☐ E10.9 Type 1 Diabetes wo complications
- ☐ E11.65 Type 2 Diabetes w complications
- ☐ E11.9 Type 2 Diabetes wo complications
- ☐ H27.0 [1 2 3] Aphakia
- ☐ H53.8 Blurred Vision
- ☐ H57.1 [1 2 3] Ocular Pain
- ☑ M06.9 Rheumatoid Arthritis
- ☐ Z79.4 Insulin Dependent
- ☐ Z79.84 Non-Insulin Dependent
- ☑ Z79.899 High Risk meds

(1-RT 2-LT 3-Bilateral)

UVEAL DISORDERS
- ☐ H20.01 [1 2 3] Primary iridocyclitis
- ☐ H21.0 [1 2 3] Hyphema
- ☐ H21.23 [1 2 3] Degeneration of Iris
- ☐ H21.26 [1 2 3] Iris Atrophy
- ☐ H21.4 [1 2 3] Pupillary membranes
- ☐ H57.05 [1 2 3] Tonic Pupil

(1-RT 2-LT 3-Bilateral)

EYELIDS
- ☐ H00.023 Hordeolum internum RT eye
- ☐ H00.026 Hordeolum internum LT eye
- ☐ H00.13 Chalazion RT eye
- ☐ H00.16 Chalazion LT eye
- ☐ H01.023 Squamous blepharitis RT eye
- ☐ H01.026 Squamous blepharitis LT eye
- ☐ H01.113 Allergic dermatitis RT eye
- ☐ H01.116 Allergic dermatitis LT eye
- ☐ H02.033 Senile entropion RT eye
- ☐ H02.036 Senile entropion LT eye
- ☐ H02.053 Trichiasis w entropion RT eye
- ☐ H02.056 Trichiasis wo entropion LT eye
- ☐ H02.133 Senile ectropion RT eye
- ☐ H02.136 Senile ectropion LT eye
- ☐ H02.40 [1 2 3] Unspec ptosis of eyelid
- ☐ H02.833 Dermatochalasis RT eye
- ☐ H02.836 Dermatochalasis LT eye

(1-RT 2-LT 3-Bilateral)

CATARACT/LENS
- ☐ H25.01 [1 2 3] Cortical age-related cat
- ☐ H25.04 [1 2 3] Post subcap polar age-related cat
- ☐ H25.1 [1 2 3] Age-related nuclear cat
- ☐ H25.89 Other age-related cat
- ☐ Z96.1 Presence of intraocular lens

(1-RT 2-LT 3-Bilateral)

DISORDER OF REFRACTION
- ☐ H52.0 [1 2 3] Hypermetropia
- ☐ H52.1 [1 2 3] Myopia
- ☐ H52.22 [1 2 3] Regular Astigmatism
- ☐ H52.4 Presbyopia

(1-RT 2-LT 3-Bilateral)

VISUAL DISORDERS
- ☐ H51.11 Convergence insufficiency
- ☐ H51.12 Convergence excess
- ☐ H52.53 [1 2 3] Spasm of accommodation
- ☐ H53.02 [1 2 3] Refractive amblyopia
- ☐ H53.03 [1 2 3] Strabismic amblyopia
- ☐ H53.14 [1 2 3] Visual discomfort
- ☐ H53.41 [1 2 3] Scotoma involving central area
- ☐ H53.42 [1 2 3] Scotoma of blind spot area
- ☐ H53.43 [1 2 3] Sector or arcuate defects
- ☐ H53.46 [1 2 3] Homonymous bilateral field defects
- ☐ H53.47 Heteronymous bilateral field defects
- ☐ H55.00 Unspec nystagmus

(1-RT 2-LT 3-Bilateral)

RETINAL DISORDERS
- ☐ E10.31 [1 9] T1 diab w unsp diab rtnop
- ☐ E10.321 [1 2 3] T1 diab w mild nonprlf diab rtnop w mac edema
- ☐ E10.329 [1 2 3] T1 diab w mild nonprlf diab rtnop wo mac edema
- ☐ E10.331 [1 2 3] T1 diab w mod nonprlf diab rtnop w mac edema
- ☐ E10.339 [1 2 3] T1 diab w mon nonprlf diab rtnop wo mac edema
- ☐ E10.341 [1 2 3] T1 diab w severe nonprlf diab rtnop w mac edema
- ☐ E10.349 [1 2 3] T1 diab w severe nonprlf diab rtnop wo mac edema
- ☐ E10.351 [1 2 3] T1 diab w prlif diab rtnop w mac edema
- ☐ E10.355 [1 2 3] T1 diab w stable prolif diab rtnop
- ☐ E10.359 [1 2 3] T1 diab w prlif diab rtnop wo mac edema
- ☐ E11.31 [1 9] T2 diab w unsp diab rtnop
- ☐ E11.321 [1 2 3] T2 diab w mild nonprlf diab rtnop w mac edema
- ☐ E11.329 [1 2 3] T2 diab w mild nonprlf diab rtnop wo mac edema
- ☐ E11.331 [1 2 3] T2 diab w mod nonprlf diab rtnop w mac edema
- ☐ E11.339 [1 2 3] T2 diab w mod nonprlf diab rtnop wo mac edema
- ☐ E11.341 [1 2 3] T2 diab w severe nonprlf diab rtnop w mac edema
- ☐ E11.349 [1 2 3] T2 diab w severe nonprlf diab rtnop wo mac edema
- ☐ E11.351 [1 2 3] T2 diab w prolif diab rtnop w mac edema
- ☐ E11.355 [1 2 3] T2 diab w stable prolif diab rtnop
- ☐ E11.359 [1 2 3] T2 diab w prolif diab rtnop wo mac edema
- ☐ H31.01 [1 2 3] Macula scars
- ☐ H31.09 [1 2 3] Other chorioretinal scars
- ☐ H32 Chorioretinal disorder
- ☐ H33.01 [1 2 3] Retinal detachment w single break
- ☐ H33.31 [1 2 3] Horseshoe tear of retina wo detachment
- ☐ H33.32 [1 2 3] Round hole
- ☐ H33.8 Other retinal detachments
- ☐ H34.1 [1 2 3] Central retinal artery occlusion
- ☐ H34.21 [1 2 3] Partial retinal artery occlusion
- ☐ H35.01 [1 2 3] Vascular sheathing
- ☐ H35.03 [1 2 3] Hypertensive retinopathy
- ☐ H35.04 [1 2 3] Retinal micro-aneurysms
- ☐ H35.34 [1 2 3] Macular cyst, hole or pseudohole
- ☐ H35.35 [1 2 3] Cystoid macular degeneration
- ☐ H35.36 [1 2 3] Drusen (degenerative) of macula
- ☐ H35.37 [1 2 3] Puckering of macule, ERM
- ☐ H35.40 Unspec peripheral retinal degeneration
- ☐ H35.41 [1 2 3] Lattice degeneration of retina
- ☐ H35.71 [1 2 3] Central serous chorioretinopathy
- ☐ H35.82 Retinal ischemia
- ☐ H43.31 [1 2 3] Vitreous membranes
- ☐ H43.81 [1 2 3] Vitreous degeneration

RT LT BI (RT-Right LT-Left BI-Bilateral)
- ☐ H34.81 [10 20 30] Central retinal vein occlusion w mac edema
- ☐ H34.81 [11 21 31] Central retinal vein occlusion w retinal neovascularization
- ☐ H34.81 [12 22 32] Central retinal vein occlusion, stable
- ☐ H34.83 [10 20 30] Tributary retinal vein occlusion w mac edema
- ☐ H34.83 [11 21 31] Tributary retinal vein occlusion w retinal neovascularization
- ☐ H34.83 [12 22 32] Tributary retinal vein occlusion, stable
- ☐ H35.31 [11 21 31] Nonexudative ARMD, early dry stage
- ☐ H35.31 [12 22 32] Nonexudative ARMD, intermediate dry stage
- ☐ H35.31 [13 23 33] Nonexudative ARMD, advanced atropic wo subfoveal inv
- ☐ H35.31 [14 24 34] Nonexudative ARMD, advanced atropic w subfoveal inv
- ☐ H35.32 [11 21 31] Exudative ARMD, active chorodial neovascularization
- ☐ H35.32 [12 22 32] Exudative ARMD, inactive chorodial neovascularization
- ☐ H35.32 [13 23 33] Exudative ARMD, inactive scar

(1-With Edema 9-Without Edema)

LACRIMAL SYSTEM
- ☐ H04.01 [1 2 3] Acute dacryoadenitis
- ☐ H04.12 [1 2 3] Dry eye syndrome
- ☐ H04.21 [1 2 3] Epiphora due to excess lacrimation

(1-RT 2-LT 3-Bilateral)

GLAUCOMA
- ☐ H40.01 [1 2 3] Open angle w borderline findings low risk
- ☐ H40.02 [1 2 3] Open angle w borderline findings high risk
- ☐ H40.05 [1 2 3] Ocular hypertension
- ☐ H40.06 [1 2 3] Primary angle closure wo glaucoma damage
- ☐ H40.21 [1 2 3] Acute angle-closure glaucoma

RT LT BI (RT-Right LT-Left BI-Bilateral)
- ☐ H40.11 [11 21 31] Primary open-angle glaucoma, mild
- ☐ H40.11 [12 22 32] Primary open-angle glaucoma, mod
- ☐ H40.11 [13 23 33] Primary open-angle glaucoma, severe
- ☐ H40.11 [14 24 34] Primary open-angle glaucoma, indeterminate
- ☐ H40.12 [11 21 31] Low-tens glaucoma, mild stage
- ☐ H40.12 [12 22 32] Low-tens glaucoma, mod stage
- ☐ H40.12 [13 23 33] Low-tens glaucoma, severe stage
- ☐ H40.13 [11 21 31] Pigmentary glaucoma, mild stage
- ☐ H40.13 [12 22 32] Pigmentary glaucoma, mod stage
- ☐ H40.13 [13 23 33] Pigmentary glaucoma, severe stage
- ☐ H40.22 [11 21 31] Chronic angle-closure glaucoma, mild stage
- ☐ H40.22 [12 22 32] Chronic angle-closure glaucoma, mod stage
- ☐ H40.22 [13 23 33] Chronic angle-closure glaucoma, severe stage

(1-RT 2-LT 3-Bilateral)

NEURO-OPHTHALMOLOGY
- ☐ H46.1 [1 2 3] Retrobulbar neuritis
- ☐ H47.01 [1 2 3] Ischemic optic neuropathy
- ☐ H47.1 [1 2 3] Papilledema assoc. w increased intracranial pressure
- ☐ H47.21 [1 2 3] Primary optic atrophy
- ☐ H47.32 [1 2 3] Drusen of optic disc

(1-RT 2-LT 3-Bilateral)

CONJUNCTIVA
- ☐ B30.0 Viral conjunctivitis
- ☐ H10.3 [1 2 3] Acute conjunctivitis
- ☑ H10.41 [1 2 3] Chronic giant papillary conjunctivitis
- ☐ H10.43 [1 2 3] Chronic follicular conjunctivitis
- ☐ H11.05 [1 2 3] Peripheral pterygium, progressive
- ☐ H11.12 [1 2 3] Conjunctival concretions
- ☐ H11.15 [1 2 3] Pinguecula
- ☐ H11.3 [1 2 3] Conjunctival hemorrhage
- ☐ S05.01X [A D S] Inj conjunctiva & corneal abrasion wo fb, RT, init
- ☐ S05.02X [A D S] Inj conjunctiva & corneal abrasion wo fb, LT, init
- ☐ T15.11X [A D S] Foreign body in conjunctival sac, RT, init
- ☐ T15.12X [A D S] Foreign body in conjunctival sac, LT init

(1-RT 2-LT 3-Bilateral)
(A-Initial D-Subsequent S-Sequela)

CORNEA
- ☐ H16.00 [1 2 3] Unspec corneal ulcer
- ☐ H16.01 [1 2 3] Central corneal ulcer
- ☐ H16.04 [1 2 3] Marginal corneal ulcer
- ☐ H16.12 [1 2 3] Filamentary keratitis
- ☐ H16.14 [1 2 3] Punctate keratitis
- ☐ H16.42 [1 2 3] Pannus (corneal)
- ☐ H18.22 [1 2 3] Idiopathic corneal edema
- ☐ H18.41 [1 2 3] Arcus senilis
- ☐ H18.51 Endothelial corneal dystrophy
- ☐ H18.59 Other hereditary corneal dystrophies
- ☐ H18.82 [1 2 3] Corneal edema due to contact lens
- ☐ H18.83 [1 2 3] Recurrent erosion of cornea
- ☐ T15.01X [A D S] Foreign body in cornea, RT, initial
- ☐ T15.02X [A D S] Foreign body in cornea, LT, initial

(1-RT 2-LT 3-Bilateral)
(A-Initial D-Subsequent S-Sequela)

STRABISMUS
- ☐ H50.00 Unspec esotropia
- ☐ H50.10 Unspec exotropia

(RT-Right LT-Left)

FEE
- ☐ S0620 _____
- ☐ S0621 _____
- ☐ 65210 _____ *
- ☐ 65222 _____ *
- ☐ 65430 _____ *
- ☐ 65435 _____ *
- ☐ 65778 _____ *
- ☐ 67820 _____ *
- ☐ 67938 _____ *
- ☐ 68761 _____ *
- ☐ 68801 _____ *
- ☐ 76510 _____
- ☐ 76514 _____
- ☐ 83516QW _____
- ☐ 83861QW _____
- ☐ 87809QW _____
- ☐ 92002 _____
- ☐ 92004 _____
- ☐ 92012 _____
- ☐ 92014 _____
- ☐ 92015 _____ +
- ☐ 92020 _____
- ☐ 92025 _____ *
- ☐ 92060 _____
- ☐ 92071 _____
- ☐ 92072 _____
- ☑ 92082 **47.26**
- ☐ 92083 _____
- ☐ 92100 _____
- ☐ 92132 _____
- ☐ 92133 _____
- ☑ 92134 **43.34**
- ☐ 92225 _____ *
- ☐ 92226 _____ *
- ☐ 92250 _____
- ☑ 92274 **123.20**
- ☐ 92284 _____
- ☐ 92285 _____
- ☐ 92286 _____
- ☐ 92310 _____ +
- ☐ 95930 _____
- ☐ 99201 _____
- ☐ 99202 _____
- ☐ 99203 _____
- ☑ 99204 **149.75**
- ☐ 99205 _____
- ☐ 99212 _____
- ☐ 99213 _____
- ☐ 99214 _____
- ☐ 99215 _____

* May Require Modifier
+ Not Paid by MC

- ☐ 5010F ☐ G8428
- ☐ G8397 ☐ 4004F
- ☐ G8398 ☐ 1036F
- ☐ 2022F ☐ G8783
- ☐ 2024F ☐ G8950
- ☐ 2026F ☐ G8784
- ☐ 3072F ☐ G8785
- ☐ 2019F ☐ G8951
- ☐ 4177F ☐ G8952
- ☐ 2027F ☐ G8730
- ☐ 3284F ☐ G8731
- ☐ 3285F ☐ G8442
- ☐ 0517F ☐ G8939
- ☐ G8427 ☐ G8732
- ☐ G8430 ☐ G8509

v2.1 Revised 3/6/17

©2017 - E. Botts, O.D.

• HIGH RISK MED •
PAGE 4

ICD-10

HEALTH INSURANCE CLAIM FORM
APPROVED BY NATIONAL UNIFORM CLAIM COMMITTEE (NUCC) 02/12

PICA		PICA

1. MEDICARE ☐ (Medicare#)   MEDICAID ☐ (Medicaid#)   TRICARE ☐ (ID#/DoD#)   CHAMPVA ☐ (Member ID#)   GROUP HEALTH PLAN ☐ (ID#)   FECA BLK LUNG ☐ (ID#)   OTHER ☐ (ID#)

1a. INSURED'S I.D. NUMBER (For Program in Item 1): **372 29 8541A**

2. PATIENT'S NAME (Last Name, First Name, Middle Initial): **Doe, Jim**

3. PATIENT'S BIRTH DATE: **06 / 07 / 47**   SEX: M ☑   F ☐

4. INSURED'S NAME (Last Name, First Name, Middle Initial):

5. PATIENT'S ADDRESS (No., Street): **201 South St**

6. PATIENT RELATIONSHIP TO INSURED: Self ☑   Spouse ☐   Child ☐   Other ☐

7. INSURED'S ADDRESS (No., Street):

CITY: **Mason**   STATE: **IL**

8. RESERVED FOR NUCC USE

CITY: STATE:

ZIP CODE: **61521**   TELEPHONE: ( )

ZIP CODE: TELEPHONE: ( )

9. OTHER INSURED'S NAME (Last Name, First Name, Middle Initial):

10. IS PATIENT'S CONDITION RELATED TO:

11. INSURED'S POLICY GROUP OR FECA NUMBER: **None**

a. OTHER INSURED'S POLICY OR GROUP NUMBER:

a. EMPLOYMENT? (Current or Previous) YES ☐ NO ☑

a. INSURED'S DATE OF BIRTH: SEX: M ☐ F ☐

b. RESERVED FOR NUCC USE

b. AUTO ACCIDENT? YES ☐ NO ☑   PLACE (State)

b. OTHER CLAIM ID (Designated by NUCC):

c. RESERVED FOR NUCC USE

c. OTHER ACCIDENT? YES ☐ NO ☑

c. INSURANCE PLAN NAME OR PROGRAM NAME

d. INSURANCE PLAN NAME OR PROGRAM NAME

10d. CLAIM CODES (Designated by NUCC)

d. IS THERE ANOTHER HEALTH BENEFIT PLAN? YES ☐ NO ☐

READ BACK OF FORM BEFORE COMPLETING & SIGNING THIS FORM.

12. PATIENT'S OR AUTHORIZED PERSON'S SIGNATURE I authorize the release of any medical or other information necessary to process this claim. I also request payment of government benefits either to myself or to the party who accepts assignment below.

SIGNED: **SOF**   DATE: **08-06-14**

13. INSURED'S OR AUTHORIZED PERSON'S SIGNATURE I authorize payment of medical benefits to the undersigned physician or supplier for services described below.

SIGNED:

14. DATE OF CURRENT ILLNESS, INJURY, or PREGNANCY (LMP):   QUAL.

15. OTHER DATE   QUAL.

16. DATES PATIENT UNABLE TO WORK IN CURRENT OCCUPATION: FROM   TO

17. NAME OF REFERRING PROVIDER OR OTHER SOURCE: **DK Eric Botts**

17a.   17b. NPI: **Individual NPI#**

18. HOSPITALIZATION DATES RELATED TO CURRENT SERVICES: FROM   TO

19. ADDITIONAL CLAIM INFORMATION (Designated by NUCC):

20. OUTSIDE LAB? YES ☐ NO ☐ $ CHARGES

21. DIAGNOSIS OR NATURE OF ILLNESS OR INJURY   ICD Ind.: **10**

A. **M06.09**   B. **Z79.899**   C. **T37.2X5A**   D.
E.   F.   G.   H.
I.   J.   K.   L.

22. RESUBMISSION CODE   ORIGINAL REF. NO.

23. PRIOR AUTHORIZATION NUMBER

24.A. DATE(S) OF SERVICE From / To	B. PLACE OF SERVICE	C. EMG	D. PROCEDURES, SERVICES, OR SUPPLIES CPT/HCPCS / MODIFIER	E. DIAGNOSIS POINTER	F. $ CHARGES	G. DAYS OR UNITS	H. EPSDT	I. ID. QUAL.	J. RENDERING PROVIDER ID. #
1	08 06 14 / 08 06 14	11		99204	ABC	149 75	1		NPI	Individual NPI #
2	08 06 14 / 08 06 14	11		92274	B	123 20	1		NPI	Individual NPI #
3	08 06 14 / 08 06 14	11		92082	B	47 26	1		NPI	Individual NPI #
4	08 06 14 / 08 06 14	11		92134	B	43 34	1		NPI	Individual NPI #
5									NPI	
6									NPI	

25. FEDERAL TAX I.D. NUMBER: **4117743621**   SSN ☐ EIN ☑

26. PATIENT'S ACCOUNT NO.

27. ACCEPT ASSIGNMENT? YES ☑ NO ☐

28. TOTAL CHARGE: $ **363 55**

29. AMOUNT PAID: $ **0**

30. Rsvd for NUCC Use: **363 55**

31. SIGNATURE OF PHYSICIAN OR SUPPLIER INCLUDING DEGREES OR CREDENTIALS
SIGNED: *E. Botts*   DATE: **08-06-14**

32. SERVICE FACILITY LOCATION INFORMATION
Eric K. Botts, O.D.
1730 East Jackson Street
Macomb, IL 61455
309-836-3373

33. BILLING PROVIDER INFO & PH # ( )
Eric K. Botts, O.D.
1730 East Jackson Street
Macomb, IL 61455
309-836-3373

NUCC Instruction Manual available at: www.nucc.org   PLEASE PRINT OR TYPE   APPROVED OMB-0938-1197 FORM 1500 (02-12)

©2014 - E. Botts, O.D.   Group NPI # if available, otherwise individual NPI #

• HIGH RISK MED •
PAGE 5

Medicare
Remittance
Notice

Eric K. Botts, OD
1730 East Jackson Street
Macomb, IL 61455-2531

NPI #: 47932761
Page #: 1 of 2
Date: 8-22-14
Check/Eft #: 115449098

PERF PROV	SERV DATE	POS	NOS	PROC	MODS	BILLED	ALLOWED	DEDUCT	COINS	GRP/RC-AMT	PROV PD
NAME DOE, JIM			HIC 36030715A		ACNT 111036P			ICN 0206222466720	ASG Y	MOA MAO 1	MA 18
47932761	0806 080614	11	1	99204		149.75	102.75	0.00	20.55	47.00	82.20
47932761	0806 080614	11	1	92274		123.20	120.57	0.00	24.11	2.63	96.46
47932761	0806 080614	11	1	92082		47.26	42.04	0.00	8.41	5.22	33.63
47932761	0806 080614	11	1	92134		43.34	34.00	0.00	6.80	9.34	27.20
PT RESP 59.87			1	CLAIM TOTALS		363.55	299.36	0.00	59.87	64.19	239.49

CLAIM INFORMATION FORWARDED TO: HCSC-BCBS OF IL (STD A & B)

239.49 NET

© 2018 - E. Botts, O.D.

Example #6
Cataract Patient

• CATARACT PATIENT •
PAGE 1
EXAMINATION

Example #6

Patient: John Doe Date: 09-05-10 Sex: (M) F DOB: 01-01-11 Age: ___ Last Exam: ___
Chief Complaint: Blurry Vision

History
HPI: Vision seems dimmer
Symptoms: Glare at night bothers
Location: Worse last 3 months
Quality: Glasses don't help
Severity:
Duration:
Timing:
Context:
Modifiers:

Allergies
Medications
Ocular ROS
Medical History & ROS from ___/___/___ reviewed: ☐ no changes
Dr. Initials ___

Examination
Head/Face ☑ nl   Psych: Mood/Affect (anxiety/depression) ☑ nl   Neuro: Oriented (person/time/place) ☑ y ☐ n

VA: sc<   cc< 70/60   ph<   near< J4/J4

K: OD ___   **OLD RX:** OD ___   add ___
OS ___   OS ___   add ___

R-scopy: OD ___   **REF:** OD -3.00 DS   20/70   add ___
OS ___   OS -2.75 DS   20/60   add +2.75

Perimetry: ☑ nl   CF ☐ nl   Color ☑ nl   ☐ RG defect   **ADNEXA** ☑ nl
Motility: ☑ Full   Stereo Animals 1/3   WD 4/9   **EYELIDS:** ☐ Blepharitis   OD OS OU
Cover Test: ☐ Eso   ☑ Exo   ☐ Ortho   ☐ Meibomianitis   OD OS OU

Pupils: ☑ no afferent defect   ☑ round OU   Size: OD 3   OS 3
☑ 20D
☑ 90D/78D
☐ 3 Mirror
☐

+3 Mature Cataract OU

SLE: OD   **OS**   **RETINA: OD**   **OS**
☑ nl ☐ FBUT:___ TEAR FILM ☑ nl ☐ FBUT:___   ☑ nl ☐ drusen   MACULA   ☑ nl ☐ drusen
☑ nl ☐ arcus   CORNEA   ☑ nl ☐ arcus   ☑ nl ☐ RPE chgs   ☑ nl ☐ RPE chgs
☑ nl ☐ pterygium   ☑ nl ☐ pterygium   ☑ nl ☐ cotton wool POST POLE ☑ nl ☐ cotton wool
☑ nl ☐ infiltrate   ☑ nl ☐ infiltrate ☑ nl ☐ hemes   ☑ nl ☐ hemes
☑ nl ☐ spk   ☑ nl ☐ spk   ☑ nl ☐ DME   ☑ nl ☐ DME
☑ nl ☐   SCLERA   ☑ nl   ☑ nl ☐   VESSELS   ☑ nl ☐
☑ nl ☐ injection CONJ.   ☑ nl ☐ injection   ☑ nl ☐ PVD   VITREOUS   ☑ nl ☐ PVD
☑ nl ☐ pinguecula   ☑ nl ☐ pinguecula ☑ nl ☐ strands   ☑ nl ☐ strands
☑ D&Q ☐   AC   ☑ D&Q ☐   ☑ nl ☐   PERIPHERY   ☑ nl ☐
☑ nl ☐ rubeosis IRIS   ☑ nl ☐ rubeosis   **OPTIC DISCS: OD**   **OS**
☐ clear ☑ cat ☐ ns LENS   ☐ clear ☑ cat ☐ ns ☑ nl   SIZE/APPEARANCE/NFL   ☑ nl
                                               ☐ .4/.4   C/D   ☐ .4/.4

NCT ___/___ @ ___   Pachymetry: OD ___
TAG 18/18 @ 4:30 pm   OS ___   Dilated: M .5% 1% (PA 1%/0.25%) C 1% 2% Ph 2.5% 10% OU@ 4:41 pm

Diagnosis/Plan   MDM 1 2 ③ 4

Cortical Cataracts
OU OD>OS

Consult with Dr. Smith
for cataract evaluation.
Appt. scheduled 9-21-10
at 3:30 pm

(Order:) ☐ HRT/GDX/OCT   RTO: ___ day
☐ Photo   ___ week
☐ VF   ___ month
☑ Consult   ___ year

Dr. E. Botts

Rev.11/11 ©2007 - E. Botts, O.D.

Confirmation of Post-operative Co-Management Arrangement

Patient Confirmation

It is my desire to have my own optometrist, Dr. *Botts* perform my post-operative follow-up care after my cataract surgery. I understand that my optometrist will contact my ophthalmologist immediately if I experience any complications related to my eye surgery.

John Doe	*09-05-10*
Patient	Date

Assistant Signature	*09-05-10*
Witness	Date

Optometrist Confirmation

I have agreed to provide follow-up care for *John Doe*. I will see the patient after surgery when Dr. *Smith* notifies me that he/she is releasing the patient to my care. I agree to notify Dr. *Smith* immediately should complication arise and to provide written progress reports regularly during my portion of the post-operative period.

E. Botts	*09-05-10*
Optometrist	Date

Rev. 11/11 ©2007 - E. Botts, O.D.

BILLING STATEMENT

• CATARACT PATIENT •
PAGE 3

Dr. Eric Botts

77

Date of Service **09/05/10**
Patient's Name **John Doe** DOB **01/01/11** ☑ Male ☐ Female
Address **2100 RedBud St.** City **Smithville** State **IL** Zip **69321**
Telephone ( ) - Insured's Name _____ Insured's DOB __/__/__
ID Number **359 26 8567A** Secondary Ins **BCBS** Total **167.75**
Special Instructions _____ Refraction Paid **18.00**
Co-Pay/Deductible Paid _____
Ins/Mcaid/Mcare Paid _____
Secondary Paid _____
Write Off _____
Balance Due _____

MODIFIERS 24 25 26 50 55 59 79 RT LT E1 E2 E3 E4 1P 2P 8P TC GW QW

MISCELLANEOUS
- ☐ E10.65 Type 1 Diabetes w complications
- ☐ E10.9 Type 1 Diabetes wo complications
- ☐ E11.65 Type 2 Diabetes w complications
- ☐ E11.9 Type 2 Diabetes wo complications
- ☐ H27.0 [1 2 3] Aphakia
- ☐ H53.8 Blurred Vision
- ☐ H57.1 [1 2 3] Ocular Pain
- ☐ M06.9 Rheumatoid Arthritis
- ☐ Z79.4 Insulin Dependent
- ☐ Z79.84 Non-Insulin Dependent
- ☐ Z79.899 High Risk meds

(1-RT 2-LT 3-Bilateral)

UVEAL DISORDERS
- ☐ H20.01 [1 2 3] Primary iridocyclitis
- ☐ H21.0 [1 2 3] Hyphema
- ☐ H21.23 [1 2 3] Degeneration of Iris
- ☐ H21.26 [1 2 3] Iris Atrophy
- ☐ H21.4 [1 2 3] Pupillary membranes
- ☐ H57.05 [1 2 3] Tonic Pupil

(1-RT 2-LT 3-Bilateral)

EYELIDS
- ☐ H00.023 Hordeolum internum RT eye
- ☐ H00.026 Hordeolum internum LT eye
- ☐ H00.13 Chalazion RT eye
- ☐ H00.16 Chalazion LT eye
- ☐ H01.023 Squamous blepharitis RT eye
- ☐ H01.026 Squamous blepharitis LT eye
- ☐ H01.113 Allergic dermatitis RT eye
- ☐ H01.116 Allergic dermatitis LT eye
- ☐ H02.033 Senile entropion RT eye
- ☐ H02.036 Senile entropion LT eye
- ☐ H02.053 Trichiasis w entropion RT eye
- ☐ H05.056 Trichiasis wo entropion LT eye
- ☐ H02.133 Senile ectropion RT eye
- ☐ H02.136 Senile ectropion LT eye
- ☐ H02.40 [1 2 3] Unspec ptosis of eyelid
- ☐ H02.833 Dermatochalasis RT eye
- ☐ H02.836 Dermatochalasis LT eye

(1-RT 2-LT 3-Bilateral)

CATARACT/LENS
- ☐ H25.01 [1 2 3] Cortical age-related cat
- ☐ H25.04 [1 2 3] Post subcap polar age-related cat
- ☑ H25.1 [1 2 ③] Age-related nuclear cat
- ☐ H25.89 Other age-related cat
- ☐ Z96.1 Presence of intraocular lens

(1-RT 2-LT 3-Bilateral)

DISORDER OF REFRACTION
- ☐ H52.0 [1 2 3] Hypermetropia
- ☐ H52.1 [1 2 3] Myopia
- ☐ H52.22 [1 2 3] Regular Astigmatism
- ☐ H52.4 Presbyopia

(1-RT 2-LT 3-Bilateral)

VISUAL DISORDERS
- ☐ H51.11 Convergence insufficiency
- ☐ H51.12 Convergence excess
- ☐ H52.53 [1 2 3] Spasm of accommodation
- ☐ H53.02 [1 2 3] Refractive amblyopia
- ☐ H53.03 [1 2 3] Strabismic amblyopia
- ☐ H53.14 [1 2 3] Visual discomfort
- ☐ H53.41 [1 2 3] Scotoma involving central area
- ☐ H53.42 [1 2 3] Scotoma of blind spot area
- ☐ H53.43 [1 2 3] Sector or arcuate defects
- ☐ H53.46 [1 2 3] Homonymous bilateral field defects
- ☐ H53.47 Heteronymous bilateral field defects
- ☐ H55.00 Unspec nystagmus

(1-RT 2-LT 3-Bilateral)

RETINAL DISORDERS
- ☐ E10.31 [1 9] T1 diab w unsp diab rtnop
- ☐ E10.321 [1 2 3] T1 diab w mild nonprlf diab rtnop w mac edema
- ☐ E10.329 [1 2 3] T1 diab w mild nonprlf diab rtnop wo mac edema
- ☐ E10.331 [1 2 3] T1 diab w mod nonprlf diab rtnop w mac edema
- ☐ E10.339 [1 2 3] T1 diab w mon nonprlf diab rtnop wo mac edema
- ☐ E10.341 [1 2 3] T1 diab w severe nonprlf diab rtnop w mac edema
- ☐ E10.349 [1 2 3] T1 diab w severe nonprlf diab rtnop wo mac edema
- ☐ E10.351 [1 2 3] T1 diab w prlif diab rtnop w mac edema
- ☐ E10.355 [1 2 3] T1 diab w stable prolif diab rtnop
- ☐ E10.359 [1 2 3] T1 diab w prlif diab rtnop wo mac edema
- ☐ E11.31 [1 9] T2 diab w unsp diab rtnop
- ☐ E11.321 [1 2 3] T2 diab w mild nonprlf diab rtnop w mac edema
- ☐ E11.329 [1 2 3] T2 diab w mild nonprlf diab rtnop wo mac edema
- ☐ E11.331 [1 2 3] T2 diab w mod nonprlf diab rtnop w mac edema
- ☐ E11.339 [1 2 3] T2 diab w mod nonprlf diab rtnop wo mac edema
- ☐ E11.341 [1 2 3] T2 diab w severe nonprlf diab rtnop w mac edema
- ☐ E11.349 [1 2 3] T2 diab w severe nonprlf diab rtnop wo mac edema
- ☐ E11.351 [1 2 3] T2 diab w prolif diab rtnop w mac edema
- ☐ E11.355 [1 2 3] T2 diab w stable prolif diab rtnop
- ☐ E11.359 [1 2 3] T2 diab w prolif diab rtnop wo mac edema
- ☐ H31.01 [1 2 3] Macula scars
- ☐ H31.09 [1 2 3] Other chorioretinal scars
- ☐ H32 Chorioretinal disorder
- ☐ H33.01 [1 2 3] Retinal detachment w single break
- ☐ H33.31 [1 2 3] Horseshoe tear of retina wo detachment
- ☐ H33.32 [1 2 3] Round hole
- ☐ H33.8 Other retinal detachments
- ☐ H34.1 [1 2 3] Central retinal artery occlusion
- ☐ H34.21 [1 2 3] Partial retinal artery occlusion
- ☐ H35.01 [1 2 3] Vascular sheathing
- ☐ H35.03 [1 2 3] Hypertensive retinopathy
- ☐ H35.04 [1 2 3] Retinal micro-aneurysms
- ☐ H35.34 [1 2 3] Macular cyst, hole or pseudohole
- ☐ H35.35 [1 2 3] Cystoid macular degeneration
- ☐ H35.36 [1 2 3] Drusen (degenerative) of macula
- ☐ H35.37 [1 2 3] Puckering of macule, ERM
- ☐ H35.40 Unspec peripheral retinal degeneration
- ☐ H35.41 [1 2 3] Lattice degeneration of retina
- ☐ H35.71 [1 2 3] Central serous chorioretinopathy
- ☐ H35.82 Retinal ischemia
- ☐ H43.31 [1 2 3] Viterous membranes
- ☐ H43.81 [1 2 3] Viterous degeneration

RT LT BI *(RT-Right LT-Left BI-Bilateral)*
- ☐ H34.81 [10 20 30] Central retinal vein occlusion w mac edema
- ☐ H34.81 [11 21 31] Central retinal vein occlusion w retinal neovascularization
- ☐ H34.81 [12 22 32] Central retinal vein occlusion, stable
- ☐ H34.83 [10 20 30] Tributary retinal vein occlusion w mac edema
- ☐ H34.83 [11 21 31] Tributary retinal vein occlusion w retinal neovascularization
- ☐ H34.83 [12 22 32] Tributary retinal vein occlusion, stable
- ☐ H35.31 [11 21 31] Nonexudative ARMD, early dry stage
- ☐ H35.31 [12 22 32] Nonexudative ARMD, intermediate dry stage
- ☐ H35.31 [13 23 33] Nonexudative ARMD, advanced atropic wo subfoveal inv
- ☐ H35.31 [14 24 34] Nonexudative ARMD, advanced atropic w subfoveal inv
- ☐ H35.32 [11 21 31] Exudative ARMD, active chorodial neovascularization
- ☐ H35.32 [12 22 32] Exudative ARMD, inactive chorodial neovascularization
- ☐ H35.32 [13 23 33] Exudative ARMD, inactive scar

(1-RT 2-LT 3-Bilateral)
(1-With Edema 9-Without Edema)

LACRIMAL SYSTEM
- ☐ H04.01 [1 2 3] Acute dacryoadenitis
- ☐ H04.12 [1 2 3] Dry eye syndrome
- ☐ H04.21 [1 2 3] Epiphora due to excess lacrimation

(1-RT 2-LT 3-Bilateral)

GLAUCOMA
- ☐ H40.01 [1 2 3] Open angle w borderline findings low risk
- ☐ H40.02 [1 2 3] Open angle w borderline findings high risk
- ☐ H40.05 [1 2 3] Ocular hypertension
- ☐ H40.06 [1 2 3] Primary angle closure wo glaucoma damage
- ☐ H40.21 [1 2 3] Acute angle-closure glaucoma

RT LT BI *(RT-Right LT-Left BI-Bilateral)*
- ☐ H40.11 [11 21 31] Primary open-angle glaucoma, mild
- ☐ H40.11 [12 22 32] Primary open-angle glaucoma, mod
- ☐ H40.11 [13 23 33] Primary open-angle glaucoma, severe
- ☐ H40.11 [14 24 34] Primary open-angle glaucoma, indeterminate
- ☐ H40.12 [11 21 31] Low-tens glaucoma, mild stage
- ☐ H40.12 [12 22 32] Low-tens glaucoma, mod stage
- ☐ H40.12 [13 23 33] Low-tens glaucoma, severe stage
- ☐ H40.13 [11 21 31] Pigmentary glaucoma, mild stage
- ☐ H40.13 [12 22 32] Pigmentary glaucoma, mod stage
- ☐ H40.13 [13 23 33] Pigmentary glaucoma, severe stage
- ☐ H40.22 [11 21 31] Chronic angle-closure glaucoma, mild stage
- ☐ H40.22 [12 22 32] Chronic angle-closure glaucoma, mod stage
- ☐ H40.22 [13 23 33] Chronic angle-closure glaucoma, severe stage

(1-RT 2-LT 3-Bilateral)

NEURO-OPHTHALMOLOGY
- ☐ H46.1 [1 2 3] Retrobulbar neuritis
- ☐ H47.01 [1 2 3] Ischemic optic neuropathy
- ☐ H47.1 [1 2 3] Papilledema assoc. w increased intracranial pressure
- ☐ H47.21 [1 2 3] Primary optic atrophy
- ☐ H47.32 [1 2 3] Drusen of optic disc

(1-RT 2-LT 3-Bilateral)

CONJUNCTIVA
- ☐ B30.0 Viral conjunctivitis
- ☐ H10.3 [1 2 3] Acute conjunctivitis
- ☐ H10.41 [1 2 3] Chronic giant papillary conjunctivitis
- ☐ H10.43 [1 2 3] Chronic follicular conjunctivitis
- ☐ H11.05 [1 2 3] Peripheral pterygium, progressive
- ☐ H11.12 [1 2 3] Conjunctival concretions
- ☐ H11.15 [1 2 3] Pinguecula
- ☐ H11.3 [1 2 3] Conjunctival hemorrhage
- ☐ S05.01X [A D S] Inj conjunctiva & corneal abrasion wo fb, RT, init
- ☐ S05.02X [A D S] Inj conjunctiva & corneal abrasion wo fb, LT, init
- ☐ T15.11X [A D S] Foreign body in conjunctival sac, RT, init
- ☐ T15.12X [A D S] Foreign body in conjunctival sac, LT, init

(1-RT 2-LT 3-Bilateral)
(A-Initial D-Subsequent S-Sequela)

CORNEA
- ☐ H16.00 [1 2 3] Unspec corneal ulcer
- ☐ H16.01 [1 2 3] Central corneal ulcer
- ☐ H16.04 [1 2 3] Marginal corneal ulcer
- ☐ H16.12 [1 2 3] Filamentary keratitis
- ☐ H16.14 [1 2 3] Punctate keratitis
- ☐ H16.42 [1 2 3] Pannus (corneal)
- ☐ H18.22 [1 2 3] Idiopathic corneal edema
- ☐ H18.41 [1 2 3] Arcus senilis
- ☐ H18.51 Endothelial corneal dystrophy
- ☐ H18.59 Other hereditary corneal dystrophies
- ☐ H18.82 [1 2 3] Corneal edema due to contact lens
- ☐ H18.83 [1 2 3] Recurrent erosion of cornea
- ☐ T15.01X [A D S] Foreign body in cornea, RT, initial
- ☐ T15.02X [A D S] Foreign body in cornea, LT, initial

(1-RT 2-LT 3-Bilateral)
(A-Initial D-Subsequent S-Sequela)

STRABISMUS
- ☐ H50.00 Unspec esotropia
- ☐ H50.10 Unspec exotropia

(RT-Right LT-Left)

FEE
- ☐ S0620 _____
- ☐ S0621 _____
- ☐ 65210 _____ *
- ☐ 65222 _____ *
- ☐ 65430 _____ *
- ☐ 65435 _____ *
- ☐ 65778 _____ *
- ☐ 67820 _____ *
- ☐ 67938 _____ *
- ☐ 68761 _____ *
- ☐ 68801 _____ *
- ☐ 76510 _____
- ☐ 76514 _____
- ☐ 83516QW _____
- ☐ 83861QW _____
- ☐ 87809QW _____
- ☐ 92002 _____
- ☐ 92004 _____
- ☐ 92012 _____
- ☐ 92014 _____
- ☑ 92015 **18.00** +
- ☐ 92020 _____
- ☐ 92025 _____ *
- ☐ 92060 _____
- ☐ 92071 _____
- ☐ 92072 _____
- ☐ 92082 _____
- ☐ 92083 _____
- ☐ 92100 _____
- ☐ 92132 _____
- ☐ 92133 _____
- ☐ 92134 _____
- ☐ 92225 _____ *
- ☐ 92226 _____ *
- ☐ 92250 _____
- ☐ 92274 _____
- ☐ 92284 _____
- ☐ 92285 _____
- ☐ 92286 _____
- ☐ 92310 _____ +
- ☐ 95930 _____
- ☐ 99201 _____
- ☐ 99202 _____
- ☐ 99203 _____
- ☑ 99204 **149.75**
- ☐ 99205 _____
- ☐ 99212 _____
- ☐ 99213 _____
- ☐ 99214 _____
- ☐ 99215 _____

* May Require Modifier
+ Not Paid by MC

☐ 5010F	☐ G8428
☐ G8397	☐ 4004F
☐ G8398	☐ 1036F
☐ 2022F	☐ G8783
☐ 2024F	☐ G8950
☐ 2026F	☐ G8784
☐ 3072F	☐ G8785
☐ 2019F	☐ G8951
☐ 4177F	☐ G8952
☐ 2027F	☐ G8730
☐ 3284F	☐ G8731
☐ 3285F	☐ G8442
☐ 0517F	☐ G8939
☐ G8427	☐ G8732
☐ G8430	☐ G8509

v2.1 Revised 3/6/17

©2017 - E. Botts, O.D.

• CATARACT PATIENT •
PAGE 4

HEALTH INSURANCE CLAIM FORM
APPROVED BY NATIONAL UNIFORM CLAIM COMMITTEE (NUCC) 02/12

ICD-10

PICA		PICA

1. MEDICARE ☐ MEDICAID ☐ TRICARE ☐ CHAMPVA ☐ GROUP HEALTH PLAN ☐ FECA BLK LUNG ☐ OTHER ☐
1a. INSURED'S I.D. NUMBER (For Program in Item 1): 359 26 8567A

2. PATIENT'S NAME (Last Name, First Name, Middle Initial): Doe, John
3. PATIENT'S BIRTH DATE: 01 01 1911 SEX: M ✓
4. INSURED'S NAME (Last Name, First Name, Middle Initial):

5. PATIENT'S ADDRESS (No., Street): 2100 Red Bud St.
6. PATIENT RELATIONSHIP TO INSURED: Self ☐ Spouse ☐ Child ☐ Other ☐
7. INSURED'S ADDRESS (No., Street):

CITY: Smithville STATE: IL
8. RESERVED FOR NUCC USE
CITY: STATE:

ZIP CODE: 69321 TELEPHONE: (000) 000-0000
ZIP CODE: TELEPHONE: ( )

9. OTHER INSURED'S NAME (Last Name, First Name, Middle Initial):
10. IS PATIENT'S CONDITION RELATED TO:
11. INSURED'S POLICY GROUP OR FECA NUMBER: None

a. OTHER INSURED'S POLICY OR GROUP NUMBER:
a. EMPLOYMENT? (Current or Previous) ☐ YES ✓ NO
a. INSURED'S DATE OF BIRTH: SEX: M ☐ F ☐

b. RESERVED FOR NUCC USE:
b. AUTO ACCIDENT? ☐ YES ✓ NO PLACE (State):
b. OTHER CLAIM ID (Designated by NUCC):

c. RESERVED FOR NUCC USE:
c. OTHER ACCIDENT? ☐ YES ✓ NO
c. INSURANCE PLAN NAME OR PROGRAM NAME:

d. INSURANCE PLAN NAME OR PROGRAM NAME:
10d. CLAIM CODES (Designated by NUCC):
d. IS THERE ANOTHER HEALTH BENEFIT PLAN? ☐ YES ☐ NO — *If yes*, complete items 9, 9a, and 9d.

READ BACK OF FORM BEFORE COMPLETING & SIGNING THIS FORM.
12. PATIENT'S OR AUTHORIZED PERSON'S SIGNATURE I authorize the release of any medical or other information necessary to process this claim. I also request payment of government benefits either to myself or to the party who accepts assignment below.
SIGNED: *John Doe* DATE: 09-05-10

13. INSURED'S OR AUTHORIZED PERSON'S SIGNATURE I authorize payment of medical benefits to the undersigned physician or supplier for services described below.
SIGNED:

14. DATE OF CURRENT ILLNESS, INJURY, or PREGNANCY (LMP): QUAL.
15. OTHER DATE QUAL. MM DD YY
16. DATES PATIENT UNABLE TO WORK IN CURRENT OCCUPATION: FROM — TO

17. NAME OF REFERRING PROVIDER OR OTHER SOURCE: DK | Joe Smith, M.D.
17a. 17b. NPI | Individual NPI#
18. HOSPITALIZATION DATES RELATED TO CURRENT SERVICES: FROM — TO

19. ADDITIONAL CLAIM INFORMATION (Designated by NUCC):
20. OUTSIDE LAB? ☐ YES ☐ NO $ CHARGES

21. DIAGNOSIS OR NATURE OF ILLNESS OR INJURY Relate A-L to service line below (24E) ICD Ind. 10
A. H25.13 B. C. D.
E. F. G. H.
I. J. K. L.

22. RESUBMISSION CODE: ORIGINAL REF. NO.:
23. PRIOR AUTHORIZATION NUMBER:

24. A. DATE(S) OF SERVICE From / To	B. PLACE OF SERVICE	C. EMG	D. PROCEDURES, SERVICES, OR SUPPLIES CPT/HCPCS	MODIFIER	E. DIAGNOSIS POINTER	F. $ CHARGES	G. DAYS OR UNITS	H. EPSDT Family Plan	I. ID. QUAL.	J. RENDERING PROVIDER ID. #
1 09 05 10 09 05 10	11		99204		A	149 75	1		NPI	Individual NPI #
2 09 05 10 09 05 10	11		92015		A	18 00	1		NPI	Individual NPI #
3									NPI	
4									NPI	
5									NPI	
6									NPI	

25. FEDERAL TAX I.D. NUMBER: 411329761 SSN ☐ EIN ✓
26. PATIENT'S ACCOUNT NO.:
27. ACCEPT ASSIGNMENT? ✓ YES ☐ NO
28. TOTAL CHARGE: $ 167 75
29. AMOUNT PAID: $ 0
30. Rsvd for NUCC Use: 167 75

31. SIGNATURE OF PHYSICIAN OR SUPPLIER INCLUDING DEGREES OR CREDENTIALS
(I certify that the statements on the reverse apply to this bill and are made a part thereof.)
SIGNED: *E. Botts* DATE: 09-05-10

32. SERVICE FACILITY LOCATION INFORMATION:
Eric K. Botts, O.D.
1730 East Jackson Street
Macomb, IL 61455
309-836-3373
a. NPI b.

33. BILLING PROVIDER INFO & PH # ( )
Eric K. Botts, O.D.
1730 East Jackson Street
Macomb, IL 61455
309-836-3373
a. NPI b.

NUCC Instruction Manual available at: www.nucc.org
PLEASE PRINT OR TYPE
APPROVED OMB-0938-1197 FORM 1500 (02-12)

©2014 - E. Botts, O.D.
Group NPI # if available, otherwise individual NPI #

• CATARACT PATIENT •
PAGE 5

Medicare
Remittance
Notice

Eric K. Botts, OD
1730 East Jackson Street
Macomb, IL 61455-2531

NPI #: 47932761
Page #: 1 of 2
Date: 9-22-10
Check/Eft #: 115449098

PERF PROV	SERV DATE	POS	NOS	PROC	MODS	BILLED	ALLOWED	DEDUCT	COINS	GRP/RC-AMT	PROV PD
NAME DOE, JOHN			HIC 36030715A		ACNT 111036P			ICN 0206222466720		ASG Y MOA MAO 1 MA 18	
47932761	0905	090510	11	1	99204		149.75	132.05	0.00	26.41	17.70	105.64
47932761	0905	090510	11	1	92015		18.00	0.00	0.00	0.00	PR-96	0.00

| PT RESP | 44.41 | | 1 | CLAIM TOTALS | 167.75 | 132.05 | 0.00 | 26.41 | 17.70 | 105.64 |

CLAIM INFORMATION FORWARDED TO: HCSC-BCBS OF IL (STD A & B)   105.64 NET

PR   Patient Responsibility. Amount that may be billed to a patient or another payer.

96   Non-covered charge(s).

• CATARACT PATIENT •
PAGE 6
EXAMINATION

Patient: **John Doe** Date: **10-21-10** Sex: (M) F DOB: **01-01-11** Age: ___ Last Exam: ___
Chief Complaint: **Blurry Vision**

History
HPI: Cataract removed 9-29-10 OD
Symptoms: Dr. Smith surgeon
Location
Quality
Severity
Duration
Timing
Context
Modifiers

Allergies
Medications
Ocular ROS
Medical History & ROS from **09 / 05 / 10** reviewed: ☐ no changes
Dr. Initials **EKB**

Examination
Head/Face ☐ nl   Psych: Mood/Affect (anxiety/depression) ☐ nl   Neuro: Oriented (person/time/place) ☐ y ☐ n

VA: sc< 20/20   cc<   ph<   near<

K: OD ___ OS ___
OLD RX: OD ___ OS ___   add ___
R-scopy: OD ___ OS ___
REF: OD **pl** 20/**20** add ___
OS **-2.75 DS** 20/**60** add **+2.75**

Perimetry:	☐ nl CF ☐ nl	Color ☐ nl ☐ RG defect	**ADNEXA** ☐ nl	
Motility:	☐ Full	Stereo Animals /3 WD /9	**EYELIDS:** ☐ Blepharitis	OD OS OU
Cover Test:	☐ Eso ___	☑ Exo ___ ☐ Ortho	☐ Meibomianitis	OD OS OU

Pupils: ☑ no afferent defect   ☑ round OU   Size: OD ___ OS ___   ☑ 20D ☑ 90D/78D ☐ 3 Mirror

Incision (OD drawing)   +3 Mature Cataract (OS drawing)

SLE: OD / OS
- ☑ nl ☐ FBUT: ___ TEAR FILM ☑ nl ☐ FBUT: ___
- ☑ nl ☐ arcus CORNEA ☑ nl ☐ arcus
- ☑ nl ☐ pterygium ☑ nl ☐ pterygium
- ☑ nl ☐ infiltrate ☑ nl ☐ infiltrate
- ☑ nl ☐ spk ☑ nl ☐ spk
- ☑ nl ☐ SCLERA ☑ nl
- ☑ nl ☐ injection CONJ. ☑ nl ☐ injection
- ☑ nl ☐ pinguecula ☑ nl ☐ pinguecula
- ☑ D&Q ☐ AC ☑ D&Q ☐
- ☑ nl ☐ rubeosis IRIS ☑ nl ☐ rubeosis
- ☑ clear ☐ cat ☐ ns LENS ☐ clear ☑ cat ☐ ns

RETINA: OD / OS
- ☑ nl ☐ drusen MACULA ☑ nl ☐ drusen
- ☑ nl ☐ RPE chgs ☑ nl ☐ RPE chgs
- ☑ nl ☐ cotton wool POST POLE ☑ nl ☐ cotton wool
- ☑ nl ☐ hemes ☑ nl ☐ hemes
- ☑ nl ☐ DME ☑ nl ☐ DME
- ☑ nl ☐ VESSELS ☑ nl ☐
- ☑ nl ☐ PVD VITREOUS ☑ nl ☐ PVD
- ☑ nl ☐ strands ☑ nl ☐ strands
- ☑ nl ☐ PERIPHERY ☑ nl ☐

OPTIC DISCS: OD ☑ nl ☐ .4/.4   SIZE/APPEARANCE/NFL   OS ☑ nl ☐ .4/.4   C/D

NCT ___ / ___ @ ___   Pachymetry: OD ___ OS ___
TAG 18 / 18 @ **1:30 pm**   Dilated: M .5% 1% (PA 1%/0.25%) C 1% 2% Ph 2.5% 10% OU @ **1:37 pm**

Diagnosis/Plan   MDM 1 2 ③ 4
Pseudophakia OD
CAT OS

RTC follow up
Cataract Post-op

Order: ☐ HRT/GDX/OCT   RTO: ___ day
☐ Photo   ___ week
☐ VF   **1** month
☐ Consult   ___ year

Dr. *E. Botts*

BILLING STATEMENT

• CATARACT PATIENT •
PAGE 6

Dr. Eric Botts
Phone 309/836-3373

Date of Service: 09/05/10
Patient's Name: John Doe
DOB: 01/01/11 ☑ Male ☐ Female
Address: 2100 RedBud St.
City: Smithville
State: IL Zip: 69321
Telephone: ( ) -
Insured's Name:
Insured's DOB: / /
ID Number: 359 26 8567A
Secondary Ins: BCBS
Total: 120.00
Special Instructions: Procedure: 66984 ($650)
Refraction Paid: 18.00
Date of Surgery: 09-29-10
Co-Pay/Deductible Paid: _____
Begin Date: 10-21-10
Ins/Mcaid/Mcare Paid: _____
Secondary Paid: _____
Write Off: _____
Balance Due: _____

MODIFIERS: 24 25 26 50 55 59 79 **RT** ☒ LT E1 E2 E3 E4 1P 2P 8P TC GW QW

MISCELLANEOUS
- E10.65 Type 1 Diabetes w complications
- E10.9 Type 1 Diabetes wo complications
- E11.65 Type 2 Diabetes w complications
- E11.9 Type 2 Diabetes wo complications
- H27.0 [1 2 3] Aphakia
- H53.8 Blurred Vision
- H57.1 [1 2 3] Ocular Pain
- M06.9 Rheumatoid Arthritis
- Z79.4 Insulin Dependent
- Z79.84 Non-Insulin Dependent
- Z79.899 High Risk meds

UVEAL DISORDERS
- H20.01 [1 2 3] Primary iridocyclitis
- H21.0 [1 2 3] Hyphema
- H21.23 [1 2 3] Degeneration of Iris
- H21.26 [1 2 3] Iris Atrophy
- H21.4 [1 2 3] Pupillary membranes
- H57.05 [1 2 3] Tonic Pupil

(1-RT 2-LT 3-Bilateral)

EYELIDS
- H00.023 Hordeolum internum RT eye
- H00.026 Hordeolum internum LT eye
- H00.13 Chalazion RT eye
- H00.16 Chalazion LT eye
- H01.023 Squamous blepharitis RT eye
- H01.026 Squamous blepharitis LT eye
- H01.113 Allergic dermatitis RT eye
- H01.116 Allergic dermatitis LT eye
- H02.033 Senile entropion RT eye
- H02.036 Senile entropion LT eye
- H02.053 Trichiasis wo entropion RT eye
- H05.056 Trichiasis wo entropion LT eye
- H02.133 Senile ectropion RT eye
- H02.136 Senile ectropion LT eye
- H02.40 [1 2 3] Unspec ptosis of eyelid
- H02.833 Dermatochalasis RT eye
- H02.836 Dermatochalasis LT eye

(1-RT 2-LT 3-Bilateral)

CATARACT/LENS
- H25.01 [1 2 3] Cortical age-related cat
- H25.04 [1 2 3] Post subcap polar age-related cat
- ☑ H25.1 (1)2 3] Age-related nuclear cat
- H25.89 Other age-related cat
- Z96.1 Presence of intraocular lens

(1-RT 2-LT 3-Bilateral)

DISORDER OF REFRACTION
- H52.0 [1 2 3] Hypermetropia
- H52.1 [1 2 3] Myopia
- H52.22 [1 2 3] Regular Astigmatism
- H52.4 Presbyopia

(1-RT 2-LT 3-Bilateral)

VISUAL DISORDERS
- H51.11 Convergence insufficiency
- H51.12 Convergence excess
- H52.53 [1 2 3] Spasm of accommodation
- H53.02 [1 2 3] Refractive amblyopia
- H53.03 [1 2 3] Strabismic amblyopia
- H53.14 [1 2 3] Visual discomfort
- H53.41 [1 2 3] Scotoma involving central area
- H53.42 [1 2 3] Scotoma of blind spot area
- H53.43 [1 2 3] Sector or arcuate defects
- H53.46 [1 2 3] Homonymous bilateral field defects
- H53.47 Heteronymous bilateral field defects
- H55.00 Unspec nystagmus

(1-RT 2-LT 3-Bilateral)

RETINAL DISORDERS
- E10.31 [1 9] T1 diab w unsp diab rtnop
- E10.321 [1 2 3] T1 diab w mild nonprlf diab rtnop w mac edema
- E10.329 [1 2 3] T1 diab w mild nonprlf diab rtnop wo mac edema
- E10.331 [1 2 3] T1 diab w mod nonprlf diab rtnop w mac edema
- E10.339 [1 2 3] T1 diab w mon nonprlf diab rtnop wo mac edema
- E10.341 [1 2 3] T1 diab w severe nonprlf diab rtnop w mac edema
- E10.349 [1 2 3] T1 diab w severe nonprlf diab rtnop wo mac edema
- E10.351 [1 2 3] T1 diab w prlif diab rtnop w mac edema
- E10.355 [1 2 3] T1 diab w stable prolif diab rtnop
- E10.359 [1 2 3] T1 diab w prlif diab rtnop wo mac edema
- E11.31 [1 9] T2 diab w unsp diab rtnop
- E11.321 [1 2 3] T2 diab w mild nonprlf diab rtnop w mac edema
- E11.329 [1 2 3] T2 diab w mild nonprlf diab rtnop wo mac edema
- E11.331 [1 2 3] T2 diab w mod nonprlf diab rtnop w mac edema
- E11.339 [1 2 3] T2 diab w mod nonprlf diab rtnop wo mac edema
- E11.341 [1 2 3] T2 diab w severe nonprlf diab rtnop w mac edema
- E11.349 [1 2 3] T2 diab w severe nonprlf diab rtnop wo mac edema
- E11.351 [1 2 3] T2 diab w prolif diab rtnop w mac edema
- E11.355 [1 2 3] T2 diab w stable prolif diab rtnop
- E11.359 [1 2 3] T2 diab w prolif diab rtnop wo mac edema
- H31.01 [1 2 3] Macula scars
- H31.09 [1 2 3] Other chorioretinal scars
- H32 Chorioretinal disorder
- H33.01 [1 2 3] Retinal detachment w single break
- H33.31 [1 2 3] Horseshoe tear of retina wo detachment
- H33.32 [1 2 3] Round hole
- H33.8 Other retinal detachments
- H34.1 [1 2 3] Central retinal artery occlusion
- H34.21 [1 2 3] Partial retinal artery occlusion
- H35.01 [1 2 3] Vascular sheathing
- H35.03 [1 2 3] Hypertensive retinopathy
- H35.04 [1 2 3] Retinal micro-aneurysms
- H35.34 [1 2 3] Macular cyst, hole or pseudohole
- H35.35 [1 2 3] Cystoid macular degeneration
- H35.36 [1 2 3] Drusen (degenerative) of macula
- H35.37 [1 2 3] Puckering of macule, ERM
- H35.40 Unspec peripheral retinal degeneration
- H35.41 [1 2 3] Lattice degeneration of retina
- H35.71 [1 2 3] Central serous chorioretinopathy
- H35.82 Retinal ischemia
- H43.31 [1 2 3] Viterous membranes
- H43.81 [1 2 3] Viterous degeneration

RT LT BI (RT-Right LT-Left BI-Bilateral)
- H34.81 [10 20 30] Central retinal vein occlusion w mac edema
- H34.81 [11 21 31] Central retinal vein occlusion w retinal neovascularization
- H34.81 [12 22 32] Central retinal vein occlusion, stable
- H34.83 [10 20 30] Tributary retinal vein occlusion w mac edema
- H34.83 [11 21 31] Tributary retinal vein occlusion w retinal neovascularization
- H34.83 [12 22 32] Tributary retinal vein occlusion, stable
- H35.31 [11 21 31] Nonexudative ARMD, early dry stage
- H35.31 [12 22 32] Nonexudative ARMD, intermediate dry stage
- H35.31 [13 23 33] Nonexudative ARMD, advanced atropic wo subfoveal inv
- H35.31 [14 24 34] Nonexudative ARMD, advanced atropic w subfoveal inv
- H35.32 [11 21 31] Exudative ARMD, active chorodial neovascularization
- H35.32 [12 22 32] Exudative ARMD, inactive chorodial neovascularization
- H35.32 [13 23 33] Exudative ARMD, inactive scar

(1-RT 2-LT 3-Bilateral)
(1-With Edema 9-Without Edema)

LACRIMAL SYSTEM
- H04.01 [1 2 3] Acute dacryoadenitis
- H04.12 [1 2 3] Dry eye syndrome
- H04.21 [1 2 3] Epiphora due to excess lacrimation

(1-RT 2-LT 3-Bilateral)

GLAUCOMA
- H40.01 [1 2 3] Open angle w borderline findings low risk
- H40.02 [1 2 3] Open angle w borderline findings high risk
- H40.05 [1 2 3] Ocular hypertension
- H40.06 [1 2 3] Primary angle closure wo glaucoma damage
- H40.21 [1 2 3] Acute angle-closure glaucoma

RT LT BI (RT-Right LT-Left BI-Bilateral)
- H40.11 [11 21 31] Primary open-angle glaucoma, mild
- H40.11 [12 22 32] Primary open-angle glaucoma, mod
- H40.11 [13 23 33] Primary open-angle glaucoma, severe
- H40.11 [14 24 34] Primary open-angle glaucoma, indeterminate
- H40.12 [11 21 31] Low-tens glaucoma, mild stage
- H40.12 [12 22 32] Low-tens glaucoma, mod stage
- H40.12 [13 23 33] Low-tens glaucoma, severe stage
- H40.13 [11 21 31] Pigmentary glaucoma, mild stage
- H40.13 [12 22 32] Pigmentary glaucoma, mod stage
- H40.13 [13 23 33] Pigmentary glaucoma, severe stage
- H40.22 [11 21 31] Chronic angle-closure glaucoma, mild stage
- H40.22 [12 22 32] Chronic angle-closure glaucoma, mod stage
- H40.22 [13 23 33] Chronic angle-closure glaucoma, severe stage

(1-RT 2-LT 3-Bilateral)

NEURO-OPHTHALMOLOGY
- H46.1 [1 2 3] Retrobulbar neuritis
- H47.01 [1 2 3] Ischemic optic neuropathy
- H47.1 [1 2 3] Papilledema assoc. w increased intracranial pressure
- H47.21 [1 2 3] Primary optic atrophy
- H47.32 [1 2 3] Drusen of optic disc

(1-RT 2-LT 3-Bilateral)

CONJUNCTIVA
- B30.0 Viral conjunctivitis
- H10.3 [1 2 3] Acute conjunctivitis
- H10.41 [1 2 3] Chronic giant papillary conjunctivitis
- H10.43 [1 2 3] Chronic follicular conjunctivitis
- H11.05 [1 2 3] Peripheral pterygium, progressive
- H11.12 [1 2 3] Conjunctival concretions
- H11.15 [1 2 3] Pinguecula
- H11.3 [1 2 3] Conjunctival hemorrhage
- S05.01X [A D S] Inj conjunctiva & corneal abrasion wo fb, RT, init
- S05.02X [A D S] Inj conjunctiva & corneal abrasion wo fb, LT, init
- T15.11X [A D S] Foreign body in conjunctival sac, RT, init
- T15.12X [A D S] Foreign body in conjunctival sac, LT init

(1-RT 2-LT 3-Bilateral)
(A-Initial D-Subsequent S-Sequela)

CORNEA
- H16.00 [1 2 3] Unspec corneal ulcer
- H16.01 [1 2 3] Central corneal ulcer
- H16.04 [1 2 3] Marginal corneal ulcer
- H16.12 [1 2 3] Filamentary keratitis
- H16.14 [1 2 3] Punctate keratitis
- H16.42 [1 2 3] Pannus (corneal)
- H18.22 [1 2 3] Idiopathic corneal edema
- H18.41 [1 2 3] Arcus senilis
- H18.51 Endothelial corneal dystrophie
- H18.59 Other hereditary corneal dystrophies
- H18.82 [1 2 3] Corneal edema due to contact lens
- H18.83 [1 2 3] Recurrent erosion of cornea
- T15.01X [A D S] Foreign body in cornea, RT, initial
- T15.02X [A D S] Foreign body in cornea, LT, initial

(1-RT 2-LT 3-Bilateral)
(A-Initial D-Subsequent S-Sequela)

STRABISMUS
- H50.00 Unspec esotropia
- H50.10 Unspec exotropia

(RT-Right LT-Left)

FEE
- S0620 _____
- S0621 _____
- 65210 _____ *
- 65222 _____ *
- 65430 _____ *
- 65435 _____ *
- 65778 _____ *
- 67820 _____ *
- 67938 _____ *
- 68761 _____ *
- 68801 _____ *
- 76510 _____
- 76514 _____
- 83516QW _____
- 83861QW _____
- 87809QW _____
- 92002 _____
- 92004 _____
- 92012 _____
- 92014 _____
- ☑ 92015 18.00 +
- 92020 _____
- 92025 _____ *
- 92060 _____
- 92071 _____
- 92072 _____
- 92082 _____
- 92083 _____
- 92100 _____
- 92132 _____
- 92133 _____
- 92134 _____
- 92225 _____ *
- 92226 _____ *
- 92250 _____
- 92274 _____
- 92284 _____
- 92285 _____
- 92286 _____
- 92310 _____ +
- 95930 _____
- 99201 _____
- 99202 _____
- 99203 _____
- 99204 _____
- 99205 _____
- 99212 _____
- 99213 _____
- 99214 _____
- 99215 _____

* May Require Modifier
+ Not Paid by MC

- 5010F G8428
- G8397 4004F
- G8398 1036F
- 2022F G8783
- 2024F G8950
- 2026F G8784
- 3072F G8785
- 2019F G8951
- 4177F G8952
- 2027F G8730
- 3284F G8731
- 3285F G8442
- 0517F G8939
- G8427 G8732
- G8430 G8509

v2.1 Revised 3/6/17

©2017 - E. Botts, O.D.

HEALTH INSURANCE CLAIM FORM

• CATARACT PATIENT •
PAGE 8

ICD-10

APPROVED BY NATIONAL UNIFORM CLAIM COMMITTEE (NUCC) 02/12

1. MEDICARE ☐ / MEDICAID ☐ / TRICARE ☐ / CHAMPVA ☐ / GROUP HEALTH PLAN ☐ / FECA BLK LUNG ☐ / OTHER ☐	1a. INSURED'S I.D. NUMBER	359 26 8567A
2. PATIENT'S NAME: Doe, John	3. PATIENT'S BIRTH DATE: 01/01/1911 SEX: M ✓	4. INSURED'S NAME:
5. PATIENT'S ADDRESS: 2100 Red Bud St.	6. PATIENT RELATIONSHIP TO INSURED: Self ✓	7. INSURED'S ADDRESS:
CITY: Smithville STATE: IL	8. RESERVED FOR NUCC USE	CITY: / STATE:
ZIP CODE: 69321 TELEPHONE: (000) 000-0000		ZIP CODE: / TELEPHONE: ( )
9. OTHER INSURED'S NAME:	10. IS PATIENT'S CONDITION RELATED TO:	11. INSURED'S POLICY GROUP OR FECA NUMBER: None
a. OTHER INSURED'S POLICY OR GROUP NUMBER:	a. EMPLOYMENT? NO ✓	a. INSURED'S DATE OF BIRTH / SEX
b. RESERVED FOR NUCC USE	b. AUTO ACCIDENT? NO ✓ PLACE (State):	b. OTHER CLAIM ID:
c. RESERVED FOR NUCC USE	c. OTHER ACCIDENT? NO ✓	c. INSURANCE PLAN NAME OR PROGRAM NAME:
d. INSURANCE PLAN NAME OR PROGRAM NAME:	10d. CLAIM CODES:	d. IS THERE ANOTHER HEALTH BENEFIT PLAN?

12. PATIENT'S OR AUTHORIZED PERSON'S SIGNATURE
SIGNED: SOF   DATE: 09-05-10

13. INSURED'S OR AUTHORIZED PERSON'S SIGNATURE
SIGNED:

14. DATE OF CURRENT ILLNESS, INJURY, or PREGNANCY (LMP):
15. OTHER DATE:
16. DATES PATIENT UNABLE TO WORK IN CURRENT OCCUPATION: FROM / TO

17. NAME OF REFERRING PROVIDER OR OTHER SOURCE: DN Joe Smith, M.D.
17b. NPI: Individual NPI#

18. HOSPITALIZATION DATES RELATED TO CURRENT SERVICES: FROM / TO

19. ADDITIONAL CLAIM INFORMATION: Begin Date 10-21-10 Relinquish Date 12-28-10 (68 days)

20. OUTSIDE LAB? ☐ YES ☐ NO $ CHARGES

21. DIAGNOSIS OR NATURE OF ILLNESS OR INJURY   ICD Ind. 10
A. H25.11   B.   C.   D.
E.   F.   G.   H.
I.   J.   K.   L.

22. RESUBMISSION CODE / ORIGINAL REF. NO.
23. PRIOR AUTHORIZATION NUMBER

24.	DATE(S) OF SERVICE From — To	B. PLACE OF SERVICE	C. EMG	D. PROCEDURES, SERVICES, OR SUPPLIES (CPT/HCPCS MODIFIER)	E. DIAGNOSIS POINTER	F. $ CHARGES	G. DAYS OR UNITS	H. EPSDT	I. ID. QUAL.	J. RENDERING PROVIDER ID. #
1	09 29 10 — 09 29 10	11		66984 RT 55	A	120 00	68		NPI	Individual NPI #
2	10 24 10 — 10 24 10	11		92015	A	18 00	1		NPI	Individual NPI #
3									NPI	
4									NPI	
5									NPI	
6									NPI	

25. FEDERAL TAX I.D. NUMBER: 411329761 EIN ✓
26. PATIENT'S ACCOUNT NO.:
27. ACCEPT ASSIGNMENT? YES ✓
28. TOTAL CHARGE: $138.00
29. AMOUNT PAID: $0
30. Rsvd for NUCC Use: 138.00

31. SIGNATURE OF PHYSICIAN OR SUPPLIER: E. Botts   10-21-10

32. SERVICE FACILITY LOCATION INFORMATION:
Eric K. Botts, O.D.
1730 East Jackson Street
Macomb, IL 61455
309-836-3373

33. BILLING PROVIDER INFO & PH #:
Eric K. Botts, O.D.
1730 East Jackson Street
Macomb, IL 61455
309-836-3373

NUCC Instruction Manual available at: www.nucc.org
PLEASE PRINT OR TYPE
APPROVED OMB-0938-1197 FORM 1500 (02-12)

©2014 - E. Botts, O.D.
Group NPI # if available, otherwise individual NPI #

• CATARACT PATIENT •
PAGE 9

Medicare
Remittance
Notice

Eric K. Botts, OD
1730 East Jackson Street
Macomb, IL 61455-2531

NPI #: 47932761
Page #: 1 of 2
Date: 11-22-10
Check/Eft #: 115449098

PERF PROV	SERV DATE	POS	NOS	PROC	MODS	BILLED	ALLOWED	DEDUCT	COINS	GRP/RC-AMT	PROV PD
NAME DOE, JOHN			HIC 36030715A		ACNT 111036P			ICN 0206222466720	ASG Y	MOA MAO 1	MA 18
47932761	0929 092910	11	1	66984	RT-55	120.00	110.00	0.00	22.00	10.00	88.00
47932761	1024 102410	11	1	92015		18.00	0.00	0.00	0.00	PR-96	0.00

| PT RESP | 40.00 | | 1 | CLAIM TOTALS | | 138.00 | 110.00 | 0.00 | 22.00 | 10.00 | 88.00 |

CLAIM INFORMATION FORWARDED TO: HCSC-BCBS OF IL (STD A & B)

88.00 NET

PR   Patient Responsibility. Amount that may be billed to a patient or another payer.

96   Non-covered charge(s).

• CATARACT PATIENT •
PAGE 10

HEALTH INSURANCE CLAIM FORM
ICD-10

APPROVED BY NATIONAL UNIFORM CLAIM COMMITTEE (NUCC) 02/12

PICA		PICA

1. MEDICARE [ ] MEDICAID [ ] TRICARE [ ] CHAMPVA [ ] GROUP HEALTH PLAN [ ] FECA BLK LUNG [ ] OTHER [ ]
1a. INSURED'S I.D. NUMBER (For Program in Item 1): 359 26 8567A

2. PATIENT'S NAME (Last Name, First Name, Middle Initial): Doe, John
3. PATIENT'S BIRTH DATE: 01 / 01 / 1911   SEX: M ✔
4. INSURED'S NAME (Last Name, First Name, Middle Initial):

5. PATIENT'S ADDRESS (No., Street): 2100 Red Bud St.
6. PATIENT RELATIONSHIP TO INSURED: Self ✔
7. INSURED'S ADDRESS (No., Street):

CITY: Smithville   STATE: IL
8. RESERVED FOR NUCC USE
CITY: STATE:

ZIP CODE: 69321   TELEPHONE: (000) 000-0000
ZIP CODE: TELEPHONE: ( )

9. OTHER INSURED'S NAME (Last Name, First Name, Middle Initial):
10. IS PATIENT'S CONDITION RELATED TO:
11. INSURED'S POLICY GROUP OR FECA NUMBER: None

a. OTHER INSURED'S POLICY OR GROUP NUMBER:
a. EMPLOYMENT? (Current or Previous) [ ] YES [✔] NO
a. INSURED'S DATE OF BIRTH: SEX: M [ ] F [ ]

b. RESERVED FOR NUCC USE:
b. AUTO ACCIDENT? [ ] YES [✔] NO   PLACE (State):
b. OTHER CLAIM ID (Designated by NUCC):

c. RESERVED FOR NUCC USE:
c. OTHER ACCIDENT? [ ] YES [✔] NO
c. INSURANCE PLAN NAME OR PROGRAM NAME:

d. INSURANCE PLAN NAME OR PROGRAM NAME:
10d. CLAIM CODES (Designated by NUCC):
d. IS THERE ANOTHER HEALTH BENEFIT PLAN? [ ] YES [ ] NO

READ BACK OF FORM BEFORE COMPLETING & SIGNING THIS FORM.
12. PATIENT'S OR AUTHORIZED PERSON'S SIGNATURE
SIGNED: SOF   DATE: 09-05-10
13. INSURED'S OR AUTHORIZED PERSON'S SIGNATURE
SIGNED:

14. DATE OF CURRENT ILLNESS, INJURY, or PREGNANCY (LMP): QUAL.
15. OTHER DATE QUAL.
16. DATES PATIENT UNABLE TO WORK IN CURRENT OCCUPATION: FROM   TO

17. NAME OF REFERRING PROVIDER OR OTHER SOURCE: DN | Joe Smith, M.D.
17a.
17b. NPI: Individual NPI#
18. HOSPITALIZATION DATES RELATED TO CURRENT SERVICES: FROM   TO

19. ADDITIONAL CLAIM INFORMATION (Designated by NUCC): Begin Date 11-9-10   Relinquish Date 1-16-11 (68 days)
20. OUTSIDE LAB? [ ] YES [ ] NO $ CHARGES

21. DIAGNOSIS OR NATURE OF ILLNESS OR INJURY   ICD Ind. 10
A. H25.12   B.   C.   D.
E.   F.   G.   H.
I.   J.   K.   L.

22. RESUBMISSION CODE: ORIGINAL REF. NO.
23. PRIOR AUTHORIZATION NUMBER:

24.	A. DATE(S) OF SERVICE From / To	B. PLACE OF SERVICE	C. EMG	D. PROCEDURES, SERVICES, OR SUPPLIES CPT/HCPCS / MODIFIER	E. DIAGNOSIS POINTER	F. $ CHARGES	G. DAYS OR UNITS	H. EPSDT	I. ID QUAL.	J. RENDERING PROVIDER ID. #
1	10 18 10 / 10 18 10	11		66984 LT 55 79	A	120 00	68		NPI	Individual NPI #
2	11 11 10 / 11 11 10	11		92015	A	18 00	1		NPI	Individual NPI #
3									NPI	
4									NPI	
5									NPI	
6									NPI	

25. FEDERAL TAX I.D. NUMBER: 411329761   SSN [ ] EIN [✔]
26. PATIENT'S ACCOUNT NO.
27. ACCEPT ASSIGNMENT? [✔] YES [ ] NO
28. TOTAL CHARGE: $ 138 00
29. AMOUNT PAID: $ 0
30. Rsvd for NUCC Use: 138 00

31. SIGNATURE OF PHYSICIAN OR SUPPLIER INCLUDING DEGREES OR CREDENTIALS
SIGNED: E. Botts   DATE: 10-21-10

32. SERVICE FACILITY LOCATION INFORMATION
Eric K. Botts, O.D.
1730 East Jackson Street
Macomb, IL 61455
309-836-3373

33. BILLING PROVIDER INFO & PH #
Eric K. Botts, O.D.
1730 East Jackson Street
Macomb, IL 61455
309-836-3373

NUCC Instruction Manual available at: www.nucc.org
PLEASE PRINT OR TYPE
APPROVED OMB-0938-1197 FORM 1500 (02-12)

©2014 - E. Botts, O.D.
Group NPI # if available, otherwise individual NPI #

• CATARACT PATIENT •
PAGE 11

Medicare
Remittance
Notice

Eric K. Botts, OD
1730 East Jackson Street
Macomb, IL 61455-2531

NPI #: 47932761
Page #: 1 of 2
Date: 11-22-10
Check/Eft #: 115449098

PERF PROV	SERV DATE	POS	NOS	PROC	MODS	BILLED	ALLOWED	DEDUCT	COINS	GRP/RC-AMT	PROV PD
NAME DOE, JOHN			HIC 36030715A		ACNT 111036P			ICN 0206222466720	ASG Y	MOA MAO 1	MA 18
47932761	1018 101810	11	1	66984	LT-55-79	120.00	110.00	0.00	22.00	10.00	88.00
47932761	1111 111110	11	1	92015		18.00	0.00	0.00	0.00	PR-96	0.00

| PT RESP | 40.00 | | 1 | CLAIM TOTALS | | 138.00 | 110.00 | 0.00 | 22.00 | 10.00 | 88.00 |

CLAIM INFORMATION FORWARDED TO: HCSC-BCBS OF IL (STD A & B)

88.00 NET

PR   Patient Responsibility. Amount that may be billed to a patient or another payer.

96   Non-covered charge(s).

Example #7
Dry Eye Patient

• DRY EYE PATIENT •
PAGE 1

EXAMINATION

Example #7

Patient: Jane Johnson   Date: 11-03-10   Sex: M (F)   DOB: 12-05-26   Age: ___   Last Exam: ___
Chief Complaint: Eyes Feel Dry

History
- **HPI:** Dry all the time
- **Symptoms:** Both eyes
- **Location:** Artificial tears don't help
- **Quality:** Feel like grit in eyes
- **Severity:** Occasional blurry vision
- **Duration:**
- **Timing:**
- **Context:**
- **Modifiers:**

Allergies:
Medications:
Ocular ROS:
Medical History & ROS from 06/14/05 reviewed: ☑ no changes
Dr. Initials: EKB

Examination
Head/Face ☑ nl   Psych: Mood/Affect (anxiety/depression) ☑ nl   Neuro: Oriented (person/time/place) ☑ y ☐ n

VA: sc< ___   cc< 25/25   ph< ___   near< ___

K: OD ___ OS ___
OLD RX: OD ___ OS ___   add ___
R-scopy: OD ___ OS ___
REF: OD 20/___ OS 20/___   add ___

- **Perimetry:** ☐ nl   CF ☐ nl   Color ☐ nl ☐ RG defect   **ADNEXA** ☑ nl
- **Motility:** ☑ Full   Stereo Animals /3 WD /9   **EYELIDS:** ☐ Blepharitis OD OS OU
- **Cover Test:** ☐ Eso ___ ☐ Exo ___ ☐ Ortho   ☐ Meibomianitis OD OS OU
- **Pupils:** ☑ no afferent defect   ☑ round OU   Size: OD ___ OS ___
  - ☐ 20D
  - ☐ 90D/78D
  - ☐ 3 Mirror
  - ☐

SLE: OD / OS
OD			OS		
☐ nl	☑ FBUT: 3	TEAR FILM	☐ nl	☑ FBUT: 3	
☑ nl	☐ arcus	CORNEA	☑ nl	☐ arcus	
☑ nl	☐ pterygium		☑ nl	☐ pterygium	
☑ nl	☐ infiltrate		☑ nl	☐ infiltrate	
☑ nl	☑ spk		☑ nl	☑ spk	
☑ nl	☐	SCLERA	☑ nl	☐	
☐ nl	☑ injection	CONJ.	☐ nl	☑ injection	
☑ nl	☐ pinguecula		☑ nl	☐ pinguecula	
☑ D&Q ☐		AC	☑ D&Q ☐		
☑ nl	☐ rubeosis	IRIS	☑ nl	☐ rubeosis	
☐ clear	☐ cat ☑ ns	LENS	☐ clear	☐ cat ☑ ns	

RETINA: OD / OS
OD			OS	
☐ nl	☐ drusen	MACULA	☐ nl	☐ drusen
☐ nl	☐ RPE chgs		☐ nl	☐ RPE chgs
☐ nl	☐ cotton wool	POST POLE	☐ nl	☐ cotton wool
☐ nl	☐ hemes		☐ nl	☐ hemes
☐ nl	☐ DME		☐ nl	☐ DME
☐ nl	☐	VESSELS	☐ nl	☐
☐ nl	☐ PVD	VITREOUS	☐ nl	☐ PVD
☐ nl	☐ strands		☐ nl	☐ strands
☐ nl	☐	PERIPHERY	☐ nl	☐

OPTIC DISCS: OD ☐ nl ☐ ___   SIZE/APPEARANCE/NFL   OS ☐ nl ☐ ___   C/D ___

NCT: ___ / ___ @ ___   **Pachymetry:** OD ___
TAG: 18 / 18 @ 2:05 pm   OS ___   Dilated: M .5% 1% PA 1%/0.25% C 1% 2% Ph 2.5% 10% OU@ ___

Diagnosis/Plan   MDM 1 2 (3) 4

Tear film insufficiency

Insert collagen plugs inferior puncta OU
Order tear osmolarity
Order ext. photo

Order:
- ☐ HRT/GDX/OCT
- ☐ Photo
- ☐ VF
- ☐ Consult

RTO: ___ day   2 week   ___ month   ___ year

Dr. E. Bolt

• *Dry Eye Patient* •
PAGE 6

Supplementary Tests

Patient: *Jane Johnson* Date: *11-03-10*

- ❏ **Visual Fields** (92081, 92082, 92083)
- ❏ **Sensorimotor Examination** (92060)
- ❏ **Scanning Computerized Ophthalmic Diagnostic Imaging** (92132, 92133, 92134) ❏ HRT ❏ OCT ❏ GDX
- ❏ **Serial Tonometry** (92100)
- ❏ **Gonioscopy** (92020)
- ❏ **Specular Microscopy** (92286)
- ❏ **Fundus Photography** (92250)
- ☒ **External Ocular Photography** (92285)
- ❏ **Corneal Topography** (92025)
- ❏ **Pattern Electroretinography** (92275)

External Ocular Photography ((92285), 92286)

	OD	OS
Findings	Diffuse punctate on epithelium	Diffuse punctate on epithelium
Diagnosis	Dry Eye Syndrome	Dry Eye Sydrome
Plan	Insert collagen plugs, RTC 2 weeks	Insert collagen plugs, RTC 2 weeks

Signature: *E. Bold*

Rev. 4/17

BILLING STATEMENT

• DRY EYE PATIENT •
PAGE 2

Dr. Eric Botts
Phone 309/836-337_

91

Date of Service **11 / 03 / 10**
Patient's Name **Jane Johnson** DOB **12 / 05 / 26** ☐ Male ☒ Female
Address **1262 Jay St.** City **Smithfield** State **IL** Zip **62555**
Telephone (____) ____ - ____ Insured's Name ____ Insured's DOB __ / __ / __
ID Number **xxx xx xxxxA** Secondary Ins **United Healthcare** Total **415.69**
Special Instructions ____

Refraction Paid ____
Co-Pay/Deductible Paid ____
Ins/Mcaid/Mcare Paid ____
Secondary Paid ____
Write Off ____
Balance Due ____

MODIFIERS: 24 [ ], 25 [X], 26 [ ], 50 [ ], 55 [ ], 59 [ ], 79 [ ], RT [X], LT [X], E1 [ ], E2 [X], E3 [ ], E4 [X], 1P [ ], 2P [ ], 8P [ ], TC [ ], GW [ ], QW [ ]

MISCELLANEOUS
- ☐ E10.65 Type 1 Diabetes w complications
- ☐ E10.9 Type 1 Diabetes wo complications
- ☐ E11.65 Type 2 Diabetes w complications
- ☐ E11.9 Type 2 Diabetes wo complications
- ☐ H27.0 [1 2 3] Aphakia
- ☐ H53.8 Blurred Vision
- ☐ H57.1 [1 2 3] Ocular Pain
- ☐ M06.9 Rheumatoid Arthritis
- ☐ Z79.4 Insulin Dependent
- ☐ Z79.84 Non-Insulin Dependent
- ☐ Z79.899 High Risk meds

(1-RT 2-LT 3-Bilateral)

UVEAL DISORDERS
- ☐ H20.01 [1 2 3] Primary iridocyclitis
- ☐ H21.0 [1 2 3] Hyphema
- ☐ H21.23 [1 2 3] Degeneration of Iris
- ☐ H21.26 [1 2 3] Iris Atrophy
- ☐ H21.4 [1 2 3] Pupillary membranes
- ☐ H57.05 [1 2 3] Tonic Pupil

(1-RT 2-LT 3-Bilateral)

EYELIDS
- ☐ H00.023 Hordeolum internum RT eye
- ☐ H00.026 Hordeolum internum LT eye
- ☐ H00.13 Chalazion RT eye
- ☐ H00.16 Chalazion LT eye
- ☐ H01.023 Squamous blepharitis RT eye
- ☐ H01.026 Squamous blepharitis LT eye
- ☐ H01.113 Allergic dermatitis RT eye
- ☐ H01.116 Allergic dermatitis LT eye
- ☐ H02.033 Senile entropion RT eye
- ☐ H02.036 Senile entropion LT eye
- ☐ H02.053 Trichiasis wo entropion RT eye
- ☐ H05.056 Trichiasis wo entropion LT eye
- ☐ H02.133 Senile ectropion RT eye
- ☐ H02.136 Senile ectropion LT eye
- ☐ H02.40 [1 2 3] Unspec ptosis of eyelid
- ☐ H02.833 Dermatochalasis RT eye
- ☐ H02.836 Dermatochalasis LT eye

(1-RT 2-LT 3-Bilateral)

CATARACT/LENS
- ☐ H25.01 [1 2 3] Cortical age-related cat
- ☐ H25.04 [1 2 3] Post subcap polar age-related cat
- ☐ H25.1 [1 2 3] Age-related nuclear cat
- ☐ H25.89 Other age-related cat
- ☐ Z96.1 Presence of intraocular lens

(1-RT 2-LT 3-Bilateral)

DISORDER OF REFRACTION
- ☐ H52.0 [1 2 3] Hypermetropia
- ☐ H52.1 [1 2 3] Myopia
- ☐ H52.22 [1 2 3] Regular Astigmatism
- ☐ H52.4 Presbyopia

(1-RT 2-LT 3-Bilateral)

VISUAL DISORDERS
- ☐ H51.11 Convergence insufficiency
- ☐ H51.12 Convergence excess
- ☐ H52.53 [1 2 3] Spasm of accommodation
- ☐ H53.02 [1 2 3] Refractive amblyopia
- ☐ H53.03 [1 2 3] Strabismic amblyopia
- ☐ H53.14 [1 2 3] Visual discomfort
- ☐ H53.41 [1 2 3] Scotoma involving central area
- ☐ H53.42 [1 2 3] Scotoma of blind spot area
- ☐ H53.43 [1 2 3] Sector or arcuate defects
- ☐ H53.46 [1 2 3] Homonymous bilateral field defects
- ☐ H53.47 Heteronymous bilateral field defects
- ☐ H55.00 Unspec nystagmus

(1-RT 2-LT 3-Bilateral)

RETINAL DISORDERS
- ☐ E10.31 [1 9] T1 diab w unsp diab rtnop
- ☐ E10.321 [1 2 3] T1 diab w mild nonprlf diab rtnop w mac edema
- ☐ E10.329 [1 2 3] T1 diab w mild nonprlf diab rtnop wo mac edema
- ☐ E10.331 [1 2 3] T1 diab w mod nonprlf diab rtnop w mac edema
- ☐ E10.339 [1 2 3] T1 diab w mon nonprlf diab rtnop wo mac edema
- ☐ E10.341 [1 2 3] T1 diab w severe nonprlf diab rtnop w mac edema
- ☐ E10.349 [1 2 3] T1 diab w severe nonprlf diab rtnop wo mac edema
- ☐ E10.351 [1 2 3] T1 diab w prlif diab rtnop w mac edema
- ☐ E10.355 [1 2 3] T1 diab w stable prolif diab rtnop
- ☐ E10.359 [1 2 3] T1 diab w prlif diab rtnop wo mac edema
- ☐ E11.31 [1 9] T2 diab w unsp diab rtnop
- ☐ E11.321 [1 2 3] T2 diab w mild nonprlf diab rtnop w mac edema
- ☐ E11.329 [1 2 3] T2 diab w mild nonprlf diab rtnop wo mac edema
- ☐ E11.331 [1 2 3] T2 diab w mod nonprlf diab rtnop w mac edema
- ☐ E11.339 [1 2 3] T2 diab w mod nonprlf diab rtnop wo mac edema
- ☐ E11.341 [1 2 3] T2 diab w severe nonprlf diab rtnop w mac edema
- ☐ E11.349 [1 2 3] T2 diab w severe nonprlf diab rtnop wo mac edema
- ☐ E11.351 [1 2 3] T2 diab w prolif diab rtnop w mac edema
- ☐ E11.355 [1 2 3] T2 diab w stable prolif diab rtnop
- ☐ E11.359 [1 2 3] T2 diab w prolif diab rtnop wo mac edema
- ☐ H31.01 [1 2 3] Macula scars
- ☐ H31.09 [1 2 3] Other chorioretinal scars
- ☐ H32 Chorioretinal disorder
- ☐ H33.01 [1 2 3] Retinal detachment w single break
- ☐ H33.31 [1 2 3] Horseshoe tear of retina wo detachment
- ☐ H33.32 [1 2 3] Round hole
- ☐ H33.8 Other retinal detachments
- ☐ H34.1 [1 2 3] Central retinal artery occlusion
- ☐ H34.21 [1 2 3] Partial retinal artery occlusion
- ☐ H35.01 [1 2 3] Vascular sheathing
- ☐ H35.03 [1 2 3] Hypertensive retinopathy
- ☐ H35.04 [1 2 3] Retinal micro-aneurysms
- ☐ H35.34 [1 2 3] Macular cyst, hole or pseudohole
- ☐ H35.35 [1 2 3] Cystoid macular degeneration
- ☐ H35.36 [1 2 3] Drusen (degenerative) of macula
- ☐ H35.37 [1 2 3] Puckering of macule, ERM
- ☐ H35.40 Unspec peripheral retinal degeneration
- ☐ H35.41 [1 2 3] Lattice degeneration of retina
- ☐ H35.71 [1 2 3] Central serous chorioretinopathy
- ☐ H35.82 Retinal ischemia
- ☐ H43.31 [1 2 3] Viterous membranes
- ☐ H43.81 [1 2 3] Viterous degeneration

RT LT BI (RT-Right LT-Left BI-Bilateral)

- ☐ H34.81 [10 20 30] Central retinal vein occlusion w mac edema
- ☐ H34.81 [11 21 31] Central retinal vein occlusion w retinal neovascularization
- ☐ H34.81 [12 22 32] Central retinal vein occlusion, stable
- ☐ H34.83 [10 20 30] Tributary retinal vein occlusion w mac edema
- ☐ H34.83 [11 21 31] Tributary retinal vein occlusion w retinal neovascularization
- ☐ H34.83 [12 22 32] Tributary retinal vein occlusion, stable
- ☐ H35.31 [11 21 31] Nonexudative ARMD, early dry stage
- ☐ H35.31 [12 22 32] Nonexudative ARMD, intermediate dry stage
- ☐ H35.31 [13 23 33] Nonexudative ARMD, advanced atropic wo subfoveal inv
- ☐ H35.31 [14 24 34] Nonexudative ARMD, advanced atropic w subfoveal inv
- ☐ H35.32 [11 21 31] Exudative ARMD, active choroidal neovascularization
- ☐ H35.32 [12 22 32] Exudative ARMD, inactive choroidal neovascularization
- ☐ H35.32 [13 23 33] Exudative ARMD, inactive scar

(1-RT 2-LT 3-Bilateral)
(1-With Edema 9-Without Edema)

LACRIMAL SYSTEM
- ☐ H04.01 [1 2 3] Acute dacryoadenitis
- ☒ H04.12 [1 2 **3**] Dry eye syndrome
- ☐ H04.21 [1 2 3] Epiphora due to excess lacrimation

(1-RT 2-LT 3-Bilateral)

GLAUCOMA
- ☐ H40.01 [1 2 3] Open angle w borderline findings low risk
- ☐ H40.02 [1 2 3] Open angle w borderline findings high risk
- ☐ H40.05 [1 2 3] Ocular hypertension
- ☐ H40.06 [1 2 3] Primary angle closure wo glaucoma damage
- ☐ H40.21 [1 2 3] Acute angle-closure glaucoma

RT LT BI (RT-Right LT-Left BI-Bilateral)

- ☐ H40.11 [11 21 31] Primary open-angle glaucoma, mild
- ☐ H40.11 [12 22 32] Primary open-angle glaucoma, mod
- ☐ H40.11 [13 23 33] Primary open-angle glaucoma, severe
- ☐ H40.11 [14 24 34] Primary open-angle glaucoma, indeterminate
- ☐ H40.12 [11 21 31] Low-tens glaucoma, mild stage
- ☐ H40.12 [12 22 32] Low-tens glaucoma, mod stage
- ☐ H40.12 [13 23 33] Low-tens glaucoma, severe stage
- ☐ H40.13 [11 21 31] Pigmentary glaucoma, mild stage
- ☐ H40.13 [12 22 32] Pigmentary glaucoma, mod stage
- ☐ H40.13 [13 23 33] Pigmentary glaucoma, severe stage
- ☐ H40.22 [11 21 31] Chronic angle-closure glaucoma, mild stage
- ☐ H40.22 [12 22 32] Chronic angle-closure glaucoma, mod stage
- ☐ H40.22 [13 23 33] Chronic angle-closure glaucoma, severe stage

(1-RT 2-LT 3-Bilateral)

NEURO-OPHTHALMOLOGY
- ☐ H46.1 [1 2 3] Retrobulbar neuritis
- ☐ H47.01 [1 2 3] Ischemic optic neuropathy
- ☐ H47.1 [1 2 3] Papilledema assoc w increased intracranial pressure
- ☐ H47.21 [1 2 3] Primary optic atrophy
- ☐ H47.32 [1 2 3] Drusen of optic disc

(1-RT 2-LT 3-Bilateral)

CONJUNCTIVA
- ☐ B30.0 Viral conjunctivitis
- ☐ H10.3 [1 2 3] Acute conjunctivitis
- ☐ H10.41 [1 2 3] Chronic giant papillary conjunctivitis
- ☐ H10.43 [1 2 3] Chronic follicular conjunctivitis
- ☐ H11.05 [1 2 3] Peripheral pterygium, progressive
- ☐ H11.12 [1 2 3] Conjunctival concretions
- ☐ H11.15 [1 2 3] Pinguecula
- ☐ H11.3 [1 2 3] Conjunctival hemorrhage
- ☐ S05.01X [A D S] Inj conjunctiva & corneal abrasion wo fb, RT, init
- ☐ S05.02X [A D S] Inj conjunctiva & corneal abrasion wo fb, LT, init
- ☐ T15.11X [A D S] Foreign body in conjunctival sac, RT, init
- ☐ T15.12X [A D S] Foreign body in conjunctival sac, LT init

(1-RT 2-LT 3-Bilateral)
(A-Initial D-Subsequent S-Sequela)

CORNEA
- ☐ H16.00 [1 2 3] Unspec corneal ulcer
- ☐ H16.01 [1 2 3] Central corneal ulcer
- ☐ H16.04 [1 2 3] Marginal corneal ulcer
- ☐ H16.12 [1 2 3] Filamentary keratitis
- ☐ H16.14 [1 2 3] Punctate keratitis
- ☐ H16.42 [1 2 3] Pannus (corneal)
- ☐ H18.22 [1 2 3] Idiopathic corneal edema
- ☐ H18.41 [1 2 3] Arcus senilis
- ☐ H18.51 Endothelial corneal dystrophie
- ☐ H18.59 Other hereditary corneal dystrophies
- ☐ H18.82 [1 2 3] Corneal edema due to contact lens
- ☐ H18.83 [1 2 3] Recurrent erosion of cornea
- ☐ T15.01X [A D S] Foreign body in cornea, RT, initial
- ☐ T15.02X [A D S] Foreign body in cornea, LT, initial

(1-RT 2-LT 3-Bilateral)
(A-Initial D-Subsequent S-Sequela)

STRABISMUS
- ☐ H50.00 Unspec esotropia
- ☐ H50.10 Unspec exotropia

(RT-Right LT-Left)

FEE
- ☐ S0620 ____
- ☐ S0621 ____
- ☐ 65210 ____*
- ☐ 65222 ____*
- ☐ 65430 ____*
- ☐ 65435 ____*
- ☐ 65778 ____*
- ☐ 67820 ____*
- ☐ 67938 ____*
- ☒ 68761 **128⁰⁰** *
- ☐ 68801 ____
- ☐ 76510 ____
- ☐ 76514 ____
- ☐ 83516QW ____
- ☒ 83861QW **22⁴⁸**
- ☐ 87809QW ____
- ☐ 92002 ____
- ☐ 92004 ____
- ☐ 92012 ____
- ☐ 92014 ____
- ☐ 92015 ____+
- ☐ 92020 ____
- ☐ 92025 ____*
- ☐ 92060 ____
- ☐ 92071 ____
- ☐ 92072 ____
- ☐ 92082 ____
- ☐ 92083 ____
- ☐ 92100 ____
- ☐ 92132 ____
- ☐ 92133 ____
- ☐ 92134 ____
- ☐ 92225 ____*
- ☐ 92226 ____*
- ☐ 92250 ____
- ☐ 92274 ____
- ☒ 92285 **18⁶⁵**
- ☐ 92286 ____
- ☐ 92310 ____+
- ☐ 95930 ____
- ☐ 99201 ____
- ☐ 99202 ____
- ☐ 99203 ____
- ☐ 99204 ____
- ☐ 99205 ____
- ☐ 99212 ____
- ☐ 99213 ____
- ☒ 99214 **95⁸⁶**
- ☐ 99215 ____

* May Require Modifier
\+ Not Paid by MC

- ☐ 5010F ☐ G8428
- ☐ G8397 ☐ 4004F
- ☐ 2022F ☐ G8398 ☐ 1036F
- ☐ 2024F ☐ G8783
- ☐ 2026F ☐ G8950
- ☐ 3072F ☐ G8784
- ☐ 2019F ☐ G8785
- ☐ 4177F ☐ G8951
- ☐ 2027F ☐ G8952
- ☐ 3284F ☐ G8730
- ☐ 3285F ☐ G8731
- ☐ 0517F ☐ G8442
- ☐ G8427 ☐ G8939
- ☐ G8430 ☐ G8732
  ☐ G8509

v2.1 Revised 3/6/17

©2017 - E. Botts, O.D.

• DRY EYE PATIENT •
PAGE 3

ICD-10

HEALTH INSURANCE CLAIM FORM
APPROVED BY NATIONAL UNIFORM CLAIM COMMITTEE (NUCC) 02/12

PICA	
1. Program	(blank)
1a. INSURED'S I.D. NUMBER	xxx xx xxxxxA
2. PATIENT'S NAME	Johnson, Jane
3. PATIENT'S BIRTH DATE	12 / 05 / 1926 SEX: F
4. INSURED'S NAME	(blank)
5. PATIENT'S ADDRESS	1262 Jay Street
6. PATIENT RELATIONSHIP TO INSURED	Self ✓
7. INSURED'S ADDRESS	(blank)
CITY	Smithville STATE: IL
ZIP CODE	62555
TELEPHONE	(000) 000-0000
9. OTHER INSURED'S NAME	(blank)
10a. EMPLOYMENT?	NO ✓
10b. AUTO ACCIDENT?	NO ✓
10c. OTHER ACCIDENT?	NO ✓
11. INSURED'S POLICY GROUP OR FECA NUMBER	None
12. PATIENT'S SIGNATURE	SOF
17. NAME OF REFERRING PROVIDER	DK Eric Botts
17b. NPI	Individual NPI#
21. DIAGNOSIS	A. H04.123 ICD Ind: 10
23. PRIOR AUTHORIZATION NUMBER	CLIA#

24. Service Lines

#	DATE FROM	DATE TO	POS	CPT/HCPCS	MOD	DX PTR	CHARGES	UNITS	ID	RENDERING PROVIDER ID
1	11 03 10	11 03 10	11	99214	25	A	95 86	1	NPI	Individual NPI #
2	11 03 10	11 03 10	11	83861	QW RT	A	22 48	1	NPI	Individual NPI #
3	11 03 10	11 03 10	11	83861	QW LT	A	22 48	1	NPI	Individual NPI #
4	11 03 10	11 03 10	11	68761	E2	A	128 11	1	NPI	Individual NPI #
5	11 03 10	11 03 10	11	68761	E4	A	128 11	1	NPI	Individual NPI #
6	11 03 10	11 03 10	11	92285		A	18 65	1	NPI	Individual NPI #

25. FEDERAL TAX I.D. NUMBER: 4171789   EIN ✓
27. ACCEPT ASSIGNMENT: YES ✓
28. TOTAL CHARGE: $415.69
29. AMOUNT PAID: $0
30. Rsvd for NUCC Use: 415.69

31. SIGNATURE OF PHYSICIAN OR SUPPLIER: E. Botts   11-03-10

32. SERVICE FACILITY LOCATION INFORMATION:
Eric K. Botts, O.D.
1730 East Jackson Street
Macomb, IL 61455
309-836-3373

33. BILLING PROVIDER INFO & PH #:
Eric K. Botts, O.D.
1730 East Jackson Street
Macomb, IL 61455
309-836-3373

NUCC Instruction Manual available at: www.nucc.org
APPROVED OMB-0938-1197 FORM 1500 (02-12)
©2014 - E. Botts, O.D.
Group NPI # if available, otherwise individual NPI #

• DRY EYE PATIENT •
PAGE 4

Medica
Remittar
Not

Eric K. Botts, OD
1730 East Jackson Street
Macomb, IL 61455-2531

NPI #: 479327
Page #: 1 o
Date: 11-22-
Check/Eft #: 1154490

PERF PROV	SERV DATE	POS	NOS	PROC	MODS	BILLED	ALLOWED	DEDUCT	COINS	GRP/RC-AMT	PROV F
NAME JOHNSON, JANE			HIC 36030715A		ACNT 111036P			ICN 0206222466720	ASG Y	MOA MAO 1	MA
47932761	1103 110310	11	1	99214	25	95.86	84.75	0.00	16.95	11.11	67.80
47932761	1103 110310	11	1	83861	QW-RT	22.48	14.57	0.00	2.91	7.91	11.66
47932761	1103 110310	11	1	83861	QW-LT	22.48	14.57	0.00	2.91	7.91	11.66
47932761	1103 110310	11	1	68761	E2	128.11	114.40	0.00	22.88	13.71	91.52
47932761	1103 110310	11	1	68761	E4	128.11	114.40	0.00	22.88	13.71	91.52
47932761	1103 110310	11	1	92285		18.65	13.12	0.00	2.62	5.53	10.50
PT RESP	71.15		1	CLAIM TOTALS		415.69	324.78	0.00	71.15	59.88	284.66

CLAIM INFORMATION FORWARDED TO: HCSC-BCBS OF IL (STD A & B)   284.66 I

• DRY EYE PATIENT •
PAGE 4

EXAMINATION

Patient **Jane Johnson**   Date **11-15-10**   Sex: M (F)   DOB **12-05-26**   Age ____   Last Exam ____
Chief Complaint **Eyes Feel Better**

History
HPI:
Symptoms
Location
Quality
Severity
Duration
Timing
Context
Modifiers

Right eye much better for several days after plugs inserted, left eye much worse

Allergies
Medications
Ocular ROS

Medical History & ROS from **06 / 14 / 05** reviewed: ☑ no changes
Dr. Initials **EKB**

Examination
Head/Face ☐ nl   Psych: Mood/Affect (anxiety/depression) ☐ nl   Neuro: Oriented (person/time/place) ☐ y ☐ n

VA: sc<   cc<   ph<   near<

K: OD _____   OLD RX: OD _____   add ____
     OS _____   OS _____   add ____
R-scopy: OD _____   REF: OD _____ 20/___ add ____
          OS _____   OS _____ 20/___ add ____

Perimetry:	☐ nl CF ☐ nl	Color ☐ nl ☐ RG defect	**ADNEXA**	☑ nl	
Motility:	☐ Full	Stereo Animals /3 WD /9	**EYELIDS:**	☐ Blepharitis	OD OS OU
Cover Test:	☐ Eso ____	☐ Exo ____ ☐ Ortho		☐ Meibomianitis	OD OS OU
Pupils:	☑ no afferent defect ☑ round OU	Size: OD **3** OS **3**		☐ 20D ☐ 90D/78D ☐ 3 Mirror ☐	

Grade 4 stain (OS diagram)

SLE: OD
☐ nl ☑ FBUT: **3**   TEAR FILM
☑ nl ☐ arcus   CORNEA
☑ nl ☐ pterygium
☑ nl ☐ infiltrate
☑ nl ☑ spk
☑ nl ☐   SCLERA
☑ nl ☑ injection   CONJ.
☑ nl ☐ pinguecula
☑ D&Q ☐   AC
☑ nl ☐ rubeosis   IRIS
☐ clear ☐ cat ☑ ns LENS

OS
☐ nl ☑ FBUT: **3**
☑ nl ☐ arcus
☑ nl ☐ pterygium
☑ nl ☐ infiltrate
☑ nl ☑ spk
☑ nl ☐
☑ nl ☑ injection
☑ nl ☐ pinguecula
☑ D&Q ☐
☑ nl ☐ rubeosis
☐ clear ☐ cat ☑ ns

RETINA: OD
☐ nl ☐ drusen   MACULA
☐ nl ☐ RPE chgs
☐ nl ☐ cotton wool POST POLE
☐ nl ☐ hemes
☐ nl ☐ DME
☐ nl ☐   VESSELS
☐ nl ☐ PVD   VITREOUS
☐ nl ☐ strands
☐ nl ☐   PERIPHERY

OS
☐ nl ☐ drusen
☐ nl ☐ RPE chgs
☐ nl ☐ cotton wool
☐ nl ☐ hemes
☐ nl ☐ DME
☐ nl ☐
☐ nl ☐ PVD
☐ nl ☐ strands
☐ nl ☐

OPTIC DISCS: OD
☐ nl   SIZE/APPEARANCE/NFL   ☐ nl
☐ ____   C/D   ☐ ____

NCT ___ / ___ @ _____   Pachymetry: OD _____
TAG 18 / 18 @ **9:32 am**   OS _____   Dilated: M .5% 1% PA 1%/0.25% C 1% 2% Ph 2.5% 10% OU@ ____

Diagnosis/Plan   MDM 1 ② 3 4

Tear film insufficiency

Order Inflammadry OU
Begin Restasis Bid OU
Insert Amniotic Membrane OS
RTC 3 days to monitor

Order: ☐ HRT/GDX/OCT   RTO: ___ day
       ☐ Photo   ___ week
       ☐ VF   **1** month
       ☐ Consult   ___ year

Dr. *E. Botts*

Rev. 11/11 ©2007 - E. Botts, O.D.

BILLING STATEMENT

• DRY EYE PATIENT •
PAGE 5

Dr. Eric Botts
Phone 309/836-3373

Date of Service **11 / 03 / 10**
Patient's Name **Jane Johnson** DOB **12 / 05 / 26** ☐ Male ☑ Female
Address **1262 Jay St.** City **Smithfield** State **IL** Zip **62555**
Telephone (___) ___-____ Insured's Name _____ Insured's DOB ___/___/___
ID Number **XXX XX XXXXA** Secondary Ins **United Healthcare** Total **1354.94**
Special Instructions _____

Refraction Paid _____
Co-Pay/Deductible Paid _____
Ins/Mcaid/Mcare Paid _____
Secondary Paid _____
Write Off _____
Balance Due _____

MODIFIERS 24 25 26 50 55 59 79 **RT** ☒ **LT** ☒ E1 E2 E3 E4 1P 2P 8P TC GW QW

MISCELLANEOUS
- E10.65 Type 1 Diabetes w complications
- E10.9 Type 1 Diabetes wo complications
- E11.65 Type 2 Diabetes w complications
- E11.9 Type 2 Diabetes wo complications
- H27.0 [1 2 3] Aphakia
- H53.8 Blurred Vision
- H57.1 [1 2 3] Ocular Pain
- M06.9 Rheumatoid Arthritis
- Z79.4 Insulin Dependent
- Z79.84 Non-Insulin Dependent
- Z79.899 High Risk meds

(1-RT 2-LT 3-Bilateral)

UVEAL DISORDERS
- H20.01 [1 2 3] Primary iridocyclitis
- H21.0 [1 2 3] Hyphema
- H21.23 [1 2 3] Degeneration of Iris
- H21.26 [1 2 3] Iris Atrophy
- H21.4 [1 2 3] Pupillary membranes
- H57.05 [1 2 3] Tonic Pupil

(1-RT 2-LT 3-Bilateral)

EYELIDS
- H00.023 Hordeolum internum RT eye
- H00.026 Hordeolum internum LT eye
- H00.13 Chalazion RT eye
- H00.16 Chalazion LT eye
- H01.023 Squamous blepharitis RT eye
- H01.026 Squamous blepharitis LT eye
- H01.113 Allergic dermatitis RT eye
- H01.116 Allergic dermatitis LT eye
- H02.033 Senile entropion RT eye
- H02.036 Senile entropion LT eye
- H02.053 Trichiasis wo entropion RT eye
- H05.056 Trichiasis wo entropion LT eye
- H02.133 Senile ectropion RT eye
- H02.136 Senile ectropion LT eye
- H02.40 [1 2 3] Unspec ptosis of eyelid
- H02.833 Dermatochalasis RT eye
- H02.836 Dermatochalasis LT eye

(1-RT 2-LT 3-Bilateral)

CATARACT/LENS
- H25.01 [1 2 3] Cortical age-related cat
- H25.04 [1 2 3] Post subcap polar age-related cat
- H25.1 [1 2 3] Age-related nuclear cat
- H25.89 Other age-related cat
- Z96.1 Presence of intraocular lens

(1-RT 2-LT 3-Bilateral)

DISORDER OF REFRACTION
- H52.0 [1 2 3] Hypermetropia
- H52.1 [1 2 3] Myopia
- H52.22 [1 2 3] Regular Astigmatism
- H52.4 Presbyopia

(1-RT 2-LT 3-Bilateral)

VISUAL DISORDERS
- H51.11 Convergence insufficiency
- H51.12 Convergence excess
- H52.53 [1 2 3] Spasm of accommodation
- H53.02 [1 2 3] Refractive amblyopia
- H53.03 [1 2 3] Strabismic amblyopia
- H53.14 [1 2 3] Visual discomfort
- H53.41 [1 2 3] Scotoma involving central area
- H53.42 [1 2 3] Scotoma of blind spot area
- H53.43 [1 2 3] Sector or arcuate defects
- H53.46 [1 2 3] Homonymous bilateral field defects
- H53.47 Heteronymous bilateral field defects
- H55.00 Unspec nystagmus

(1-RT 2-LT 3-Bilateral)

RETINAL DISORDERS
- E10.31 [1 9] T1 diab w unsp diab rtnop
- E10.321 [1 2 3] T1 diab w mild nonprlf diab rtnop w mac edema
- E10.329 [1 2 3] T1 diab w mild nonprlf diab rtnop wo mac edema
- E10.331 [1 2 3] T1 diab w mod nonprlf diab rtnop w mac edema
- E10.339 [1 2 3] T1 diab w mon nonprlf diab rtnop wo mac edema
- E10.341 [1 2 3] T1 diab w severe nonprlf diab rtnop w mac edema
- E10.349 [1 2 3] T1 diab w severe nonprlf diab rtnop wo mac edema
- E10.351 [1 2 3] T1 diab w prlif diab rtnop w mac edema
- E10.355 [1 2 3] T1 diab w stable prolif diab rtnop
- E10.359 [1 2 3] T1 diab w prolif diab rtnop wo mac edema
- E11.31 [1 9] T2 diab w unsp diab rtnop
- E11.321 [1 2 3] T2 diab w mild nonprlf diab rtnop w mac edema
- E11.329 [1 2 3] T2 diab w mild nonprlf diab rtnop wo mac edema
- E11.331 [1 2 3] T2 diab w mod nonprlf diab rtnop w mac edema
- E11.339 [1 2 3] T2 diab w mod nonprlf diab rtnop wo mac edema
- E11.341 [1 2 3] T2 diab w severe nonprlf diab rtnop w mac edema
- E11.349 [1 2 3] T2 diab w severe nonprlf diab rtnop wo mac edema
- E11.351 [1 2 3] T2 diab w prlif diab rtnop w mac edema
- E11.355 [1 2 3] T2 diab w stable prolif diab rtnop
- E11.359 [1 2 3] T2 diab w prolif diab rtnop wo mac edema
- H31.01 [1 2 3] Macula scars
- H31.09 [1 2 3] Other chorioretinal scars
- H32 Chorioretinal disorder
- H33.01 [1 2 3] Retinal detachment w single break
- H33.31 [1 2 3] Horseshoe tear of retina wo detachment
- H33.32 [1 2 3] Round hole
- H33.8 Other retinal detachments
- H34.1 [1 2 3] Central retinal artery occlusion
- H34.21 [1 2 3] Partial retinal artery occlusion
- H35.01 [1 2 3] Vascular sheathing
- H35.03 [1 2 3] Hypertensive retinopathy
- H35.04 [1 2 3] Retinal micro-aneurysms
- H35.34 [1 2 3] Macular cyst, hole or pseudohole
- H35.35 [1 2 3] Cystoid macular degeneration
- H35.36 [1 2 3] Drusen (degenerative) of macula
- H35.37 [1 2 3] Puckering of macule, ERM
- H35.40 Unspec peripheral retinal degeneration
- H35.41 [1 2 3] Lattice degeneration of retina
- H35.71 [1 2 3] Central serous chorioretinopathy
- H35.82 Retinal ischemia
- H43.31 [1 2 3] Viterous membranes
- H43.81 [1 2 3] Viterous degeneration

RT LT BI *(RT-Right LT-Left BI-Bilateral)*

- H34.81 [10 20 30] Central retinal vein occlusion w mac edema
- H34.81 [11 21 31] Central retinal vein occlusion w retinal neovascularization
- H34.81 [12 22 32] Central retinal vein occlusion, stable
- H34.83 [10 20 30] Tributary retinal vein occlusion w mac edema
- H34.83 [11 21 31] Tributary retinal vein occlusion w retinal neovascularization
- H34.83 [12 22 32] Tributary retinal vein occlusion, stable
- H35.31 [11 21 31] Nonexudative ARMD, early dry stage
- H35.31 [12 22 32] Nonexudative ARMD, intermediate dry stage
- H35.31 [13 23 33] Nonexudative ARMD, advanced atropic wo subfoveal inv
- H35.31 [14 24 34] Nonexudative ARMD, advanced atropic w subfoveal inv
- H35.32 [11 21 31] Exudative ARMD, active chorodial neovascularization
- H35.32 [12 22 32] Exudative ARMD, inactive chorodial neovascularization
- H35.32 [13 23 33] Exudative ARMD, inactive scar

(1-RT 2-LT 3-Bilateral)
(1-With Edema 9-Without Edema)

LACRIMAL SYSTEM
- ☐ H04.01 [1 2 3] Acute dacryoadenitis
- ☑ H04.12 [1 2 ③] Dry eye syndrome
- ☐ H04.21 [1 2 3] Epiphora due to excess lacrimation

(1-RT 2-LT 3-Bilateral)

GLAUCOMA
- H40.01 [1 2 3] Open angle w borderline findings low risk
- H40.02 [1 2 3] Open angle w borderline findings high risk
- H40.05 [1 2 3] Ocular hypertension
- H40.06 [1 2 3] Primary angle closure wo glaucoma damage
- H40.21 [1 2 3] Acute angle-closure glaucoma

RT LT BI *(RT-Right LT-Left BI-Bilateral)*

- H40.11 [11 21 31] Primary open-angle glaucoma, mild
- H40.11 [12 22 32] Primary open-angle glaucoma, mod
- H40.11 [13 23 33] Primary open-angle glaucoma, severe
- H40.11 [14 24 34] Primary open-angle glaucoma, indeterminate
- H40.12 [11 21 31] Low-tens glaucoma, mild stage
- H40.12 [12 22 32] Low-tens glaucoma, mod stage
- H40.12 [13 23 33] Low-tens glaucoma, severe stage
- H40.13 [11 21 31] Pigmentary glaucoma, mild stage
- H40.13 [12 22 32] Pigmentary glaucoma, mod stage
- H40.13 [13 23 33] Pigmentary glaucoma, severe stage
- H40.22 [11 21 31] Chronic angle-closure glaucoma, mild stage
- H40.22 [12 22 32] Chronic angle-closure glaucoma, mod stage
- H40.22 [13 23 33] Chronic angle-closure glaucoma, severe stage

(1-RT 2-LT 3-Bilateral)

NEURO-OPHTHALMOLOGY
- H46.1 [1 2 3] Retrobulbar neuritis
- H47.01 [1 2 3] Ischemic optic neuropathy
- H47.1 [1 2 3] Papilledema assoc. w increased intracranial pressure
- H47.21 [1 2 3] Primary optic atrophy
- H47.32 [1 2 3] Drusen of optic disc

(1-RT 2-LT 3-Bilateral)

CONJUNCTIVA
- B30.0 Viral conjunctivitis
- H10.3 [1 2 3] Acute conjunctivitis
- H10.41 [1 2 3] Chronic giant papillary conjunctivitis
- H10.43 [1 2 3] Chronic follicular conjunctivitis
- H11.05 [1 2 3] Peripheral pterygium, progressive
- H11.12 [1 2 3] Conjunctival concretions
- H11.15 [1 2 3] Pinguecula
- H11.3 [1 2 3] Conjunctival hemorrhage
- S05.01X [A D S] Inj conjunctiva & corneal abrasion wo fb, RT, init
- S05.02X [A D S] Inj conjunctiva & corneal abrasion wo fb, LT, init
- T15.11X [A D S] Foreign body in conjunctival sac, RT, init
- T15.12X [A D S] Foreign body in conjunctival sac, LT, init

(1-RT 2-LT 3-Bilateral)
(A-Initial D-Subsequent S-Sequela)

CORNEA
- H16.00 [1 2 3] Unspec corneal ulcer
- H16.01 [1 2 3] Central corneal ulcer
- H16.04 [1 2 3] Marginal corneal ulcer
- H16.12 [1 2 3] Filamentary keratitis
- H16.14 [1 2 3] Punctate keratitis
- H16.42 [1 2 3] Pannus (corneal)
- H18.22 [1 2 3] Idiopathic corneal edema
- H18.41 [1 2 3] Arcus senilis
- H18.51 Endothelial corneal dystrophy
- H18.59 Other hereditary corneal dystrophies
- H18.82 [1 2 3] Corneal edema due to contact lens
- H18.83 [1 2 3] Recurrent erosion of cornea
- T15.01X [A D S] Foreign body in cornea, RT, initial
- T15.02X [A D S] Foreign body in cornea, LT, initial

(1-RT 2-LT 3-Bilateral)
(A-Initial D-Subsequent S-Sequela)

STRABISMUS
- H50.00 Unspec esotropia
- H50.10 Unspec exotropia

(RT-Right LT-Left)

FEE
- S0620
- S0621
- 65210
- 65222 *
- 65430 *
- 65435 *
- ☑ 65778 **132 3⁵⁴**
- 67820 *
- 67938 *
- 68761 *
- 68801 *
- 76510
- 76514
- ☑ 83516QW **15⁷⁰**
- 83861QW
- 87809QW
- 92002
- 92004
- 92012
- 92014
- 92015 +
- 92020
- 92025 *
- 92060
- 92071
- 92072
- 92082
- 92083
- 92100
- 92132
- 92133
- 92134
- 92225 *
- 92226 *
- 92250
- 92275
- 92284
- 92285
- 92286
- 92310 +
- 95930
- 99201
- 99202
- 99203
- 99204
- 99205
- 99212
- 99213
- 99214
- 99215

* May Require Modifier
+ Not Paid by MC

5010F	G8428
G8397	4004F
G8398	1036F
2022F	G8783
2024F	G8950
2026F	G8784
3072F	G8785
2019F	G8951
4177F	G8952
2027F	G8730
3284F	G8731
3285F	G8442
0517F	G8939
G8427	G8732
G8430	G8509

v2.1 Revised 3/6/17

©2017 - E. Botts, O.D.

• DRY EYE PATIENT •
PAGE 7

HEALTH INSURANCE CLAIM FORM
APPROVED BY NATIONAL UNIFORM CLAIM COMMITTEE (NUCC) 02/12

ICD-10

PICA		PICA

1. MEDICARE / MEDICAID / TRICARE / CHAMPVA / GROUP HEALTH PLAN / FECA BLK LUNG / OTHER — (blank)
1a. INSURED'S I.D. NUMBER (For Program in Item 1): xxx xx xxxxA

2. PATIENT'S NAME (Last Name, First Name, Middle Initial): Johnson, Jane
3. PATIENT'S BIRTH DATE: 12 / 05 / 1926 **SEX**: F ✓
4. INSURED'S NAME: (blank)

5. PATIENT'S ADDRESS: 1262 Jay Street
6. PATIENT RELATIONSHIP TO INSURED: Self ✓
7. INSURED'S ADDRESS: (blank)

CITY: Smithville   **STATE**: IL
8. RESERVED FOR NUCC USE

ZIP CODE: 62555   **TELEPHONE**: (000) 000-0000

9. OTHER INSURED'S NAME: (blank)
10. IS PATIENT'S CONDITION RELATED TO:
 a. EMPLOYMENT? NO ✓
 b. AUTO ACCIDENT? NO ✓
 c. OTHER ACCIDENT? NO ✓
11. INSURED'S POLICY GROUP OR FECA NUMBER: None

a. OTHER INSURED'S POLICY OR GROUP NUMBER: (blank)
a. INSURED'S DATE OF BIRTH: (blank)

b. RESERVED FOR NUCC USE
b. OTHER CLAIM ID (Designated by NUCC)

c. RESERVED FOR NUCC USE
c. INSURANCE PLAN NAME OR PROGRAM NAME

d. INSURANCE PLAN NAME OR PROGRAM NAME
10d. CLAIM CODES
d. IS THERE ANOTHER HEALTH BENEFIT PLAN? (blank)

12. PATIENT'S OR AUTHORIZED PERSON'S SIGNATURE
 SIGNED: SOF   DATE: _____
13. INSURED'S OR AUTHORIZED PERSON'S SIGNATURE
 SIGNED: _____

14. DATE OF CURRENT ILLNESS, INJURY, or PREGNANCY (LMP): (blank)   QUAL.
15. OTHER DATE: (blank)
16. DATES PATIENT UNABLE TO WORK IN CURRENT OCCUPATION: FROM ___ TO ___

17. NAME OF REFERRING PROVIDER OR OTHER SOURCE: DK | Eric Botts
 17b. NPI: Individual NPI#
18. HOSPITALIZATION DATES RELATED TO CURRENT SERVICES: FROM ___ TO ___

19. ADDITIONAL CLAIM INFORMATION
20. OUTSIDE LAB? (blank)   **$ CHARGES**

21. DIAGNOSIS OR NATURE OF ILLNESS OR INJURY — ICD Ind. 10
 A. H04.123   B. ___   C. ___   D. ___
 E. ___   F. ___   G. ___   H. ___
 I. ___   J. ___   K. ___   L. ___

22. RESUBMISSION CODE / **ORIGINAL REF. NO.**
23. PRIOR AUTHORIZATION NUMBER: CLIA#

24. DATE(S) OF SERVICE / PLACE OF SERVICE / EMG / CPT/HCPCS / MODIFIER / DIAGNOSIS POINTER / $ CHARGES / DAYS OR UNITS / EPSDT / ID QUAL / RENDERING PROVIDER ID.#

#	From	To	POS	EMG	CPT	MOD	DX	Charges	Units	NPI
1	11 15 10	11 15 10	11		65778	LT	A	1323 54	1	Individual NPI #
2	11 15 10	11 15 10	11		83516	QW	B	15 70	2	Individual NPI #
3										
4										
5										
6										

25. FEDERAL TAX I.D. NUMBER: 4171789   **EIN** ✓
26. PATIENT'S ACCOUNT NO.
27. ACCEPT ASSIGNMENT? YES ✓
28. TOTAL CHARGE: $ 1354 94
29. AMOUNT PAID: $ 0
30. Rsvd for NUCC Use: 1354 94

31. SIGNATURE OF PHYSICIAN OR SUPPLIER: E. Botts   11-15-10
32. SERVICE FACILITY LOCATION INFORMATION:
 Eric K. Botts, O.D.
 1730 East Jackson Street
 Macomb, IL 61455
 309-836-3373
33. BILLING PROVIDER INFO & PH #:
 Eric K. Botts, O.D.
 1730 East Jackson Street
 Macomb, IL 61455
 309-836-3373

NUCC Instruction Manual available at: www.nucc.org   PLEASE PRINT OR TYPE   APPROVED OMB-0938-1197 FORM 1500 (02-12)

©2014 - E. Botts, O.D.   Group NPI # if available, otherwise individual NPI #

DRY EYE PATIENT
PAGE 8

Medicare
Remittance
Notice

Eric K. Botts, OD
1730 East Jackson Street
Macomb, IL 61455-2531

NPI #: 47932761
Page #: 1 of 2
Date: 12-22-10
Check/Eft #: 115449098

PERF PROV	SERV DATE	POS	NOS	PROC	MODS	BILLED	ALLOWED	DEDUCT	COINS	GRP/RC-AMT	PROV PD
NAME JOHNSON, JANE			HIC 36030715A		ACNT 111036P			ICN 0206222466720	ASG Y	MOA MAO 1	MA 18
47932761	1115 111510	11	2	83516	QW	31.40	30.00	0.00	6.00	1.40	24.00
47932761	1115 111510	11	1	65778	LT	1323.54	1214.40	0.00	242.88	109.14	971.52
PT RESP	248.88		1	CLAIM TOTALS		1354.94	1244.40	0.00	248.88	110.54	995.52

CLAIM INFORMATION FORWARDED TO: HCSC-BCBS OF IL (STD A & B)

995.52 NET

Example #8
Trichiasis Epilation

TRICHIASIS/EPILATION PATIENT
PAGE 1

EXAMINATION

Patient: Joe Jackson   Date: 11-13-10   Sex: M F   DOB: 04-16-19   Age: ___   Last Exam: ___
Chief Complaint: Eyes Hurt

History
HPI: Both eyes
Symptoms: Past 2 weeks
Location: Feels better when eyes are closed
Quality: Occasional redness
Severity:
Duration:
Timing:
Context:
Modifiers:

Allergies:
Medications:
Ocular ROS:
Medical History & ROS from 12/02/05 reviewed: ✓ no changes
Dr. Initials: EKB

Examination
Head/Face ✓ nl   Psych: Mood/Affect (anxiety/depression) ✓ nl   Neuro: Oriented (person/time/place) ✓ y ☐ n

VA: sc< 40/30   cc<   ph<   near<

K: OD ___   OS ___
OLD RX: OD ___ add ___   OS ___ add ___
R-scopy: OD ___   OS ___
REF: OD 20/___ add ___   OS 20/___ add ___

Perimetry: ☐ nl CF ☐ nl	Color ☐ nl ☐ RG defect	**ADNEXA** ✓ nl		
Motility: ☐ Full	Stereo Animals /3 WD /9	**EYELIDS:** ☐ Blepharitis OD OS OU		
Cover Test: ☐ Eso	☐ Exo ☐ Ortho	☐ Meibomianitis OD OS OU		

Pupils: ✓ no afferent defect   ✓ round OU   Size: OD 3 OS 3
☐ 20D ☐ 90D/78D ☐ 3 Mirror

SLE: OD / **OS**
- ✓ nl ☐ FBUT:___ TEAR FILM ✓ nl ☐ FBUT:___
- ✓ nl ☐ arcus   CORNEA   ✓ nl ☐ arcus
- ✓ nl ☐ pterygium   ✓ nl ☐ pterygium
- ✓ nl ☐ infiltrate   ✓ nl ☐ infiltrate
- ☐ nl ✓ spk   ☐ nl ✓ spk
- ✓ nl ☐   SCLERA   ✓ nl ☐
- ☐ nl ✓ injection CONJ.   ☐ nl ✓ injection
- ✓ nl ☐ pinguecula   ✓ nl ☐ pinguecula
- ✓ D&Q ☐   AC   ✓ D&Q ☐
- ✓ nl ☐ rubeosis IRIS   ✓ nl ☐ rubeosis
- ✓ clear ☐ cat ☐ ns LENS   ✓ clear ☐ cat ☐ ns

RETINA: OD / **OS**
- ☐ nl ☐ drusen   MACULA   ☐ nl ☐ drusen
- ☐ nl ☐ RPE chgs   ☐ nl ☐ RPE chgs
- ☐ nl ☐ cotton wool POST POLE ☐ nl ☐ cotton wool
- ☐ nl ☐ hemes   ☐ nl ☐ hemes
- ☐ nl ☐ DME   ☐ nl ☐ DME
- ☐ nl ☐   VESSELS   ☐ nl ☐
- ☐ nl ☐ PVD   VITREOUS   ☐ nl ☐ PVD
- ☐ nl ☐ strands   ☐ nl ☐ strands
- ☐ nl ☐   PERIPHERY   ☐ nl ☐

OPTIC DISCS: OD ☐ nl SIZE/APPEARANCE/NFL OS ☐ nl
☐ ___ C/D ☐ ___

NCT / @ ___   Pachymetry: OD ___
TAG 18/18 @ 11:30 am   OS ___   Dilated: M .5% 1% PA 1%/0.25% C 1% 2% Ph 2.5% 10% OU@ ___

Diagnosis/Plan   MDM 1 2 ③ 4

SPK
Trichiasis

Epilate lashes both eyes, inferior lids with forceps

Order: ☐ HRT/GDX/OCT   RTO: ___ day
☐ Photo   1 week
☐ VF   ___ month
☐ Consult   ___ year

Dr. E. Botts

BILLING STATEMENT

• *TRICHIASIS/EPILATION PATIENT* •
PAGE 2

Dr. Eric Botts
Phone 309/836-3373

Date of Service **11 / 13 / 10**
Patient's Name **Joe Jackson** DOB **04/ 16 / 19** ☑ Male ☐ Female
Address **1347 S. State St.** City **Union City** State **AR** Zip **62510**
Telephone (___)___-____ Insured's Name _____ Insured's DOB ___/___/___
ID Number **xxx xx xxxxA** Secondary Ins **BCBS** Total **189.34**
Special Instructions _____

Refraction Paid ____
Co-Pay/Deductible Paid ____
Ins/Mcaid/Mcare Paid ____
Secondary Paid ____
Write Off ____
Balance Due ____

MODIFIERS 24 [25:X] 26 50 55 59 79 RT LT E1 [E2:X] [E3:X] E4 1P 2P 8P TC GW QW

MISCELLANEOUS
- E10.65 Type 1 Diabetes w complications
- E10.9 Type 1 Diabetes wo complications
- E11.65 Type 2 Diabetes w complications
- E11.9 Type 2 Diabetes wo complications
- H27.0 [1 2 3] Aphakia
- H53.8 Blurred Vision
- H57.1 [1 2 3] Ocular Pain
- M06.9 Rheumatoid Arthritis
- Z79.4 Insulin Dependent
- Z79.84 Non-Insulin Dependent
- Z79.899 High Risk meds

(1-RT 2-LT 3-Bilateral)

UVEAL DISORDERS
- H20.01 [1 2 3] Primary iridocyclitis
- H21.0 [1 2 3] Hyphema
- H21.23 [1 2 3] Degeneration of Iris
- H21.26 [1 2 3] Iris Atrophy
- H21.4 [1 2 3] Pupillary membranes
- H57.05 [1 2 3] Tonic Pupil

(1-RT 2-LT 3-Bilateral)

EYELIDS
- H00.023 Hordeolum internum RT eye
- H00.026 Hordeolum internum LT eye
- H00.13 Chalazion RT eye
- H00.16 Chalazion LT eye
- H01.023 Squamous blepharitis RT eye
- H01.026 Squamous blepharitis LT eye
- H01.113 Allergic dermatitis RT eye
- H01.116 Allergic dermatitis LT eye
- H02.033 Senile entropion RT eye
- ☑ H02.036 Senile entropion LT eye
- ☑ H02.053 Trichiasis wo entropion RT eye
- H05.056 Trichiasis wo entropion LT eye
- H02.133 Senile ectropion RT eye
- H02.136 Senile ectropion LT eye
- H02.40 [1 2 3] Unspec ptosis of eyelid
- H02.833 Dermatochalasis RT eye
- H02.836 Dermatochalasis LT eye

(1-RT 2-LT 3-Bilateral)

CATARACT/LENS
- H25.01 [1 2 3] Cortical age-related cat
- H25.04 [1 2 3] Post subcap polar age-related cat
- H25.1 [1 2 3] Age-related nuclear cat
- H25.89 Other age-related cat
- Z96.1 Presence of intraocular lens

(1-RT 2-LT 3-Bilateral)

DISORDER OF REFRACTION
- H52.0 [1 2 3] Hypermetropia
- H52.1 [1 2 3] Myopia
- H52.22 [1 2 3] Regular Astigmatism
- H52.4 Presbyopia

(1-RT 2-LT 3-Bilateral)

VISUAL DISORDERS
- H51.11 Convergence insufficiency
- H51.12 Convergence excess
- H52.53 [1 2 3] Spasm of accommodation
- H53.02 [1 2 3] Refractive amblyopia
- H53.03 [1 2 3] Strabismic amblyopia
- H53.14 [1 2 3] Visual discomfort
- H53.41 [1 2 3] Scotoma invloving central area
- H53.42 [1 2 3] Scotoma of blind spot area
- H53.43 [1 2 3] Sector or arcuate defects
- H53.46 [1 2 3] Homonymous bilateral field defects
- H53.47 Heteronymous bilateral field defects
- H55.00 Unspec nystagmus

(1-RT 2-LT 3-Bilateral)

RETINAL DISORDERS
- E10.31 [1 9] T1 diab w unsp diab rtnop
- E10.321 [1 2 3] T1 diab w mild nonprlf diab rtnop w mac edema
- E10.329 [1 2 3] T1 diab w mild nonprlf diab rtnop wo mac edema
- E10.331 [1 2 3] T1 diab w mod nonprlf diab rtnop w mac edema
- E10.339 [1 2 3] T1 diab w mon nonprlf diab rtnop wo mac edema
- E10.341 [1 2 3] T1 diab w severe nonprlf diab rtnop w mac edema
- E10.349 [1 2 3] T1 diab w severe nonprlf diab rtnop wo mac edema
- E10.351 [1 2 3] T1 diab w prlif diab rtnop w mac edema
- E10.355 [1 2 3] T1 diab w stable prolif diab rtnop
- E10.359 [1 2 3] T1 diab w prlif diab rtnop wo mac edema
- E11.31 [1 9] T2 diab w unsp diab rtnop
- E11.321 [1 2 3] T2 diab w mild nonprlf diab rtnop w mac edema
- E11.329 [1 2 3] T2 diab w mild nonprlf diab rtnop wo mac edema
- E11.331 [1 2 3] T2 diab w mod nonprlf diab rtnop w mac edema
- E11.339 [1 2 3] T2 diab w mod nonprlf diab rtnop wo mac edema
- E11.341 [1 2 3] T2 diab w severe nonprlf diab rtnop w mac edema
- E11.349 [1 2 3] T2 diab w severe nonprlf diab rtnop wo mac edema
- E11.351 [1 2 3] T2 diab w prolif diab rtnop w mac edema
- E11.355 [1 2 3] T2 diab w stable prolif diab rtnop
- E11.359 [1 2 3] T2 diab w prolif diab rtnop wo mac edema
- H31.01 [1 2 3] Macula scars
- H31.09 [1 2 3] Other chorioretinal scars
- H32 Chorioretinal disorder
- H33.01 [1 2 3] Retinal detachment w single break
- H33.31 [1 2 3] Horseshoe tear of retina wo detachment
- H33.32 [1 2 3] Round hole
- H33.8 Other retinal detachments
- H34.1 [1 2 3] Central retinal artery occlusion
- H34.21 [1 2 3] Partial retinal artery occlusion
- H35.01 [1 2 3] Vascular sheathing
- H35.03 [1 2 3] Hypertensive retinopathy
- H35.04 [1 2 3] Retinal micro-aneurysms
- H35.34 [1 2 3] Macular cyst, hole or pseudohole
- H35.35 [1 2 3] Cystoid macular degeneration
- H35.36 [1 2 3] Drusen (degenerative) of macula
- H35.37 [1 2 3] Puckering of macule, ERM
- H35.40 Unspec peripheral retinal degeneration
- H35.41 [1 2 3] Lattice degeneration of retina
- H35.71 [1 2 3] Central serous chorioretinopathy
- H35.82 Retinal ischemia
- H43.31 [1 2 3] Viterous membranes
- H43.81 [1 2 3] Viterous degeneration

RT LT BI *(RT-Right LT-Left BI-Bilateral)*
- H34.81 [10 20 30] Central retinal vein occlusion w macular edema
- H34.81 [11 21 31] Central retinal vein occlusion w retinal neovascularization
- H34.81 [12 22 32] Central retinal vein occlusion, stable
- H34.83 [10 20 30] Tributary retinal vein occlusion w mac edema
- H34.83 [11 21 31] Tributary retinal vein occlusion w retinal neovascularization
- H34.83 [12 22 32] Tributary retinal vein occlusion, stable
- H35.31 [11 21 31] Nonexudative ARMD, early dry stage
- H35.31 [12 22 32] Nonexudative ARMD, intermediate dry stage
- H35.31 [13 23 33] Nonexudative ARMD, advanced atropic wo subfoveal inv
- H35.31 [14 24 34] Nonexudative ARMD, advanced atropic w subfoveal inv
- H35.32 [11 21 31] Exudative ARMD, active choroidal neovascularization
- H35.32 [12 22 32] Exudative ARMD, inactive choroidal neovascularization
- H35.32 [13 23 33] Exudative ARMD, inactive scar

(1-RT 2-LT 3-Bilateral)
(1-With Edema 9-Without Edema)

LACRIMAL SYSTEM
- H04.01 [1 2 3] Acute dacryoadenitis
- ☑ H04.12 [1 2 (3)] Dry eye syndrome
- H04.21 [1 2 3] Epiphora due to excess lacrimation

(1-RT 2-LT 3-Bilateral)

GLAUCOMA
- H40.01 [1 2 3] Open angle w borderline findings low risk
- H40.02 [1 2 3] Open angle w borderline findings high risk
- H40.05 [1 2 3] Ocular hypertension
- H40.06 [1 2 3] Primary angle closure wo glaucoma damage
- H40.21 [1 2 3] Acute angle-closure glaucoma

RT LT BI *(RT-Right LT-Left BI-Bilateral)*
- H40.11 [11 21 31] Primary open-angle glaucoma, mild
- H40.11 [12 22 32] Primary open-angle glaucoma, mod
- H40.11 [13 23 33] Primary open-angle glaucoma, severe
- H40.11 [14 24 34] Primary open-angle glaucoma, indeterminate
- H40.12 [11 21 31] Low-tens glaucoma, mild stage
- H40.12 [12 22 32] Low-tens glaucoma, mod stage
- H40.12 [13 23 33] Low-tens glaucoma, severe stage
- H40.13 [11 21 31] Pigmentary glaucoma, mild stage
- H40.13 [12 22 32] Pigmentary glaucoma, mod stage
- H40.13 [13 23 33] Pigmentary glaucoma, severe stage
- H40.22 [11 21 31] Chronic angle-closure glaucoma, mild stage
- H40.22 [12 22 32] Chronic angle-closure glaucoma, mod stage
- H40.22 [13 23 33] Chronic angle-closure glaucoma, severe stage

(1-RT 2-LT 3-Bilateral)

NEURO-OPHTHALMOLOGY
- H46.1 [1 2 3] Retrobulbar neuritis
- H47.01 [1 2 3] Ischemic optic neuropathy
- H47.1 [1 2 3] Papilledema assoc. w increased intracranial pressure
- H47.21 [1 2 3] Primary optic atrophy
- H47.32 [1 2 3] Drusen of optic disc

(1-RT 2-LT 3-Bilateral)

CONJUNCTIVA
- B30.0 Viral conjunctivitis
- H10.3 [1 2 3] Acute conjunctivitis
- H10.41 [1 2 3] Chronic giant papillary conjunctivitis
- H10.43 [1 2 3] Chronic follicular conjunctivitis
- H11.05 [1 2 3] Peripheral pterygium, progressive
- H11.12 [1 2 3] Conjunctival concretions
- H11.15 [1 2 3] Pinguecula
- H11.3 [1 2 3] Conjunctival hemorrhage
- S05.01X [A D S] Inj conjunctiva & corneal abrasion wo fb, RT, init
- S05.02X [A D S] Inj conjunctiva & corneal abrasion wo fb, LT, init
- T15.11X [A D S] Foreign body in conjunctival sac, RT, init
- T15.12X [A D S] Foreign body in conjunctival sac, LT init

(1-RT 2-LT 3-Bilateral)
(A-Initial D-Subsequent S-Sequela)

CORNEA
- H16.00 [1 2 3] Unspec corneal ulcer
- H16.01 [1 2 3] Central corneal ulcer
- H16.04 [1 2 3] Marginal corneal ulcer
- H16.12 [1 2 3] Filamentary keratitis
- H16.14 [1 2 3] Punctate keratitis
- H16.42 [1 2 3] Pannus (corneal)
- H18.22 [1 2 3] Idiopathic corneal edema
- H18.41 [1 2 3] Arcus senilis
- H18.51 Endothelial corneal dystrophy
- H18.59 Other hereditary corneal dystrophies
- H18.82 [1 2 3] Corneal edema due to contact lens
- H18.83 [1 2 3] Recurrent erosion of cornea
- T15.01X [A D S] Foreign body in cornea, RT, initial
- T15.02X [A D S] Foreign body in cornea, LT, initial

(1-RT 2-LT 3-Bilateral)
(A-Initial D-Subsequent S-Sequela)

STRABISMUS
- H50.00 Unspec esotropia
- H50.10 Unspec exotropia

(RT-Right LT-Left)

FEE
- S0620 ____
- S0621 ____
- 65210 ____ *
- 65222 ____ *
- 65430 ____ *
- 65435 ____ *
- 65778 ____ *
- ☑ 67820 **4677** *
- 67938 ____ *
- 68761 ____ *
- 68801 ____ *
- 76510 ____
- 76514 ____
- 83516QW ____
- 83861QW ____
- 87809QW MC ____
- 92002 ____
- 92004 ____
- 92012 ____
- 92014 ____
- 92015 ____ +
- 92020 ____
- 92025 ____ *
- 92060 ____
- 92071 ____
- 92072 ____
- 92082 ____
- 92083 ____
- 92100 ____
- 92132 ____
- 92133 ____
- 92134 ____
- 92225 ____ *
- 92226 ____ *
- 92250 ____
- 92274 ____
- 92284 ____
- 92285 ____
- 92286 ____
- 92310 ____ +
- 95930 ____
- 99201 ____
- 99202 ____
- 99203 ____
- 99204 ____
- 99205 ____
- 99212 ____
- 99213 ____
- ☑ 99214 **9580**
- 99215 ____

* May Require Modifier
+ Not Paid by MC

- 5010F / G8428
- G8397 / 4004F
- G8398 / 1036F
- 2022F / G8783
- 2024F / G8950
- 2026F / G8784
- 3072F / G8785
- 2019F / G8951
- 4177F / G8952
- 2027F / G8730
- 3284F / G8731
- 3285F / G8442
- 0517F / G8939
- G8427 / G8732
- G8430 / G8509

v2.1 Revised 3/6/17

©2017 - E. Botts, O.D.

• TRICHIASIS/EPILATION PATIENT •
PAGE 3

ICD-10

HEALTH INSURANCE CLAIM FORM
APPROVED BY NATIONAL UNIFORM CLAIM COMMITTEE (NUCC) 02/12

1. MEDICARE / MEDICAID / TRICARE / CHAMPVA / GROUP HEALTH PLAN / FECA BLK LUNG / OTHER	**1a. INSURED'S I.D. NUMBER** (For Program in Item 1)	
	XXX XX XXXXX A	
2. PATIENT'S NAME (Last Name, First Name, Middle Initial)	**3. PATIENT'S BIRTH DATE** 04 / 16 / 19 SEX: M ✓	**4. INSURED'S NAME** (Last Name, First Name, Middle Initial)
Jackson, Joe		
5. PATIENT'S ADDRESS (No., Street)	**6. PATIENT RELATIONSHIP TO INSURED** Self ✓	**7. INSURED'S ADDRESS** (No., Street)
1347 S. State St.		
CITY: Union City **STATE**: IL	**8. RESERVED FOR NUCC USE**	**CITY** / **STATE**
ZIP CODE: 62510 **TELEPHONE**: (000) 000-0000		**ZIP CODE** / **TELEPHONE**
9. OTHER INSURED'S NAME	**10. IS PATIENT'S CONDITION RELATED TO:**	**11. INSURED'S POLICY GROUP OR FECA NUMBER**: None
a. OTHER INSURED'S POLICY OR GROUP NUMBER	a. EMPLOYMENT? NO ✓	a. INSURED'S DATE OF BIRTH / SEX
b. RESERVED FOR NUCC USE	b. AUTO ACCIDENT? NO ✓ PLACE (State)	b. OTHER CLAIM ID (Designated by NUCC)
c. RESERVED FOR NUCC USE	c. OTHER ACCIDENT? NO ✓	c. INSURANCE PLAN NAME OR PROGRAM NAME
d. INSURANCE PLAN NAME OR PROGRAM NAME	10d. CLAIM CODES (Designated by NUCC)	d. IS THERE ANOTHER HEALTH BENEFIT PLAN?

READ BACK OF FORM BEFORE COMPLETING & SIGNING THIS FORM.

12. PATIENT'S OR AUTHORIZED PERSON'S SIGNATURE
SIGNED: SOF   DATE:

13. INSURED'S OR AUTHORIZED PERSON'S SIGNATURE
SIGNED:

14. DATE OF CURRENT ILLNESS, INJURY, or PREGNANCY (LMP)   **15. OTHER DATE**   **16. DATES PATIENT UNABLE TO WORK IN CURRENT OCCUPATION**

17. NAME OF REFERRING PROVIDER OR OTHER SOURCE: DK Eric Botts   17b. NPI: Individual NPI#

18. HOSPITALIZATION DATES RELATED TO CURRENT SERVICES

19. ADDITIONAL CLAIM INFORMATION (Designated by NUCC)

20. OUTSIDE LAB? $ CHARGES

21. DIAGNOSIS OR NATURE OF ILLNESS OR INJURY   ICD Ind. 10
A. H04.123   B. H02.053   C. H02.056   D.

22. RESUBMISSION CODE / ORIGINAL REF. NO.

23. PRIOR AUTHORIZATION NUMBER

24. A. DATE(S) OF SERVICE From / To	B. PLACE OF SERVICE	C. EMG	D. PROCEDURES, SERVICES, OR SUPPLIES CPT/HCPCS / MODIFIER	E. DIAGNOSIS POINTER	F. $ CHARGES	G. DAYS OR UNITS	H. EPSDT	I. ID. QUAL.	J. RENDERING PROVIDER ID. #
11 13 10 - 11 13 10	11		99214 / 25	A	95 80	1		NPI	Individual NPI #
11 13 10 - 11 13 10	11		67820 / E4	B	46 77	1		NPI	Individual NPI #
11 13 10 - 11 13 10	11		67820 / E2	C	46 77	1		NPI	Individual NPI #

25. FEDERAL TAX I.D. NUMBER: 4171789 EIN ✓
26. PATIENT'S ACCOUNT NO.
27. ACCEPT ASSIGNMENT? YES ✓
28. TOTAL CHARGE: $ 189.34
29. AMOUNT PAID: $ 0
30. Rsvd for NUCC Use: 189.34

31. SIGNATURE OF PHYSICIAN OR SUPPLIER INCLUDING DEGREES OR CREDENTIALS
E. Botts 11-13-10

32. SERVICE FACILITY LOCATION INFORMATION
Eric K. Botts, O.D.
1730 East Jackson Street
Macomb, IL 61455
309-836-3373

33. BILLING PROVIDER INFO & PH #
Eric K. Botts, O.D.
1730 East Jackson Street
Macomb, IL 61455
309-836-3373

NUCC Instruction Manual available at: www.nucc.org   APPROVED OMB-0938-1197 FORM 1500 (02-12)

©2014 - E. Botts, O.D.   Group NPI # if available, otherwise individual NPI #

• TRICHIASIS/EPILATION PATIENT •
PAGE 4

Medicare Remittance Notice

Eric K. Botts, OD
1730 East Jackson Street
Macomb, IL 61455-2531

NPI #: 47932761
Page #: 1 of 2
Date: 12-22-10
Check/Eft #: 115449098

PERF PROV	SERV DATE	POS	NOS	PROC	MODS	BILLED	ALLOWED	DEDUCT	COINS	GRP/RC-AMT	PROV PD
NAME JACKSON, JOE			HIC 36030715A		ACNT 111036P			ICN 0206222466720	ASG Y	MOA MAO 1 MA 18	
47932761	1113 111310	11	1	99214	25	95.80	94.75	0.00	18.95	1.05	75.80
47932761	1113 111310	11	1	68720	E4	46.77	44.40	0.00	8.88	2.37	35.52
47932761	1113 111310	11	1	68720	E2	46.77	44.40	0.00	8.88	2.37	35.52
PT RESP 36.71			1	CLAIM TOTALS		147.34	183.55	0.00	36.71	5.79	146.84

CLAIM INFORMATION FORWARDED TO: HCSC-BCBS OF IL (STD A & B)

146.84 NET

Example #9
Cornea Foreign Body

• **CORNEA FOREIGN BODY PATIENT** •
PAGE 1

EXAMINATION

Patient: James Peterson Date: 09-17-10 Sex: (M) F DOB: 03-29-21 Age: ___ Last Exam: ___
Chief Complaint: Eyes feel like something in them

History
HPI: Both eyes hurt and red
Symptoms: Grinding on metal and it flew in both eyes
Location: Incident occurred 1 day ago
Quality: Not wearing safety glasses
Severity:
Duration:
Timing:
Context:
Modifiers:

Allergies:
Medications:
Ocular ROS:

Medical History & ROS from 10 / 23 / 08 reviewed: ☑ no changes
Dr. Initials: EKB

Examination Head/Face ☑ nl   Psych: Mood/Affect (anxiety/depression) ☑ nl   Neuro: Oriented (person/time/place) ☑ y ☐ n

VA: sc<___   cc< 30/30   ph<___   near<___

K: OD____ OLD RX: OD____ add____
   OS____   OS____ add____
R-scopy: OD____ REF: OD____ 20/____ add____
         OS____   OS____ 20/____ add____

Perimetry: ☐ nl CF ☐ nl   Color ☐ nl ☐ RG defect   ADNEXA ☑ nl
Motility: ☐ Full   Stereo Animals /3 WD /9   EYELIDS: ☐ Blepharitis OD OS OU
Cover Test: ☐ Eso____   ☐ Exo____ ☐ Ortho   ☐ Meibomianitis OD OS OU

Pupils: ☑ no afferent defect   ☑ round OU   Size: OD 3 OS 3   ☐ 20D
                                                                 ☐ 90D/78D
                                                                 ☐ 3 Mirror
                                                                 ☐

small metal fragments embedded in cornea
rust rings OU

SLE: OD   OS   RETINA: OD   OS
☑ nl ☐ FBUT:___ TEAR FILM ☑ nl ☐ FBUT:___   ☐ nl ☐ drusen   MACULA   ☐ nl ☐ drusen
☑ nl ☐ arcus   CORNEA   ☑ nl ☐ arcus   ☐ nl ☐ RPE chgs   ☐ nl ☐ RPE chgs
☑ nl ☐ pterygium   ☑ nl ☐ pterygium   ☐ nl ☐ cotton wool POST POLE ☐ nl ☐ cotton wool
☑ nl ☐ infiltrate   ☑ nl ☐ infiltrate   ☐ nl ☐ hemes   ☐ nl ☐ hemes
☐ nl ☑ spk   ☐ nl ☑ spk   ☐ nl ☐ DME   ☐ nl ☐ DME
☑ nl ☐   SCLERA   ☑ nl   ☐ nl ☐   VESSELS   ☐ nl ☐
☐ nl ☑ injection CONJ.   ☐ nl ☑ injection   ☐ nl ☐ PVD   VITREOUS   ☐ nl ☐ PVD
☑ nl ☐ pinguecula   ☑ nl ☐ pinguecula   ☐ nl ☐ strands   ☐ nl ☐ strands
☑ D&Q ☐   AC   ☑ D&Q ☐   ☐ nl ☐   PERIPHERY   ☐ nl ☐
☑ nl ☐ rubeosis IRIS   ☑ nl ☐ rubeosis   OPTIC DISCS: OD   OS
☑ clear ☐ cat ☐ ns LENS   ☑ clear ☐ cat ☐ ns   ☐ nl   SIZE/APPEARANCE/NFL ☐ nl
                                                     ☐ ____ C/D   ☐ ____

NCT 18 / 18 @ 3:32 pm   Pachymetry: OD____
TAG /   @____   OS____   Dilated: M .5% 1% PA 1%/0.25% C 1% 2% Ph 2.5% 10% OU@____

Diagnosis/Plan   MDM 1 2 3 4   Order: ☐ HRT/GDX/OCT   RTO: 1 day
                                                     ☐ Photo   ___ week
Metal FB Cornea OU   Removed with forceps and alger brush   ☐ VF   ___ month
Corneal abrasion OU   Vigamox oph. sol. OU Tid x 5 days   ☐ Consult   ___ year
                      Bandage contact lenses OU
                                                             Dr. E. Botts

Rev.11/11 ©2007 - E. Botts, O.D.

BILLING STATEMENT

CORNEA FOREIGN BODY PATIENT
PAGE 2

Dr. Eric Botts
Phone 309/836-3373

Date of Service: 09/17/10
Patient's Name: James Peterson
DOB: 03/29/21
☒ Male ☐ Female
Address: 12212 S. Dove Lane
City: Biggsville
State: IL Zip: 62491
Telephone: (   )   -
Insured's Name:
Insured's DOB: /   /
ID Number: xxx xx xxxxA
Secondary Ins:
Total: 137.40
Special Instructions:
Refraction Paid:
Co-Pay/Deductible Paid:
Ins/Mcaid/Mcare Paid:
Secondary Paid:
Write Off:
Balance Due:

MODIFIERS: 24 25 26 50 55 59 79 **RT ☒** **LT ☒** E1 E2 E3 E4 1P 2P 8P TC GW QW

Selected Codes

- **65222** — Foreign body, cornea (fee ~$67.80)
- **T15.00X [A]** — Foreign body in cornea, RT, initial
- **T15.00X [A]** — Foreign body in cornea, LT, initial

108

• CORNEA FOREIGN BODY PATIENT •
PAGE 3

HEALTH INSURANCE CLAIM FORM
ICD-10

APPROVED BY NATIONAL UNIFORM CLAIM COMMITTEE (NUCC) 02/12

PICA	PICA

1. MEDICARE / MEDICAID / TRICARE / CHAMPVA / GROUP HEALTH PLAN / FECA BLK LUNG / OTHER

1a. INSURED'S I.D. NUMBER (For Program in Item 1): XXX XX XXXXA

2. PATIENT'S NAME (Last Name, First Name, Middle Initial): Peterson, James

3. PATIENT'S BIRTH DATE: 03 / 29 / 21 **SEX**: M ✔

4. INSURED'S NAME (Last Name, First Name, Middle Initial):

5. PATIENT'S ADDRESS (No., Street): 1221 S. Dove Ln.

6. PATIENT RELATIONSHIP TO INSURED: Self / Spouse / Child / Other

7. INSURED'S ADDRESS (No., Street):

CITY: Biggsville   **STATE**: IL

8. RESERVED FOR NUCC USE

CITY: **STATE**:

ZIP CODE: 62491   **TELEPHONE** (Include Area Code): (000) 000-0000

ZIP CODE: **TELEPHONE**: ( )

9. OTHER INSURED'S NAME (Last Name, First Name, Middle Initial):

10. IS PATIENT'S CONDITION RELATED TO:

11. INSURED'S POLICY GROUP OR FECA NUMBER: None

a. OTHER INSURED'S POLICY OR GROUP NUMBER:

a. EMPLOYMENT? (Current or Previous): YES / NO ✔

a. INSURED'S DATE OF BIRTH: MM / DD / YY   **SEX**: M / F

b. RESERVED FOR NUCC USE

b. AUTO ACCIDENT?: YES / NO ✔   **PLACE (State)**:

b. OTHER CLAIM ID (Designated by NUCC):

c. RESERVED FOR NUCC USE

c. OTHER ACCIDENT?: YES / NO ✔

c. INSURANCE PLAN NAME OR PROGRAM NAME:

d. INSURANCE PLAN NAME OR PROGRAM NAME

10d. CLAIM CODES (Designated by NUCC):

d. IS THERE ANOTHER HEALTH BENEFIT PLAN?: YES / NO — *If yes*, complete items 9, 9a, and 9d.

READ BACK OF FORM BEFORE COMPLETING & SIGNING THIS FORM.

12. PATIENT'S OR AUTHORIZED PERSON'S SIGNATURE I authorize the release of any medical or other information necessary to process this claim. I also request payment of government benefits either to myself or to the party who accepts assignment below.

SIGNED: SOF   DATE:

13. INSURED'S OR AUTHORIZED PERSON'S SIGNATURE I authorize payment of medical benefits to the undersigned physician or supplier for services described below.

SIGNED:

14. DATE OF CURRENT ILLNESS, INJURY, or PREGNANCY (LMP): MM / DD / YY   QUAL.:

15. OTHER DATE: QUAL. / MM / DD / YY

16. DATES PATIENT UNABLE TO WORK IN CURRENT OCCUPATION FROM / TO

17. NAME OF REFERRING PROVIDER OR OTHER SOURCE: DK Eric Botts   **17a.**:   **17b. NPI**: Individual NPI#

18. HOSPITALIZATION DATES RELATED TO CURRENT SERVICES FROM / TO

19. ADDITIONAL CLAIM INFORMATION (Designated by NUCC):

20. OUTSIDE LAB?: YES / NO   **$ CHARGES**:

21. DIAGNOSIS OR NATURE OF ILLNESS OR INJURY Relate A-L to service line below (24E)   **ICD Ind.**: 10

A. T15.01XA   B. T15.02XA   C.   D.
E.   F.   G.   H.
I.   J.   K.   L.

22. RESUBMISSION CODE: **ORIGINAL REF. NO.**:

23. PRIOR AUTHORIZATION NUMBER:

24.

	A. DATE(S) OF SERVICE From – To	B. PLACE OF SERVICE	C. EMG	D. PROCEDURES, SERVICES, OR SUPPLIES CPT/HCPCS	MODIFIER	E. DIAGNOSIS POINTER	F. $ CHARGES	G. DAYS OR UNITS	H. EPSDT Family Plan	I. ID. QUAL.	J. RENDERING PROVIDER ID. #
1	09 17 10 – 09 17 10	11		65222	RT	A	67 80	1		NPI	Individual NPI #
2	09 17 10 – 09 17 10	11		65222	LT	B	67 80	1		NPI	Individual NPI #
3										NPI	
4										NPI	
5										NPI	
6										NPI	

25. FEDERAL TAX I.D. NUMBER: 41714981   **SSN / EIN**: EIN ✔

26. PATIENT'S ACCOUNT NO.:

27. ACCEPT ASSIGNMENT? (For govt. claims, see back): YES ✔ / NO

28. TOTAL CHARGE: $ 137 40   **29. AMOUNT PAID**: $ 0   **30. Rsvd for NUCC Use**: 137 40

31. SIGNATURE OF PHYSICIAN OR SUPPLIER INCLUDING DEGREES OR CREDENTIALS (I certify that the statements on the reverse apply to this bill and are made a part thereof.)

SIGNED: E. Botts   DATE: 09-17-10

32. SERVICE FACILITY LOCATION INFORMATION:
Eric K. Botts, O.D.
1730 East Jackson Street
Macomb, IL 61455
309-836-3373

a. NPI   b.

33. BILLING PROVIDER INFO & PH #: ( )
Eric K. Botts, O.D.
1730 East Jackson Street
Macomb, IL 61455
309-836-3373

a. NPI   b.

NUCC Instruction Manual available at: www.nucc.org   **PLEASE PRINT OR TYPE**   APPROVED OMB-0938-1197 FORM 1500 (02-12)

©2014 - E. Botts, O.D.   Group NPI # if available, otherwise individual NPI #

• *CORNEA FOREIGN BODY PATIENT* •
PAGE 4

Medica
Remittanc
Notic

Eric K. Botts, OD
1730 East Jackson Street
Macomb, IL 61455-2531

NPI #: 4793276
Page #: 1 of
Date: 10-22-1
Check/Eft #: 1154490¢

PERF PROV	SERV DATE	POS	NOS	PROC	MODS	BILLED	ALLOWED	DEDUCT	COINS	GRP/RC-AMT	PROV PC
NAME PETERSON, JAMES			HIC 36030715A		ACNT 111036P			ICN 0206222466720	ASG Y	MOA MAO 1	MA 1
47932761	0917 091710	11	1	65222	RT	67.80	64.75	0.00	12.95	3.05	51.80
47932761	0917 091710	11	1	65222	LT	67.80	64.75	0.00	12.95	3.05	51.80
PT RESP	25.90		1	CLAIM TOTALS		135.60	129.50	0.00	25.90	6.10	103.60

CLAIM INFORMATION FORWARDED TO: HCSC-BCBS OF IL (STD A & B)

103.60 NE

Example #10
Conjunctivitis

• CONJUNCTIVITIS PATIENT •
PAGE 1

EXAMINATION

Patient: John Doe Date: 07-15-10 Sex: (M) F DOB: xx-xx-xx Age: 43 Last Exam: _____
Chief Complaint: Red Eye

History
HPI: Hurt when woke up this AM
Symptoms: Excessive tearing
Location: Vision is blurry x 1 day
Quality: Sensitive to light
Severity: Both eyes affected
Duration:
Timing:
Context:
Modifiers:

Allergies:
Medications:
Ocular ROS:
Medical History & ROS from 11 / 02 / 04 reviewed: ☑ no changes
Dr. Initials: EKB

Examination
Head/Face ☑ nl   Psych: Mood/Affect (anxiety/depression) ☑ nl   Neuro: Oriented (person/time/place) ☑ y ☐ n

VA: sc< 30/30   cc<   ph<   near<

K: OD _____   OLD RX: OD _____ add _____
OS _____   OS _____ add _____
R-scopy: OD _____   REF: OD _____ 20/____ add _____
OS _____   OS _____ 20/____ add _____

Perimetry: ☐ nl CF ☐ nl   Color ☐ nl ☐ RG defect   **ADNEXA** ☑ nl
Motility: ☑ Full   Stereo Animals /3 WD /9   **EYELIDS:** ☐ Blepharitis OD OS (OU)
Cover Test: ☐ Eso _____   ☐ Exo _____   ☐ Ortho   ☐ Meibomianitis OD OS (OU)
Pupils: ☑ no afferent defect   ☑ round OU   Size: OD _____ OS _____
☐ 20D
☐ 90D/78D
☐ 3 Mirror

diffuse spk OU

SLE: OD   **OS**   **RETINA: OD**   **OS**
☑ nl ☐ FBUT: ___ TEAR FILM ☑ nl ☐ FBUT: ___   ☐ nl ☐ drusen   MACULA   ☐ nl ☐ drusen
☑ nl ☐ arcus   CORNEA   ☑ nl ☐ arcus   ☐ nl ☐ RPE chgs   ☐ nl ☐ RPE chgs
☑ nl ☐ pterygium   ☑ nl ☐ pterygium   ☐ nl ☐ cotton wool POST POLE ☐ nl ☐ cotton wool
☑ nl ☐ infiltrate   ☑ nl ☐ infiltrate ☐ nl ☐ hemes   ☐ nl ☐ hemes
☐ nl ☑ spk   ☐ nl ☑ spk   ☐ nl ☐ DME   ☐ nl ☐ DME
☑ nl ☐   SCLERA   ☑ nl ☐   ☐ nl ☐   VESSELS   ☐ nl ☐
☐ nl ☑ injection CONJ.   ☐ nl ☑ injection   ☐ nl ☐ PVD   VITREOUS ☐ nl ☐ PVD
☑ nl ☐ pinguecula   ☑ nl ☐ pinguecula ☐ nl ☐ strands   ☐ nl ☐ strands
☑ D&Q ☐   AC   ☑ D&Q ☐   ☐ nl ☐   PERIPHERY ☐ nl ☐
☑ nl ☐ rubeosis   IRIS   ☑ nl ☐ rubeosis   **OPTIC DISCS: OD**   **OS**
☑ clear ☐ cat ☐ ns LENS   ☑ clear ☐ cat ☐ ns   ☐ nl   SIZE/APPEARANCE/NFL   ☐ nl
                                                        ☐ ____   C/D   ☐ ____

NCT 16 / 16 @ 3:45 pm   Pachymetry: OD _____
TAG ___ / ___ @ _____   OS _____   Dilated: M .5% 1% PA 1%/0.25% C 1% 2% Ph 2.5% 10% OU@ _____

Diagnosis/Plan MDM 1 2 (3) 4
Viral Conjunctivitis OU

Order adeno detector
Order external photos
Betadine lavage
RTC 1 week

Order: ☐ HRT/GDX/OCT   RTO: ___ day
☐ Photo   1 week
☐ VF   ___ month
☐ Consult   ___ year

Dr. E. Botts

CONJUNCTIVITIS PATIENT
PAGE 2
EXAMINATION
Supplementary Tests

Patient **John Doe** Date **07-15-10**

OD OS
External Ocular Photography (92285, 92286)

Findings: 2+ injection bulbar conj. 360° | 2+ injection bulbar conj. 360°
Diagnosis: Limbal encroachment | Limbal encroachment
Plan: Central SPK | Central SPK
Viral conjunctivitis | Viral conjunctivitis

Signature: E. Botts

OD OS
Scanning Computerized Ophthalmic Diagnostic Imaging (92132, 92133, 92134)

☐ HRT ☐ OCT ☐ GDX

Findings
Diagnosis
Plan

Signature

Extended Ophthalmoscopy (92225, 92226)

☐ 78D Lens ☐ 90D Lens ☐ 20D Lens ☐ 2.2D Lens ☐ 3-Mirror ☐ Scleral depression

OD **OS**

Findings
Diagnosis
Plan

Signature

©2007 - E. Botts, O.D.

BILLING STATEMENT

• *CONJUNCTIVITIS PATIENT* •
PAGE 3

Dr. Eric Botts
Phone 309/836-3373

Date of Service **07/15/10**
Patient's Name **John Doe** DOB __/__/__ ☒ Male ☐ Female
Address **2100 RedBud St.** City **Smithville** State **IL** Zip **69321**
Telephone (___)___-____ Insured's Name _____ Insured's DOB __/__/__
ID Number **359 26 8567A** Secondary Ins _____ Total **167.84**
Special Instructions _____
Refraction Paid _____
Co-Pay/Deductible Paid **33.57**
Ins/Mcaid/Mcare Paid _____
Secondary Paid _____
Write Off _____
Balance Due _____

MODIFIERS 24 25 26 50 55 59 79 **RT**☒ **LT**☒ E1 E2 E3 E4 1P 2P 8P TC GW QW

MISCELLANEOUS
- E10.65 — Type 1 Diabetes w complications
- E10.9 — Type 1 Diabetes wo complications
- E11.65 — Type 2 Diabetes w complications
- E11.9 — Type 2 Diabetes wo complications
- H27.0 [1 2 3] — Aphakia
- H53.8 — Blurred Vision
- H57.1 [1 2 3] — Ocular Pain
- M06.9 — Rheumatoid Arthritis
- Z79.4 — Insulin Dependent
- Z79.84 — Non-Insulin Dependent
- Z79.899 — High Risk meds

(1-RT 2-LT 3-Bilateral)

UVEAL DISORDERS
- H20.01 [1 2 3] — Primary iridocyclitis
- H21.0 [1 2 3] — Hyphema
- H21.23 [1 2 3] — Degeneration of Iris
- H21.26 [1 2 3] — Iris Atrophy
- H21.4 [1 2 3] — Pupillary membranes
- H57.05 [1 2 3] — Tonic Pupil

(1-RT 2-LT 3-Bilateral)

EYELIDS
- H00.023 — Hordeolum internum RT eye
- H00.026 — Hordeolum internum LT eye
- H00.13 — Chalazion RT eye
- H00.16 — Chalazion LT eye
- H01.023 — Squamous blepharitis RT eye
- H01.026 — Squamous blepharitis LT eye
- H01.113 — Allergic dermatitis RT eye
- H01.116 — Allergic dermatitis LT eye
- H02.033 — Senile entropion RT eye
- H02.036 — Senile entropion LT eye
- H02.053 — Trichiasis wo entropion RT eye
- H05.056 — Trichiasis wo entropion LT eye
- H02.133 — Senile ectropion RT eye
- H02.136 — Senile ectropion LT eye
- H02.40 [1 2 3] — Unspec ptosis of eyelid
- H02.833 — Dermatochalasis RT eye
- H02.836 — Dermatochalasis LT eye

(1-RT 2-LT 3-Bilateral)

CATARACT/LENS
- H25.01 [1 2 3] — Cortical age-related cat
- H25.04 [1 2 3] — Post subcap polar age-related cat
- H25.1 [1 2 3] — Age-related nuclear cat
- H25.89 — Other age-related cat
- Z96.1 — Presence of intraocular lens

(1-RT 2-LT 3-Bilateral)

DISORDER OF REFRACTION
- H52.0 [1 2 3] — Hypermetropia
- H52.1 [1 2 3] — Myopia
- H52.22 [1 2 3] — Regular Astigmatism
- H52.4 — Presbyopia

(1-RT 2-LT 3-Bilateral)

VISUAL DISORDERS
- H51.11 — Convergence insufficiency
- H51.12 — Convergence excess
- H52.53 [1 2 3] — Spasm of accommodation
- H53.02 [1 2 3] — Refractive amblyopia
- H53.03 [1 2 3] — Strabismic amblyopia
- H53.14 [1 2 3] — Visual discomfort
- H53.41 [1 2 3] — Scotoma involving central area
- H53.42 [1 2 3] — Scotoma of blind spot area
- H53.43 [1 2 3] — Sector or arcuate defects
- H53.46 [1 2 3] — Homonymous bilateral field defects
- H53.47 — Heteronymous bilateral field defects
- H55.00 — Unspec nystagmus

(1-RT 2-LT 3-Bilateral)

RETINAL DISORDERS
- E10.31 [1 9] — T1 diab w unsp diab rtnop
- E10.321 [1 2 3] — T1 diab w mild nonprlf diab rtnop w mac edema
- E10.329 [1 2 3] — T1 diab w mild nonprlf diab rtnop wo mac edema
- E10.331 [1 2 3] — T1 diab w mod nonprlf diab rtnop w mac edema
- E10.339 [1 2 3] — T1 diab w mon nonprlf diab rtnop wo mac edema
- E10.341 [1 2 3] — T1 diab w severe nonprlf diab rtnop w mac edema
- E10.349 [1 2 3] — T1 diab w severe nonprlf diab rtnop wo mac edema
- E10.351 [1 2 3] — T1 diab w prlif diab rtnop w mac edema
- E10.355 [1 2 3] — T1 diab w stable prlif diab rtnop
- E10.359 [1 2 3] — T1 diab w prlif diab rtnop wo mac edema
- E11.31 [1 9] — T2 diab w unsp diab rtnop
- E11.321 [1 2 3] — T2 diab w mild nonprlf diab rtnop w mac edema
- E11.329 [1 2 3] — T2 diab w mild nonprlf diab rtnop wo mac edema
- E11.331 [1 2 3] — T2 diab w mod nonprlf diab rtnop w mac edema
- E11.339 [1 2 3] — T2 diab w mod nonprlf diab rtnop wo mac edema
- E11.341 [1 2 3] — T2 diab w severe nonprlf diab rtnop w mac edema
- E11.349 [1 2 3] — T2 diab w severe nonprlf diab rtnop wo mac edema
- E11.351 [1 2 3] — T2 diab w prolif diab rtnop w mac edema
- E11.355 [1 2 3] — T2 diab w stable prolif diab rtnop
- E11.359 [1 2 3] — T2 diab w prolif diab rtnop wo mac edema
- H31.01 [1 2 3] — Macula scars
- H31.09 [1 2 3] — Other chorioretinal scars
- H32 — Chorioretinal disorder
- H33.01 [1 2 3] — Retinal detachment w single break
- H33.31 [1 2 3] — Horseshoe tear of retina wo detachment
- H33.32 [1 2 3] — Round hole
- H33.8 — Other retinal detachments
- H34.1 [1 2 3] — Central retinal artery occlusion
- H34.21 [1 2 3] — Partial retinal artery occlusion
- H35.01 [1 2 3] — Vascular sheathing
- H35.03 [1 2 3] — Hypertensive retinopathy
- H35.04 [1 2 3] — Retinal micro-aneurysms
- H35.34 [1 2 3] — Macular cyst, hole or pseudohole
- H35.35 [1 2 3] — Cystoid macular degeneration
- H35.36 [1 2 3] — Drusen (degenerative) of macula
- H35.37 [1 2 3] — Puckering of macule, ERM
- H35.40 — Unspec peripheral retinal degeneration
- H35.41 [1 2 3] — Lattice degeneration of retina
- H35.71 [1 2 3] — Central serous chorioretinopathy
- H35.82 — Retinal ischemia
- H43.31 [1 2 3] — Viterous membranes
- H43.81 [1 2 3] — Viterous degeneration

RT LT BI *(RT-Right LT-Left BI-Bilateral)*
- H34.81 [10 20 30] — Central retinal vein occlusion w mac edema
- H34.81 [11 21 31] — Central retinal vein occlusion w retinal neovascularization
- H34.81 [12 22 32] — Central retinal vein occlusion, stable
- H34.83 [10 20 30] — Tributary retinal vein occlusion w mac edema
- H34.83 [11 21 31] — Tributary retinal vein occlusion w retinal neovascularization
- H34.83 [12 22 32] — Tributary retinal vein occlusion, stable
- H35.31 [11 21 31] — Nonexudative ARMD, early dry stage
- H35.31 [12 22 32] — Nonexudative ARMD, intermediate dry stage
- H35.31 [13 23 33] — Nonexudative ARMD, advanced atropic wo subfoveal inv
- H35.31 [14 24 34] — Nonexudative ARMD, advanced atropic w subfoveal inv
- H35.32 [11 21 31] — Exudative ARMD, active chorodial neovascularization
- H35.32 [12 22 32] — Exudative ARMD, inactive chorodial neovascularization
- H35.32 [13 23 33] — Exudative ARMD, inactive scar

(1-RT 2-LT 3-Bilateral)
(1-With Edema 9-Without Edema)

LACRIMAL SYSTEM
- H04.01 [1 2 3] — Acute dacryoadenitis
- H04.12 [1 2 3] — Dry eye syndrome
- H04.21 [1 2 3] — Epiphora due to excess lacrimation

(1-RT 2-LT 3-Bilateral)

GLAUCOMA
- H40.01 [1 2 3] — Open angle w borderline findings low risk
- H40.02 [1 2 3] — Open angle w borderline findings high risk
- H40.05 [1 2 3] — Ocular hypertension
- H40.06 [1 2 3] — Primary angle closure wo glaucoma damage
- H40.21 [1 2 3] — Acute angle-closure glaucoma

RT LT BI *(RT-Right LT-Left BI-Bilateral)*
- H40.11 [11 21 31] — Primary open-angle glaucoma, mild
- H40.11 [12 22 32] — Primary open-angle glaucoma, mod
- H40.11 [13 23 33] — Primary open-angle glaucoma, severe
- H40.11 [14 24 34] — Primary open-angle glaucoma, indeterminate
- H40.12 [11 21 31] — Low-tens glaucoma, mild stage
- H40.12 [12 22 32] — Low-tens glaucoma, mod stage
- H40.12 [13 23 33] — Low-tens glaucoma, severe stage
- H40.13 [11 21 31] — Pigmentary glaucoma, mild stage
- H40.13 [12 22 32] — Pigmentary glaucoma, mod stage
- H40.13 [13 23 33] — Pigmentary glaucoma, severe stage
- H40.22 [11 21 31] — Chronic angle-closure glaucoma, mild stage
- H40.22 [12 22 32] — Chronic angle-closure glaucoma, mod stage
- H40.22 [13 23 33] — Chronic angle-closure glaucoma, severe stage

(1-RT 2-LT 3-Bilateral)

NEURO-OPHTHALMOLOGY
- H46.1 [1 2 3] — Retrobulbar neuritis
- H47.01 [1 2 3] — Ischemic optic neuropathy
- H47.1 [1 2 3] — Papilledema assoc. w increased intracranial pressure
- H47.21 [1 2 3] — Primary optic atrophy
- H47.32 [1 2 3] — Drusen of optic disc

(1-RT 2-LT 3-Bilateral)

CONJUNCTIVA
- ☒ B30.0 — Viral conjunctivitis
- H10.3 [1 2 3] — Acute conjunctivitis
- H10.41 [1 2 3] — Chronic giant papillary conjunctivitis
- H10.43 [1 2 3] — Chronic follicular conjunctivitis
- H11.05 [1 2 3] — Peripheral pterygium, progressive
- H11.12 [1 2 3] — Conjunctival concretions
- H11.15 [1 2 3] — Pinguecula
- H11.3 [1 2 3] — Conjunctival hemorrhage
- S05.01X [A D S] — Inj conjunctiva & corneal abrasion wo fb, RT, init
- S05.02X [A D S] — Inj conjunctiva & corneal abrasion wo fb, LT, init
- T15.11X [A D S] — Foreign body in conjunctival sac, RT, init
- T15.12X [A D S] — Foreign body in conjunctival sac, LT, init

(1-RT 2-LT 3-Bilateral)
(A-Initial D-Subsequent S-Sequela)

CORNEA
- H16.00 [1 2 3] — Unspec corneal ulcer
- H16.01 [1 2 3] — Central corneal ulcer
- H16.04 [1 2 3] — Marginal corneal ulcer
- H16.12 [1 2 3] — Filamentary keratitis
- H16.14 [1 2 3] — Punctate keratitis
- H16.42 [1 2 3] — Pannus (corneal)
- H18.22 [1 2 3] — Idiopathic corneal edema
- H18.41 [1 2 3] — Arcus senilis
- H18.51 — Endothelial corneal dystrophie
- H18.59 — Other hereditary corneal dystrophies
- H18.82 [1 2 3] — Corneal edema due to contact lens
- H18.83 [1 2 3] — Recurrent erosion of cornea
- T15.01X [A D S] — Foreign body in cornea, RT, initial
- T15.02X [A D S] — Foreign body in cornea, LT, initial

(1-RT 2-LT 3-Bilateral)
(A-Initial D-Subsequent S-Sequela)

STRABISMUS
- H50.00 — Unspec esotropia
- H50.10 — Unspec exotropia

(RT-Right LT-Left)

FEE
- S0620 _____
- S0621 _____
- 65210 _____ *
- 65222 _____ *
- 65430 _____ *
- 65435 _____ *
- 65778 _____ *
- 67820 _____ *
- 67938 _____ *
- 68761 _____ *
- 68801 _____ *
- 76510 _____
- 76514 _____
- 83516QW _____
- 83861QW _____
- ☒ 87809QW **17.00**
- 92002 _____
- 92004 _____
- 92012 _____
- 92014 _____
- 92015 _____ +
- 92020 _____
- 92025 _____ *
- 92060 _____
- 92071 _____
- 92072 _____
- 92082 _____
- 92083 _____
- 92100 _____
- 92132 _____
- 92133 _____
- 92134 _____
- 92225 _____ *
- 92226 _____ *
- 92250 _____
- 92274 _____
- 92284 _____
- ☒ 92285 **38.04**
- 92286 _____
- 92310 _____ +
- 95930 _____
- 99201 _____
- 99202 _____
- 99203 _____
- 99204 _____
- 99205 _____
- 99212 _____
- 99213 _____
- ☒ 99214 **95.80**
- 99215 _____

* May Require Modifier
\+ Not Paid by MC

- 5010F / G8428
- G8397 / 4004F
- G8398 / 1036F
- 2022F / G8783
- 2024F / G8950
- 2026F / G8784
- 3072F / G8785
- 2019F / G8951
- 4177F / G8952
- 2027F / G8730
- 3284F / G8731
- 3285F / G8442
- 0517F / G8939
- G8427 / G8732
- G8430 / G8509

v2.1 Revised 3/6/17

©2017 - E. Botts, O.D.

• CONJUNCTIVITIS PATIENT •
PAGE 4

HEALTH INSURANCE CLAIM FORM
APPROVED BY NATIONAL UNIFORM CLAIM COMMITTEE (NUCC) 02/12

ICD-10

	PICA								PICA	

1. MEDICARE ☐ (Medicare#) | MEDICAID ☐ (Medicaid#) | TRICARE ☐ (ID#/DoD#) | CHAMPVA ☐ (Member ID#) | GROUP HEALTH PLAN ☐ (ID#) | FECA BLK LUNG ☐ (ID#) | OTHER ☐ (ID#) | 1a. INSURED'S I.D. NUMBER (For Program in Item 1): **359 26 8567A**

2. PATIENT'S NAME (Last Name, First Name, Middle Initial): **Doe, John**
3. PATIENT'S BIRTH DATE: XX XX XXXX SEX: M ☑ F ☐
4. INSURED'S NAME (Last Name, First Name, Middle Initial):

5. PATIENT'S ADDRESS (No., Street): **2100 Red Bud St.**
6. PATIENT RELATIONSHIP TO INSURED: Self ☐ Spouse ☐ Child ☐ Other ☐
7. INSURED'S ADDRESS (No., Street):

CITY: **Smithville** STATE: **IL**
8. RESERVED FOR NUCC USE
CITY: | STATE:

ZIP CODE: **69321** TELEPHONE: **(000) 000-0000**
ZIP CODE: | TELEPHONE: ( )

9. OTHER INSURED'S NAME (Last Name, First Name, Middle Initial):
10. IS PATIENT'S CONDITION RELATED TO:
11. INSURED'S POLICY GROUP OR FECA NUMBER: **None**

a. OTHER INSURED'S POLICY OR GROUP NUMBER:
a. EMPLOYMENT? (Current or Previous): YES ☐ NO ☑
a. INSURED'S DATE OF BIRTH: | SEX: M ☐ F ☐

b. RESERVED FOR NUCC USE:
b. AUTO ACCIDENT? YES ☐ NO ☑ PLACE (State):
b. OTHER CLAIM ID (Designated by NUCC):

c. RESERVED FOR NUCC USE:
c. OTHER ACCIDENT? YES ☐ NO ☑
c. INSURANCE PLAN NAME OR PROGRAM NAME:

d. INSURANCE PLAN NAME OR PROGRAM NAME:
10d. CLAIM CODES (Designated by NUCC):
d. IS THERE ANOTHER HEALTH BENEFIT PLAN? YES ☐ NO ☐ *If yes*, complete items 9, 9a, and 9d.

READ BACK OF FORM BEFORE COMPLETING & SIGNING THIS FORM.
12. PATIENT'S OR AUTHORIZED PERSON'S SIGNATURE: I authorize the release of any medical or other information necessary to process this claim. I also request payment of government benefits either to myself or to the party who accepts assignment below.
SIGNED: *John Doe*   DATE: **03-02-10**

13. INSURED'S OR AUTHORIZED PERSON'S SIGNATURE: I authorize payment of medical benefits to the undersigned physician or supplier for services described below.
SIGNED:

14. DATE OF CURRENT ILLNESS, INJURY, or PREGNANCY (LMP): QUAL.:
15. OTHER DATE: QUAL.: MM DD YY:
16. DATES PATIENT UNABLE TO WORK IN CURRENT OCCUPATION: FROM | TO

17. NAME OF REFERRING PROVIDER OR OTHER SOURCE: **DK | Eric Botts**
17a.
17b. NPI: **Individual NPI#**
18. HOSPITALIZATION DATES RELATED TO CURRENT SERVICES: FROM | TO

19. ADDITIONAL CLAIM INFORMATION (Designated by NUCC):
20. OUTSIDE LAB? YES ☐ NO ☐ $ CHARGES:

21. DIAGNOSIS OR NATURE OF ILLNESS OR INJURY Relate A-L to service line below (24E) ICD Ind. **10**
A. **B30.0** B. C. D.
E. F. G. H.
I. J. K. L.

22. RESUBMISSION CODE: | ORIGINAL REF. NO.:
23. PRIOR AUTHORIZATION NUMBER:

#	24.A. DATE(S) OF SERVICE From MM DD YY	To MM DD YY	B. PLACE OF SERVICE	C. EMG	D. PROCEDURES, SERVICES, OR SUPPLIES CPT/HCPCS | MODIFIER	E. DIAGNOSIS POINTER	F. $ CHARGES	G. DAYS OR UNITS	H. EPSDT Family Plan	I. ID. QUAL.	J. RENDERING PROVIDER ID. #
1	07 15 10	07 15 10	11		99214	A	95 80	1		NPI	Individual NPI #
2	07 15 10	07 15 10	11		92285	A	38 04	1		NPI	Individual NPI #
3	07 15 10	07 15 10	11		87809 | QW RT	A	17 00	1		NPI	Individual NPI #
4	07 15 10	07 15 10	11		87809 | QW LT	A	17 00	1		NPI	Individual NPI #
5										NPI	
6										NPI	

25. FEDERAL TAX I.D. NUMBER: **411743621** SSN ☐ EIN ☑
26. PATIENT'S ACCOUNT NO.:
27. ACCEPT ASSIGNMENT? YES ☑ NO ☐
28. TOTAL CHARGE: $ **167 84**
29. AMOUNT PAID: $ **33 57**
30. Rsvd for NUCC Use: **134 27**

31. SIGNATURE OF PHYSICIAN OR SUPPLIER INCLUDING DEGREES OR CREDENTIALS
SIGNED: *E. Botts*   DATE: **07-15-10**

32. SERVICE FACILITY LOCATION INFORMATION:
Eric K. Botts, O.D.
1730 East Jackson Street
Macomb, IL 61455
309-836-3373
a. NPI | b.

33. BILLING PROVIDER INFO & PH # ( )
Eric K. Botts, O.D.
1730 East Jackson Street
Macomb, IL 61455
309-836-3373
a. NPI | b.

NUCC Instruction Manual available at: www.nucc.org PLEASE PRINT OR TYPE APPROVED OMB-0938-1197 FORM 1500 (02-12)

©2014 - E. Botts, O.D. Group NPI # if available, otherwise individual NPI #

• CONJUNCTIVITIS PATIENT •
PAGE 5

Medicare
Remittance
Notice

Eric K. Botts, OD
1730 East Jackson Street
Macomb, IL 61455-2531

NPI #: 47932761
Page #: 1 of 2
Date: 8-22-10
Check/Eft #: 115449098

PERF PROV	SERV DATE	POS	NOS	PROC	MODS	BILLED	ALLOWED	DEDUCT	COINS	GRP/RC-AMT	PROV PD
NAME DOE, JOHN	HIC 36030715A			ACNT 111036P				ICN 0206222466720	ASG Y	MOA MAO 1	MA 18
47932761	0715 071510	11	1	99214		95.80	84.75	0.00	16.95	11.05	67.80
47932761	0715 071510	11	1	92285		38.04	34.75	0.00	6.95	3.29	27.80
47932761	0715 071510	11	1	87809	QW-RT	17.00	14.57	0.00	2.91	2.43	11.66
47932761	0715 071510	11	1	87809	QW-LT	17.00	14.57	0.00	2.91	2.43	11.66
PT RESP	29.72		1	CLAIM TOTALS		167.84	148.64	0.00	29.72	19.20	118.92

CLAIM INFORMATION FORWARDED TO: HCSC-BCBS OF IL (STD A & B)

118.92 NET

Made in the
USA
Lexington, KY